The Influence of Race and Racial Identity in Psychotherapy

Toward a Racially Inclusive Model

Robert T. Carter

A WILEY-INTERSCIENCE PUBLICATION

JOHN WILEY & SONS, INC.

New York • Chichester • Brisbane • Toronto • Singapore

Extracts in Chapters 5, 6, and 7 are reprinted with permission of
Greenwood Publishing Group, Inc., Wesport, CT. Copyright © 1990.
Janet E. Helms, *Black and White Racial Identity: Theory, Research, and Practice.*

Extracts in Chapter 6, from John A. Ordway, "Some emotional consequences of racism for
whites," and Jeanne Spurlock, "Some consequences of racism for children," in *Racism and
Mental Health,* Charles V. Willie, Bernard M. Kramer, & Bertram S. Brown, (Eds.),
copyright © 1973 by the University -of Pittsburgh Press.

This text is printed on acid-free paper.

This publication is designed to provide accurate and authoritative
information in regard to the subject matter covered. It is sold
with the understanding that the publisher is not engaged in
rendering professional services. If legal, accounting, medical,
psychological, or any other expert assistance is required, the
services of a competent professional person should be sought.

Library of Congress Cataloging-in-Publication Data:

Carter, Robert T., 1948–
   The influence of race and racial identity in psychotherapy :
toward a racially inclusive model / Robert T. Carter.
        p.   cm. — (The Wiley series on personality processes)
   "A Wiley-Interscience publication."
   Includes bibliographical references.
   ISBN 0-471-57111-3
   1. Psychotherapy—Social aspects. 2. Race awareness.
3. Ethnopsychology. 4. Ethnicity. 5. Psychotherapy—Social
aspects—United States. 6. Intercultural communication.   I. Title.
II. Series.
RC455.4.E8C37   1995
616.89′14′ 08693—dc20   95-5145

Printed in the United States of America

10 9 8 7 6 5 4 3 2 1

Dedicated to Wilhelmina, Florice,
Anita, Morrell, Pat, and Walter

Acknowledgments

The completion of this book was not a singular activity. Many people were involved in various ways. I would like to thank them and acknowledge their contributions. I would first like to thank Janet E. Helms for her mentoring, guidance, support, and encouragement, without which this project would not have been possible. Janet, I also want to thank you for remembering my childhood dream of becoming an author and for helping me to make it a reality. A. J. Franklin and Nancy Boyd-Franklin, Sam D. Johnson, Jr., and Kay Jackson provided invaluable feedback on drafts of the manuscript. I also want to thank each of you for letting me know that you believed I had something to offer. I also would like to thank all of my friends who were encouraging and supportive; you know who you are.

Tamara Buckley and Evangeline Sicalides provided essential and thoughtful editorial assistance. Caroline Clauss, Leah DeSole, and Patricia Clark-Brown helped with other aspects of manuscript preparation. Betty Engel and Robert Schwarz of the Teachers College Word Processing Center produced various drafts and helped prepare the final manuscript.

Nadine Revheim, Donald Lee, and Elizabeth Parks helped with research activities associated with the case studies. Students who worked with me gave critical assistance in that they allowed me the opportunity to focus on the book while other research activities were going on. They also put up with my sporadic inattention. I thank them for their patience and support. In addition to those listed above, I would like to thank George Gushue, Stephanie Irby-Coard, Michelle Harap, Lauren Platt, Elizabeth Smailes, Jay Wade, David Watts, Sharon Bowers, Adeyinka Akinsulure, Hawthorne Smith, Kenneth Glass, Deidre Franklin, and Edna Van Harte.

I also thank my family for their love and encouragement without which I would not produce anything of value. Especially my children who are my source of strength: thank you, Theresa, Robert, Bryant, and Nakir, and my brother and sister-in-law, Jimmy and Mary.

Last, but in no way least, I thank Herb Reich, Senior Editor at John Wiley & Sons.

R.T.C.

Contents

An Overview of Race and Mental Health

Race is an elusive, perplexing, troubling, and enduring aspect of life in the United States. Race has been a critical factor in the economic, social, and political structure of American society from its precolonial beginnings to the present. Any examination of American social history points to the legacy of America's fascination with skin color, caste, and social status. Race and beliefs about race have had crucial effects on the course of American history. For instance, European Americans used duplicitous means to obtain land held by American Indians. Throughout American history, Black Americans have been at the center of several controversies arising from fundamental constitutional questions: the debates over slavery during the framing of the Constitution and the Constitutional Convention of 1787, the Civil War, and the civil rights movement of the 1950s and 1960s to end the denial of Blacks' basic rights as citizens. The history of Asian Americans in the United States provides other examples of race's influence, specifically the Exclusion Act of 1882 against Chinese immigration and the forced internment of Japanese American citizens during World War II. These examples demonstrate the broad-based and fundamental significance of race in the United States. "In view of this history, race is likely to retain much of its saliency as a feature of American society for some time" (Jaynes & Williams, 1989, p. 5).

Yet, despite the central and enduring significance of race in North American society, psychology, psychiatry, and mental health disciplines relegate race to, at best, a marginal status in models of human development and in treatment approaches. According to the traditional psychotherapeutic perspectives (psychoanalytic, psychodynamic, humanistic, behavioral, cognitive-behavioral, and integrative models), it seems that race is considered only when a person of color brings it into treatment. For instance, in White/White dyads, race is typically thought not to matter or to exist as an aspect of mental health. However, in a mixed race dyad, when a Black or Hispanic person raises race-related issues in psychotherapy, it is often interpreted by clinicians as a defense or an avoidance of more critical intrapsychic material. More often than not, race is thought by mental health professionals to be an unimportant aspect of personality development and interpersonal relationships. Consequently, how race influences the therapeutic process is not well understood by psychological theorists, clinicians, and clinical scholars. Race as a personality and treatment factor has, at best, been treated as marginal. It can be argued that the marginal status of race in psychological thought and the paucity of theories to guide psychological thinking and research about race and its influences on human life and interactions in the United States (Yee, Fairchild, Weizmann, & Wyatt, 1993) are functions of the marginal status of people of color.

Yee et al. (1993) contend that race is a legally sanctioned social category used to direct public policy to allocate resources (based on census data) and to comply with legal statutes (e.g., voting rights). They also point to evidence of race's long history in America and to its current significance, which is reflected in the steady stream of books and articles addressing the crisis of race in America (D'Souza, 1992; Fairchild, 1991; Jencks, 1992; Smedley, 1993; Solinger, 1992; Steele, 1990; Terkel, 1992; West, 1993). Yee et al. (1993) argue for a clearer and more precise definition of race, and they call on psychologists and mental health professionals to address the role of race and its use within the discipline.

Race has many dimensions and levels of complexity. When analyzing race's impact on the development of an individual, the examination becomes complicated and often unwieldy. In this book, I try to balance the various levels of complexity that seem to impinge on how race affects the therapy process. As A. J. Franklin (personal communication, December 10, 1993) notes, when writing about race one constantly struggles with the questions of how much emphasis to give historical, socioeconomic, sociopolitical, intrapsychic, and contemporary events that relate to the topic.

In discussing and describing race's influence in the psychotherapeutic process, I also find myself in a dilemma concerning emphasis. My resolution to this dilemma is to provide an introduction and overview of the myriad levels and dimensions of racial influences in society and the mental health discipline. I also provide some historical information concerning race in American society and then discuss the history of race in mental health assessment and treatment. I describe briefly the traditional models of psychotherapy that were used to characterize and explain human and personality development and to guide treatment, and I discuss how these approaches addressed race. Race in psychotherapy is salient as it relates to client referral, descriptions, conceptualizations, patient–therapist dynamics, and treatment planning. Against this backdrop, I describe the current state of knowledge pertaining to race in psychotherapy and point to its limitations, including many mental health professionals' tendency to avoid race or to argue that race is less salient than ethnicity or culture.

I assume that race has been and is the variable that matters most in the United States. This text is written from a Race-based approach which is contrasted with the Universal, Ubiquitous, Traditional, and Pan-national perspectives. It assumes that the experiences associated with belonging to a racial group transcends/supersedes all other experiences in the United States. This approach is predicated on the belief that race is perhaps the most visible of all cultural differences and on America's history of racial segregation and racism. In addition, race has been and continues to be the ultimate measure of social exclusion and inclusion, because it is a visible factor that historically and currently determines the rules and bounds of social and cultural interaction (Kovel, 1984; Smedley, 1993).

The Universal approach with its individual difference viewpoint is the foundation for many traditional psychological theories and practices. This perspective's main assumption is that our experiences and identities are minimally derived from our reference groups (e.g., race, gender, age, religion). The primary benefit of the Universal approach is that it reminds us that all human beings not only have many common characteristics and attributes, but also are unique. This orientation, however, downplays the significance and impact of North American sociopolitical history and intergroup power dynamics on one's personality by positing that all group membership are equivalent.

The Ubiquitous approach proposes that any human difference (e.g., race, income level, sexual orientation) can be seen as cultural, and people can belong to multiple cultural groups which are situationally determined. The advantage of this perspective is that social group differences are not seen as pathological. The main shortcomings of the Ubiquitous approach are that it is ahistorical and often ignores or denies the histories of various groups and intergroup dynamics. Consequently, this viewpoint tends to minimize the relative importance of different reference group memberships by conceptualizing them as equal.

The Traditional approach is anthropologically based and equates culture with country, that is, the combination of a common language, kinship, history, values, beliefs, symbols, and epistemology constitutes a culture. Culture, then, is not a matter of social differences or domains of difference, because one is a member of a cultural group by birth, upbringing, and environment. According to the Traditional perspective, domains of difference (e.g., gender, social class) exist, but they do not solely constitute the cultural experience.

And finally, the Pan-national perspective, unlike the Race-based approach, posits that racial group membership determines culture regardless of geo-social contingencies. This approach, with few exceptions, deems European and American culture as antithetical to non-European culture. According to the Pan-national perspective, White (European) culture is based on violence, that is, colonialism and slavery, as well as their legacies. For non-European (non-White) people the primary consequence of White oppression is the alienation from themselves and their original cultures.

One might argue that, in part, race has become less salient because mental health clinicians, scholars, and researchers are more comfortable examining presumed cultural and ethnic issues than addressing racial issues. Many writers seem to suggest that race is included within analyses and explanations of culture and ethnicity. *I contend that race is not understood when culture and ethnicity are assumed to encompass racial issues.* When race is subsumed in ethnic and cultural phenomena, our history as Americans, our current sociopolitical climate, and the operation of our institutions are ignored. Emphasis on ethnicity and culture, particularly when it is grounded in broad definitions of culture, obscures and distorts how central race is in American life, in the delivery of mental health services, and in psychotherapeutic encounters.

To understand how race affects people's lives and their intrapsychic dynamics, I believe it is essential to have a psychotherapeutic model that includes race. Recently, theories of racial identity development have emerged and seem to be the only psychological models of within-racial-group variation. The strength of these theories for racial/ethnic people (i.e., Black, White, Asian, Hispanic, Indian) is that they provide a framework for conceptualizing individual differences in the context of race and, through race, culture. Racial identity theories suggest that people's racial identities vary—that is, how and to what extent they identify with their respective group(s)—and that a person's race is more than his or her skin color, or physical features. Moreover, racial identity theories posit that a person's resolution is psychological and it seems to guide that person's feelings, thoughts, perceptions, and level of investment in his or her racial group's cultural patterns. The integration of (1) some traditional psychotherapeutic principles, (2) the basic tenets of the racial identity theories, and (3) the research generated by these theories results in a Racially Inclusive Model of Psychotherapy that can be used to guide clinical practice and training.

Going beyond the most widely used constructs (transference and countertransference) for explaining race's influence in psychotherapy, I argue that race and racial identity (i.e., an individual's level of psychological maturation associated with his or her racial group membership) are integral aspects of personality and human development. To support my contention, I present models of racial identity for all racial-ethnic group people—those who are classified as belonging to a visible racial-ethnic group (i.e., Asian, Indian, Hispanic, and Black/African Americans), Biracial people and Whites, who typically deny or avoid race as a personal and group characteristic. Furthermore, I argue that racial identity has a powerful effect on psychotherapeutic interactions on a covert and an overt level. I describe how, in therapy, each participant's racial identity and worldview combine to form particular types of relationships that result in varying processes, such as therapist and client strategies, affective responses, and outcomes. Lastly, I include empirical evidence to support my contentions. The combination of the elements described above forms the basis of the *Racially Inclusive Model of Psychotherapy*. This model is built on the notion that race is a psychological factor, not just a social or cultural factor, and, from this perspective, weaves together racial identity theory and the therapeutic interaction model.

A part of this book is devoted to describing empirical studies that validate the notion of variable psychosocial resolutions within racial groups, where each resolution operates as a racial worldview. Two research studies, which I conducted, are presented as evidence for some propositions of the racially inclusive model. One study investigates how racial identity resolutions affect psychotherapy process in racially similar and mixed therapy pairs. A second study explores the notion that participants' racial identities, rather than their race, exclusively, combine to create four distinct types of therapeutic relationships. Lastly, four case studies are presented where the overt psychotherapeutic processes and the racial identity dynamics were examined. The research part of the book is offered to validate the models presented and discussed as well as to demonstrate how race and racial identity appear in therapy exchanges, presenting problems, and therapeutic interventions.

Although I believe that racial issues in psychotherapy are complex and have been reduced historically to somewhat simplistic explanations, I, nonetheless, think racial issues should be understood in all their complexity. So, my intent in this book is to help people understand the complexities of racial issues within helping relationships. I believe that a racially inclusive model will allow readers to come away from this book with a way to understand racial issues and to use this understanding in their clinical work. Armed with theory, research evidence, and clinical applications, readers will be able to incorporate their new knowledge and insight into clinical practice.

I intend this book to serve several purposes. First, I hope to fill a void in the social science and mental health literature by presenting a theoretical model about how psychotherapy and counseling processes are influenced by race. Second, there is a need to advance our understanding of the complex, mutual influences involved in interactions. This is accomplished herein by using research to examine the interplay of race in the counseling process and its outcome. The use of research to test a theory about racial dynamics in therapy can help clinicians move away from speculation, and it can promote effective prevention programs and treatment strategies in mental health and educational practice. Lastly, I hope that this book will be a catalyst for scholars, researchers, and practitioners to think more about the complex psychotherapeutic dynamics that occur as a result of race.

By connecting racial and cultural psychology with the psychotherapeutic process, this book opens up new territory. I hope this bridge will help readers become aware of and work to overcome the racial barriers in psychotherapy and other helping relationships.

The book is divided into four parts. **Part One: What Do We Know?** provides an overview of what is known about race in psychotherapy, what shortcomings are found in the present state of the psychotherapy literature, and how race has been used as a demographic variable with little or no psychological variability. The overview also shows how race was excluded from theories of personality and human development. Lastly, the substitution of ethnicity and culture for race is reviewed. From the state of knowledge pertaining to race in psychotherapy, it is apparent that race has been an issue in mental health from the beginnings of efforts to provide services to psychologically distressed populations in the United States. The information in Part One illustrates the need for the various elements of the Racially Inclusive Model of Psychotherapy. This part of the book is organized using the dominant social science paradigms to describe and explain racial differences. Each chapter presents the tenets of a particular paradigm and describes the literature reflective of that paradigm. Chapter 1 defines terms and places issues of race in psychotherapy in the context of psychological theory and practice. Chapter 2 continues the review and traces race in psychotherapy to its roots in history. Chapter 3 covers the contemporary literature.

Part Two: Where Do We Go? consists of five chapters that discusses a new direction away from the current state of our knowledge about race in psychotherapy. This part lays the foundation and sets the first building blocks of the Racially Inclusive Model of Psychotherapy. Chapter 4 describes how race is incorporated into personality through developmental processes. Chapters 5 and 6 present theoretical frameworks that facilitate our knowledge and understanding of how race influences individual psychological development. Chapter 7 deals with general concerns and questions that often arise regarding racial identity theories, and it addresses the issue of biracial identity. Chapter 8 presents a model of psychotherapeutic process that builds on the theories of racial identity.

The four chapters of **Part Three: How Do We Know?** present empirical evidence and case studies that test whether the theories work. It is unusual to find research studies in a clinical book. But as the review of the state of knowledge about race in psychotherapy shows, much of what is known is grounded in a mixture of supposition, speculation, racism, and personal bias. Little information about race in psychotherapy is derived from theory, and less has been supported by empirical evidence. It is absolutely imperative that race as a psychological characteristic be treated as a construct capable of systematic investigation. Moreover, it is equally imperative that I show that the propositions of the Racially Inclusive Model of Psychotherapy have merit beyond theory. Chapter 9 reviews studies that show the psychological and social correlates of the various levels of racial identity development. Chapter 10 reports the results of a cross-racial dyad study. Chapter 11 tests the interactional psychotherapeutic process notion, and Chapter 12 reports on four psychotherapy cases and examines process dynamics associated with race.

Part Four: What Do We Do with Race? addresses the question of what to do with the knowledge gained from theory and research. Applications of theory to clinical practice are presented in Chapters 13 and 14, along with suggestions for training. Finally, Chapters 15 and 16 challenge and call on psychologists and other mental health professionals to deal with race in therapy. Part Four is intended to provide integration and closure for the reader, utilizing information from previous chapters. Thus, the last part of the book will have the most significance for clinicians who wish to improve their understanding of how race influences psychotherapy.

The Appendix is provided for researchers and clinicians who desire more specific information about the process constructs and measures used in the empirical sections of the book.

PART ONE

What Do We Know?
The Psychotherapy Literature

Part One is an overview of how race is and has been used in psychother-apy. It discusses how race has and has not been used in the mental health literature as a construct and diagnostic tool. The social scientific para-digms are the conceptual frameworks used to organize the review across Part One of the book. The first chapter focuses on how race has been used in traditional theories of human development and personality. It pre-sents definitions of the terms used in the text and begins to sketch the rationale for the Racially Inclusive Model of Psychotherapy. The second chapter traces the roots of race in psychotherapy and the third chapter brings the review to the present.

CHAPTER 1

Race in Psychological Theory and Practice

The work of mental health professionals, educators, and social scientists is to help people learn, grow, and cope with their intrapsychic and interpersonal lives. However, racial boundaries limit mental health professionals' capacity to help visible racial/ethnic group members (i.e., Black, Asian, Hispanic, and Indian Americans), and some White individuals, on their terms and from their perspectives. Consequently, at least one third, if not more, of the nation's residents are inadequately served by mental health providers' efforts to help them learn, grow, and cope with life in the United States. Smedley (1993) notes this about race as a barrier:

> Where race is the more powerful divider, it does not matter what one's sociocultural background may be or how similar ethnically two so-called racial groups are. In fact, the reality of ethnic, or social class, similarities and differences is irrelevant in situations in which race is the prime and irreducible factor for social differentiation. The best example of this are blacks and whites in the United States whose cultural similarities are so obvious to outsiders but internally are obfuscated by the racial world view. When the racial world view is operant, there can never be an alteration of an individual's or group's status, as both status and behavior are presumed to be biologically fixed. (p. 32)

Racial barriers exist in psychotherapy and counseling in large part because traditional theories have not considered race in human and personality development. Neither have the personal meaning and significance of race been extended to White Americans. There also has not been theory to guide our understanding about how race influences psychotherapy interactions and personal development.

Author's note: The terms *psychotherapy* and *counseling* are used interchangeably throughout the text, as are the terms *client* and *patient*.

DEFINING TERMS

Conceptual and sociopolitical complexity is associated with race and racism, and the literature on cross-cultural or multicultural counseling over the past few decades has often used terms interchangeably. Therefore, before exploring race in psychotherapy further, it is necessary to define *culture, ethnicity,* and *race* as they will be used in this volume.

Culture

During the past two decades, clinicians and mental health scholars have increasingly acknowledged the salience of ethnic and cultural differences (at least that seems to be the basis of the rhetoric). Nevertheless, more often than not, race is subsumed in this literature under the rubric of ethnicity and culture, or race, ethnicity, and culture are used interchangeably (Betancourt & Lopez, 1993). I believe that each term has a distinct but related meaning. Johnson (1990) uses the notion of context to distinguish race, ethnicity, and culture. He argues that the larger sociocultural system determines the superordinate cultural framework that gives meaning to people's behavior, language, communication style, and thinking pattern. Concurring with Johnson, Betancourt and Lopez (1993) argues that culture represents learned systems of meaning that are shared by people in a particular context where the meanings are transmitted from generation to generation. Brislin (1990) argues that culture best describes recurring behavioral patterns that vary from location to location (usually, from country to country) and are observable in many generations. Furthermore, he notes that adults have the primary responsibility for socializing children such that the behaviors indicative of the group are learned. In this way, the child becomes a well-accepted socialized adult. Similarly, Smedley (1993) points out that culture is learned, not inherited, and that one learns how to behave and think during the process of development in a particular society. Thus, the term *culture,* in this book, is defined as the transmission of knowledge, skills, attitudes, behaviors, and language from one generation to the next, usually within the confines of a physical environment. According to this view, culture is a *learned behavior.* Johnson points out that "culture is an analogue for the physical-social contexts of development and interactions that account for environmental contributions to human behavior. Culture is represented as the product of human interaction on a large-system level" (p. 43). Cultures or subcultures may arise as a consequence of distinct physical-social contexts. These contexts may be chosen or imposed. Therefore, within a country, it is possible, as a result of group separation and isolation, for several (i.e., racial) groups to have some distinct cultural patterns while at the same time sharing some cultural patterns, particularly those needed to function in the larger society.

Ethnicity

A great deal of confusion surrounds the meaning of the term *ethnic* or *ethnicity.* Many uses and definitions abound. The extent of the confusion can be discerned in the definition in *Merriam-Webster's Collegiate Dictionary, Tenth Edition* (1994), which defines *ethnic* as "of or relating to large groups of people classed according to common racial, national, tribal, religious, linguistic, or cultural origin or background" (p. 398). As is apparent from this definition, *race, ethnicity,* and *culture* are used in similar ways, thus obscuring their meanings. Like *culture,* the term *ethnicity* or *ethnic* refers to a group and a social-physical context based on common experiences that come, in time, to distinguish one group from another. The basis for group commonness may vary widely, depending on many considerations. Smedley (1993) suggests that *ethnic* or *ethnicity* be used as an analytic term to refer to a group of people seen by others and themselves as having distinct cultural features and history and a clearly defined sociocultural history.

Rotheram and Phinney (1987) state that "the term ethnic group has been used to refer to minority groups within a larger culture" (p. 12). Some would argue that any group may think of themselves as an ethnic group. Johnson points out that, in China, the Chinese are not ethnic people because they are the dominant cultural group, but, in the United States, Chinese people are ethnic because they are a nondominant cultural group in this context. Thus, the term *ethnic group* can refer to one's national origin, religious affiliation, or other type of socially or geographically defined group. However, in the United States, ethnicity has been used as a euphemism for race when referring to people of color and as a nonracial designation for Whites (Betancourt & Lopez, 1993). Nevertheless, *ethnic group* will be defined here as a group with a specific national or religious identity.

Race

Race has a long history in psychological thinking and writing. In its original use, race referred to a biological taxonomy that was applied to humans and represented the assumption that a group's shared genetic heritage was evident from physical characteristics (Guthrie, 1976; Johnson, 1990). According to *Merriam-Webster's Collegiate Dictionary* (1994), race is defined as follows:

1 : a breeding stock of animals   2   a : a family, tribe, people, or nation belonging to the same stock   b : a class or kind of people unified by community of interests, habits, or characteristics . . .   3   a : an actually or potentially interbreeding group within a species; *also:* a taxonomic category (as a subspecies) representing such a group   b : BREED   c : a division of mankind possessing traits that are transmissible by descent and sufficient to characterize it as a distinct human type . . . (p. 961)

However, the validity of race as a purely biological variable has been hotly debated and rejected, and race has come to have a social and political meaning that, in part, is related to its original biological roots (Yee et al., 1993). Race as a social and social scientific construct refers "to group characteristics that in popular ideology [not in fact] are carried in the blood (i.e., skin-color)" (Johnson, 1990, p. 41). Thus, in the United States, race is primarily determined by skin color, physical features, and, for some, language, and is associated with powerful social and psychological meaning. Race has been used to make psychological and cultural inferences about one's ascribed membership in a designated group. However, this judgment about what is desirable is associated with a group's particular cultural values. Because groups were thought to have particular characteristics due to their race, this notion leads directly to ranking and evaluating human groups on physical and behavioral traits, a practice that was considered an appropriate classificatory schema. These various elements made race quite distinct when applied to human groups. Smedley (1993) makes this observation:

Unlike other terms for classifying people . . . the term "race" places emphasis on innateness, on the inbred nature of whatever is being judged. Whatever is inheritable is also permanent and unalterable . . . whether it be body size, horn length, fur length or color, or aggressiveness, fearsomeness, docility, dullness, intelligence, or any other states of being that humans attribute to animals. The term "race" made possible an easy analogy of inheritable and unchangeable features from breeding animals to human groups. (pp. 39–40)

Pinderhughes (1989) summarizes the powerful historical, emotional, and psychological meaning associated with race when she notes that

[r]ace constitutes a different level of cultural meaning than ethnicity. Originally carrying a meaning that referred to biological origin and physical appearance, the concept of race was always more inclusive, embracing a number of ethnic groups within a given racial category. Over time, race has acquired a social meaning in which these biological differences, via the mechanism of stereotyping, have become markers for status assignment

within the social system. The status assignment based on skin color identity has evolved into complex social structures that promote a power differential between Whites and various people-of-color. (p. 71)

Race, then, is defined as a concept that refers to a *presumed* classification of all human groups on the basis of *visible physical traits or phe-
notype and behavioral differences.* Inherent in classifying groups in this
way is also the presumption of rank order where one group, typically
Whites (the creators of the concept of races), is the standard by which all
others are judged and ranked (Allen, 1994). When race, in North America, is used as a social classification system, physical characteristics of
different human groups are believed to reflect emotional, cognitive, psychological, intellectual, and moral qualities (Fredrickson, 1989; Gould,
1981; Smedley, 1993). The qualities, both external and internal, are presumed to be inheritable unlike ethnicity or culture which are fluid and
flexible and subject to change, and

> the most critical element of all [to the definition of race] was the belief
> that each exclusive group (race) so differentiated was created unique
> and distinct by nature or God so that the imputed differences, believed
> fixed and unalterable, could never be bridged or transcended. (Smedley,
> 1993, p. 27)

Later, as the term began to be widely used, these elements took on sociopolitical meaning. Today, race's sociopolitical meaning still carries
most, if not all, of its earlier elements.

Race is defined as a sociopolitical designation in which individuals are
assigned to a particular racial group based on presumed biological or visible characteristics such as skin color, physical features, and, in some
cases, language. For example, *Hispanic* is a sociopolitical racial category
assigned to a group of people who share a language and some common
cultural and historical elements. In fact, Hispanics vary in terms of skin
color and physical features, and therefore do not constitute a distinct
racial group on the basis of visible characteristics alone. Nevertheless,
White people are designated White non-Hispanic to separate the groups.
For historically disenfranchised Americans, including Blacks, American
Indians, Asian Americans, and people of Latin descent, racial classification is thought to reflect individual members' and the group's psychological and social status. The reader should be careful not to confuse
genetics or biology with race as noted by Smedley (1993):

> It [Race] was the cultural invention of arbitrary meaning applied to what
> appeared to be natural divisions within the human species. The mean-
> ings has social value but no intrinsic relationship to the biological

diversity itself. Race has a reality created in the human mind, not a reflection of objective truths. It was fabricated as an existential reality out of a combination of recognizable physical differences and some incontrovertible social facts: the conquest of indigenous peoples, their domination and exploitation, and the importation of a vulnerable and controllable population from Africa to service the insatiable greed of some European entrepreneurs. The physical differences were a major tool by which the dominant whites constructed and maintained social barriers and economic inequalities; that is they consciously sought to create social stratification based on visible differences. (Smedley, 1993, p. 22)

MENTAL HEALTH THEORY AND AMERICAN SOCIETY

I contend that race should not be subsumed under culture or ethnicity, but rather confronted directly. At the same time, I recognize that there have been no useful or productive ways to discuss race, particularly because race is associated with a profound social and psychological silence, strong emotional reactions, and polemic. Moreover, psychology has operated from a universal approach to difference. Also, race is often discussed and dismissed (in the clinical literature) as irrelevant because many Whites do not think of themselves in racial terms. Thinking of oneself in racial terms seems to be reserved for visible racial/ethnic group members, particularly Black people (Wilkerson, 1992). However, to assume that race does not have meaning for all American people, including Whites, reflects an ahistorical understanding of being an American, and ignores assumptions about race in the mental health literature. Race, primarily determined by skin color, has been and continues to divide American society. This social division also exists in the mental health delivery system. Societal racial conflicts are inherent in the mental health profession, but the assumptions about race that pervade the mental health literature reflect a profound denial of the reality of race. Assumptions about how humans develop and what is meaningful to their development; what elements influence and contribute to one's personality, identity, and community; and how individual psychological perspectives are formed—all of these obscure the relevance of race by conceptualizing personality in decontextualized and ahistorical terms.

It is virtually impossible to discuss race without also including racism (i.e., individual, institutional, cultural), and it is equally difficult to talk about racism without including interrelated topics and disciplines such as history, economics, politics, education, anthropology, sociology, law, language, and communication patterns. With respect to race and racism, these interrelated issues and domains operate as a complex and dynamic system that has come to characterize the structure and institutional functions of

American society. As a consequence, race affects the social and psychological life of all its citizens. Kovel (1984) puts it this way:

> The prejudice against race is a special psychological issue in which people may handle their specific problems by drawing on the nuclear racist fantasies. Racism includes this, but also the more fundamental phenomenon of the generation and sustaining of these fantasies. Prejudice is the surfacing of racism. Racism is the activity within history and culture through which races are created, oppressed, and fantasized about without the aid of bigots. . . . It pervades the history of our culture at the deepest of levels at which the primary fantasies are generated. The problem of racism is part of the problem of Western culture. (p. 95)

Kovel also notes that:

> Racism served as a stabilizing function in American culture for many generations. Indeed it was a source of gratification to Whites. It defined a social universe, absorbed aggression, and facilitated a sense of virtue in White America—a trait which contributed to America's material success. Racism was an integral part of a stable and productive cultural order. (p. 4)

Although some scholars and clinicians acknowledge race and racism as integral aspects of American society and culture, human development and personality theorists seldom, if ever, include race as an important personality or psychological variable. Because human development and personality theories constitute the foundational perspectives on which psychotherapy is constructed, it follows that the literature in treatment also rarely conceives of race as a central variable.

RACE IN THE CLINICAL LITERATURE:
TRANSFERENCE AND COUNTERTRANSFERENCE

Psychotherapy and, more specifically, the psychodynamic approach to treatment have evolved from Sigmund Freud's pioneering work. Freud's psychoanalytical models are the most influential in applied psychology, including the practice of psychotherapy. Garfield and Bergin (1986) believed that Freud was the most significant figure in the history of psychotherapy. They suggested:

> Although the roots of psychotherapy can be traced back to antiquity, we usually think of it as having taken on its modern form in the latter part of the nineteenth century. Although there were others, Sigmund Freud

was the most significant figure, and his creation, psychoanalysis, was the first distinctively recognized form of psychotherapy. In our opinion it has also been the most influential, and it clearly dominated psychotherapeutic thought through about the 1960's. (p. 3)

Freud's psychoanalytic theories led to the development of a psychoanalytic treatment that sought to uncover unconscious conflicts using transference (i.e., positive and negative) and countertransference (i.e., positive and negative). Psychoanalysis and other psychodynamic approaches to therapy that followed characterize patient/therapist interactions in terms of transference and countertransference, where transference is defined as a form of projection from patient to therapist and countertransference is a similar type of projection from therapist to patient.

One of Freud's first references to transference appeared during the early 1900s. He stated:

It remains the first aim of the treatment to attach him (the patient) to it and to the person of the doctor. To ensure this, nothing need be done but to give him time. If one exhibits a serious interest in him, carefully clears away the resistances that crop up at the beginning and avoids making certain mistakes, he will of himself form such an attachment and link the doctor up with one of the images of the people by whom he was accustomed to be treated with affection. (cited in Thompson, 1987, p. 212)

The term *transference* was not specifically used here, but it is fair to say that Freud was referring to infantile feelings, attitudes, and beliefs that in various disguised forms were transferred to the therapist. Later, Anna Freud expanded the concept of transference by including the idea that transference could be used as a defense to ward off unwanted childhood experiences and wishes. According to Anna Freud, transference could be "externalized" and the person's unwanted wishes and desires would appear to be the therapist's (Thompson, 1987).

Other clinicians and theorists expanded the concept of transference (e.g., Greenson, 1965; Klein, 1952). Greenson offered the following definition of transference, which is used by many clinicians:

Transference is the experiencing of feelings, drives, attitudes, fantasies, and defenses toward a person in the present which are inappropriate to that person and are a repetition, a displacement of reactions originating in regard to significant persons in early childhood. (p. 156)

A similar definition was offered by Basch (1980) and Kernberg, Selzer, Koenigsburg, Carr, and Appelbaum (1980). It should be noted, however, that the precise definition of *transference* is not universally agreed on.

Nevertheless, it usually refers to the client's projection of earlier experiences to the present situation with the therapist.

Countertransference is the flip side of transference, wherein the therapist's own unconscious feelings, thoughts, and actions are stimulated by the patient's therapeutic material. Initially, Sigmund Freud thought these reactions constituted therapeutic errors that should be avoided at all costs. In fact, Thompson (1987) notes that:

> The concept of countertransference and the attitude that it was a therapeutic "error" formed much of the argument for requiring analysts to have a personal or didactic analysis in which they would become aware of their own instinctual impulses and their defenses against them. (p. 239)

As with the concept of transference, countertransference has grown and expanded. Currently, its specific definition is debated, although most would agree that countertransference refers to the manner in which the therapist's own life experiences and personality influence the therapeutic process. Some writers have suggested that countertransference and transference affect psychotherapy in a dynamic way by operating together to shape the type of interactions that occur during the course of treatment.

Most schools of psychotherapy recognize the importance of the therapist-patient relationship. In fact, psychodynamic clinicians and scholars have contributed the most to understanding various dimensions of race in psychotherapy. Nevertheless, historically, psychoanalysis was unavailable to several classes of people, such as those who were thought to be less intelligent and not sufficiently verbal, those who could not devote sufficient time to treatment, or could not afford the treatment. Based on these criteria, people of color were often judged unsuitable for psychoanalysis and many other psychodynamic approaches.

Psychoanalytic and other psychodynamic psychotherapies are guided by the assumption that the individual experiences distortions and unconscious conflicts in his or her intrapsychic structure, and has difficulty with internal object relations (Strupp, 1992). In discussing the history and future of psychodynamic therapy, Strupp (1992) writes:

> [P]sychodynamic psychotherapy remains firmly anchored in psychoanalytic theory and psychotherapeutic principles enunciated by Freud many decades ago. . . . However, as psychodynamic thinking has evolved, considerable attention has been paid to various aspects of personality, which includes prominently internal structures that are no longer seen as solely the products of conflicts between basic drives (sex and aggression) but are significantly influenced by interpersonal experiences with significant figures, primarily those of one's early childhood. Deficiencies and problems

in personality development affect the strengths and weaknesses of intrapsychic structures that are the dynamic psychotherapist's major concern. (p. 21)

The therapist's focus is on the person's internal world. In psychoanalysis, patients who present with psychological concerns that stem from racial or social experiences would be thought to have a deficiency in their internal life or intrapsychic structures.

Similarly, humanistic-existential psychotherapy stems from the work of existential philosophers and others. This therapeutic category includes the theoretical work and treatment approaches of Carl Rogers, Viktor Frankl, and Fritz Perls. The primary focus of humanistic-existential thought and psychotherapy centers on the person's experience and perception of the world. Ivey, Ivey, and Simek-Downing (1980) state that "a central task of the counselor is to understand and empathize with the unique experiential world of the client" (p. 273). Again, the emphasis is on one's subjective world experience. Some scholars have argued that these humanistic-existential principles are appropriate for treating visible racial/ethnic group people, and Blacks in particular. Jenkins (1991), for instance, writes that a therapist who takes a humanistic-existential perspective is able to see the Black client from his or her point of view. Thus, the therapist is more inclined to see and understand the person's potential intelligence, strengths, and individuality. The advantage of the humanistic-existential perspective is that it helps the therapist to see an individual as separate from his or her racial group membership; however, a clinician may then miss important information relating to the client's racial group membership and ways that he or she integrates racial information into his or her identity structure.

Another important therapeutic approach is behavior theory, which evolved in reaction to the tenets of psychoanalytic theories. Behavioral theorists argue that actions are the most important behavior in that they are objective and measurable. Wilson and Agras (1992) believe that behavior therapy was derived from experimental psychology. They describe the history, development, and principles of behavior therapy this way:

In the 1950s and 1960s behavior therapy was informed primarily by the principles and procedures of classical and operant conditioning. In the 1970s behavior therapy began to embrace cognitive and social psychology (Meichenbaum & Cameron, 1982; Wilson, 1986). The 1980s were heralded as the time for integrating affective with cognitive and behavioral process. (p. 40)

The focus of behavior therapy is on influencing and shaping behavior and on helping the patient to acquire or develop better control of his or her behavior. A cognitive-behavioral therapy relies on the relationship between thought and behavior to facilitate and achieve the therapeutic goals. The action-oriented and concrete techniques of behavior therapy and cognitive-behavioral therapy have been suggested as ideal for cross-racial therapy (e.g., Acosta, Yamamoto, & Evans, 1982; Hayes, 1991). Some clinicians may argue that behavior and cognitive-behavioral therapies, because they focus on behaviors and thoughts, are not racially biased. However, it is important to note that behavioral therapy emerged out of the same Euro-American cultural traditions as other theories. It is on the other extreme from psychodynamic models in its focus, but it nevertheless places emphasis on analysis of the person and the environment in terms of significantly smaller influences than social beliefs and group memberships. It is also quite individualistic in orientation.

Most theoretical and clinical orientations have not considered the psychological meaning and importance of race. Because race has been thought of as a sociological or anthropological construct, it has been deemed irrelevant to psychology. Traditionally, groups defined in racial terms have been thought to have psychosocial experiences that affect personality traits and behaviors, impede growth, create obstacles to treatment, or serve as permanent sources of dysfunction. Therefore, race has been seen as unimportant to universal and traditional notions of human development, usually drawn from a Eurocentric worldview. Consequently, as practitioners learn about personality theories and human development, the influence of race is virtually absent.

THERAPY INTO PRACTICE: THE ABSENCE OF RACE

Most mental health practitioners have been taught that psychotherapy should be guided by a single theoretical orientation, such as psychoanalytic, psychodynamic, humanistic, client-centered, behavioral, or cognitive-behavioral, or by an integration or use of various theories and techniques (i.e., eclecticism).

Many of these major theories of personality development have evolved and been expanded or altered since they were originally articulated. Each theoretical model has its own ideas about personality and human development and how to approach developmental issues when they arise. Nonetheless, critics have suggested that all traditional models are grounded in Euro-American worldviews or cultural assumptions (Sue & Sue, 1990). Therefore, few theories have meaningfully incorporated race.

Theorists often mention culture and social factors (Erikson, 1963), but few note how historically ingrained racial beliefs affect personality development for all people. As a result of the civil rights movement, increasing attention has been given to the mental health needs of people from visible racial/ethnic groups.

During the 1960s, the federal government, in response to a report from the Joint Commission on Mental Health, began funding initiatives in community mental health. This report (Garfield & Bergin, 1986) found that psychoanalysis was not available to people who suffered from psychosis or were described as underprivileged. As a result of these federal initiatives, many new therapeutic approaches were used and popularized. Theorists began to acknowledge that traditional psychotherapeutic approaches did not help practitioners work with or understand the mental health needs of people from visible racial/ethnic groups. This realization generated several decades of research focusing on the needs of various groups ill-served by the mental health system. Researchers investigated many variables that were thought to facilitate or inhibit a client's or therapist's behavior in psychotherapy, such as characteristics that may influence whether a client would seek or remain in treatment. As additional studies examined the various predictors associated with the quality of the therapeutic relationship and the possible benefits of treatment, racial influences in psychotherapy were incorporated.

SUMMARY

In the mental health literature, race has received the most attention from psychoanalytic and psychodynamic theorists and clinicians. Psychodynamic characterizations of race have focused, almost exclusively, on the transferential and countertransferential aspects of racial difference in treatment. Typically, it has been argued that visible racial/ethnic group clients have numerous transferential reactions to White therapists. For instance, Kennedy (1952) noted that Whites' and Blacks' transference phenomena are distinctly different. He suggested that "the initial transference in a White patient can be either positive or negative. . . . [T]he Negro patient in our culture . . . enters treatment with fear, suspicion, and distrust of the therapist, whether the therapist be Negro or White" (p. 313). After treating two Black women, Kennedy observed that "the cause of the neuroses of these two patients appeared to be the conflicts arising from a hostile white ego ideal. The self-hatred generated by the fact of not being white started with earliest infancy" (p. 325). Later in the 20th century, race was seen by some writers as a source of resistance or an impediment to treatment. Waite (1968), for example, listed at least five types of resistance often used by Black clients with regard to race. Others argued that one's race and societal racism are associated with experiences that have implications for one's mental health regardless of one's particular racial group (Petti-grew, 1981; Thomas & Sillen, 1972).

Countertransference reactions stimulated by race were considered to be obstacles for visible racial/ethnic group and White therapists working with visible racial/ethnic group patients. For example, it was believed that a therapist would be prone to societal attitudes regarding the patient or would have reactions to the patient because of his or her limited knowl-edge of the patient's worldview and communication style. Nevertheless, it was thought that a therapist would need to guard against, rather than ex-plore and understand, the pitfalls associated with unconscious, racially based attitudes and beliefs prevalent in society. To clearly understand how race and racism were thought to influence transference and coun-tertransference, an exploration of societal racism is needed.

CONCLUSION

Typically, many trainees and professionals are strongly encouraged to adopt a specific theoretical orientation or framework that guides practice. These same professionals are not trained to understand how sociopoliti-cal circumstances shape and guide a theoretical orientation. The impor-tance of race has been denied in personality and human development despite the fact that theory building comes from knowledge of, and in-teractions with, people who have distinct racial legacies. Also, despite recent interest in diversity, cross-cultural, transcultural, ethnocultural, multicultural, or ethnic issues in treatment, racial influences have not been well elaborated (Yee et al., 1993).

As a consequence, most psychotherapists adopt one of many treatment approaches, or a combination thereof, for working with clients. Although these approaches for understanding human behavior and motivation offer unique perspectives, they all are grounded in a Euro-American world-view that focuses on an individual's intrapsychic or interpersonal life to the exclusion of other factors (e.g., race) that may shape the individual's psychological perspective.

When these other factors that shape one's identity are excluded from the therapeutic process, therapy may be ineffective: it can be difficult to assess the client, to conceptualize the problem, and to form a therapeu-tic relationship. Moreover, a clinician may adhere to his or her theoreti-cal orientation and be unable to see the patient as a unique individual in the context of his or her group memberships.

Even though race is an integral aspect of sociopolitical life in the United States and can influence one's life course (e.g., where one lives, learns, finds job opportunities), psychological theorists have built and promoted models of personality and human development absent of race.

The idea that the tasks and processes of development are not differentially affected by race is curious, given the central role of race in American history and sociopolitical life.

When one examines the history of mental health theorizing, it becomes apparent that definite ideas exist and have existed about race as a factor in mental health. However, these racial ideas have been applied singularly to victims of racism. Whites were seldom explicitly included in the discussion of racial effects on individuals and society.

CHAPTER 2

Overview of the Social and Historical
Basis of Beliefs about Race in Psychotherapy

A brief overview of what is known about race in psychotherapy is in order here. The present chapter describes the historical and social development of race and racism in American society and its mental health profession as it was articulated through the 1950s and 1960s. The discussion of societal racism is followed by a description of how the basic premises of racism permeated mental health service and treatment strategies. Chapter 3 picks up the debate about the influence of race in psychotherapy.

Societal meanings and mechanisms associated with race provided the context for basic assumptions that grounded the debate about race in psychotherapy. Writings about race in America are numerous and cover a wide spectrum. They date from the earliest contacts by missionaries in the 1400s to the present. Given the scope of this literature, it is possible to discuss only the general issues that informed and shaped the way mental health professionals thought about race.

Three paradigms—(a) inferiority, (b) cultural and social deprivation, and (c) cultural difference—have been used to understand mental health where race is concerned. According to Banks (1988), the term *paradigm* is

> an interrelated set of facts, concepts, generalizations, and theories that attempt to explain human behavior or social phenomena and that imply policy and action. . . . [I]t is also a set of explanations, [with] specific goals, assumptions, and values, that can be described. (p. 84)

When a paradigm is dominant, its adherents seldom seek alternative views or explanations. Rather, they use the concepts and policies of their point of view to guide problem solving and to create and establish policies, procedures, programs, and interventions (Carter & Goodwin, 1994). In the present chapter, paradigms of inferiority and of cultural and social deprivation are presented, and their underlying assumptions are discussed in terms of how they influenced what was known about the mental health status of visible racial/ethnic group members. The third paradigm, cultural difference, is presented in Chapter 3. It is important to remember that although each paradigm has been associated with a particular period in the nation's history, none has been confined to that period. Therefore, these paradigms overlap and are often used simultaneously. In addition, the underlying assumptions for each paradigm are embedded, to varying degrees, in current social, political, educational, and mental health institutions and practices (Carter & Goodwin, 1994).

HISTORICAL AND SOCIAL CONTEXT

Since the Europeans arrived on the shores of the New World and encountered indigenous people, race and its counterpart, culture, have been salient in human relations in the Americas and the Caribbean islands. The importance of racial differences, thought to reflect cultural differences, was accelerated by the arrival of Africans. Racial issues have been endemic and ingrained in all aspects of North American life, first as custom, then as law and tradition. An elusive, enigmatic, and deeply troubling aspect of the United States' social, political, and economic life, race has secured its effect on the nation's efforts to deliver mental health services.

Members of colonial settlements, while initially predisposed to racism, became more racist through custom rather than by ideology (Fredrickson, 1989; Smedley, 1993). In fact, race has been and continues to be used to determine the social order. Historically and presently, the White race has been thought of as superior, and White culture has been seen as normative. Thus, status and achievement have often resulted from White privilege rather than greater effort or ability (McIntosh, 1995). Conversely, the American Indians and other people of color have been disenfranchised and forced to assimilate American cultural norms to obtain social status or remain on their reservations; Blacks and Hispanics have been segregated and oppressed throughout history, thus limiting their social mobility. Fredrickson (1989), in an essay on the social origins of American racism, observes:

> The United States has been a genuinely racist society. On the whole it has treated blacks as if they were inherently inferior, and for at least a century of its history this pattern of rigid racial stratification was buttressed and strengthened by a widely accepted racist ideology. Although few would deny that explicit or ideological racism—the formal doctrine of inherent biological inferiority—became popular at a relatively late

date in American history, recent historians have tended to see implicit or societal racism as having sprung up very early, partly because of certain pre-existing European attitudes towards blacks which gave a special character to the natural antipathy of English settlers toward any people who were obviously strange and different. (pp. 190–191)

Race has become so powerful a force in the minds and hearts of Americans that, as Edsall and Edsall (1991) note:

> When the official subject is presidential politics, taxes, welfare, crime, rights or values . . . the real subject is race, . . . race is no longer a straightforward, morally unambiguous force in American politics; instead, considerations of race are now deeply imbedded in the strategy and tactics of politics, in competing concepts of function and responsibility of government, and in each voter's conceptual structure of . . . identity. Race helps define liberal and conservative ideologies, . . . provides a harsh new dimension of concern over taxes and crime. In terms of policy, race has played a critical role in the creation of a political system that has tolerated, if not supported, the growth of the disparity between rich and poor over the past fifteen years. Race-coded images and language changed the course of the 1980, 1984, . . . 1988 [and 1992] presidential elections. The political role of race is subtle and complex, requiring listening to those whose views are deeply repellent to some and deeply resonant for others. The debate over racial policy has been skewed and distorted by a profound failure to listen. (p. 53)

RACE IN MENTAL HEALTH

Because any institution in a society is shaped by social and cultural forces, it is reasonable to assume that racist notions have been incorporated into the mental health system. Race is a factor that shapes the personality and affects developmental processes and tasks and the life path of all Americans (Carter & Cook, 1992). As such, race has powerful implications for personality development and mental health.

Jackson (1990), summarizing how race has been addressed in the mental health literature, presents five conceptual and clinical approaches to psychotherapy treatment: (a) Differential, (b) Parallel, (c) Collaborative, (d) Culture-free, and (e) Culture-specific. According to Jackson, Differential models pay little or no attention to cultural or racial factors. "Parallel treatment models involve the use of interpreters and the use of mental health professionals of the same racial group in the provision of traditional psychotherapy. Collaborative treatment models involve cooperative efforts between traditional and indigenous health care providers" (p. 428). Culture-free models are believed to be applicable to all individuals regardless of race or culture because they ignore these variables, and Culture-specific models of treatment are believed to incorporate the norms and values of the client's particular culture in identifying abnormal behavior and treatment approaches. It should be noted that four of the five models described by Jackson rely on traditional theories and approaches and universal or traditional assumptions about difference. Culture-specific models that presume to be guided by a group's particular racial patterns are the only treatment approaches that do not rely solely on traditional theories and approaches. Rather Culture-specific models tend to assume or adopt an ubiquitous, or pan-national approach. Nonetheless, these models can operate from assumptions of inferiority or deprivation.

Jackson (1990) points out that sociopolitical factors seem to determine which treatment model holds sway in the mental health field at any one time:

> The progression of ethnocultural models has been influenced markedly by the level of racism in the general society. At the time that Differential treatment models were predominant, theories of racial inferiority were endemic. At the present time racism, while still prevalent, is more subtle and there is reasonably strong advocacy for the inclusion of cultural models in treatment. Progression in cultural sensitivity has increased as well through training and collaboration among mental health professionals. The peaks and valleys in this process parallel the waxing and waning of overt racism, economic prosperity and political conservatism/liberalism in our society as well as the increasing levels of ethnic cultural diversity. (p. 428)

Jackson argues that when politically conservative ideas are dominant, racism becomes more overt and explicit, and traditional models of treatment (i.e., Differential, Parallel, Collaborative) become more popular. In this climate, Jackson (1990) notes, "Stereotypes are likely to be unquestioned and racist practices thoroughly enmeshed in institutional practices" (p. 428). In contrast, she suggests that Culture-specific models are likely to be endorsed when culturally diverse groups increase in size, economic conditions are stable, and political and racial issues are less evident in social systems and interactions. Jackson's analysis of treatment models highlights the influence and role of race, racism, and the sociopolitical climate on psychotherapy. Implicit in each model are the ideas and concepts about race that are communicated in the mental health literature and produced by its adherents.

INFERIORITY PARADIGM

The inferiority paradigm assumes that visible racial/ethnic group people are biologically limited and genetically inferior when compared to Whites. Therefore, it follows that the mental health and treatment of Whites and of visible racial/ethnic group people are different.

Of the two paradigms presented in this chapter, the inferiority perspective has the longer history (Sims, 1981) and continues to be expressed in numerous forms. Many scientific and social disciplines, such as medicine, psychiatry, psychology, and education, have contributed to the social and scientific "evidence" that promotes the idea of White racial superiority and visible racial/ethnic group inferiority. Many esteemed scientists from the country's most prestigious institutions have supported and given credence to the inferiority paradigm.

The belief that African, Indian, and other visible racial/ethnic group people were inferior to Europeans was taken for granted during the country's colonial era. Historians suggest that Western Europeans were predisposed, prior to actual contact, to consider Africans, Indians, and Mexicans with disfavor because of the numerous language referents that connected darkness with evil. The development of a theory or ideology of biological inferiority did not evolve to support these beliefs until the 19th century. Before the 1800s, the inferior status of Indians, Mexicans, and Africans was taken for granted as a socially accepted custom (Fredrickson, 1971; Smedley, 1993). As Fredrickson (1989) notes, "Although societal racism—the treatment of Blacks [and people of color] as if they were inherently inferior for reasons of race—dates from the late seventeenth and early eighteenth centuries, a rationalized racist ideology did not develop until the nineteenth century" (p. 201). For example, during the 1840s and 1850s, scholars debated whether Whites and Negroes were created equal. During the same period, White scholars from America and Europe argued whether other racial groups represented a separate species or subspecies. Nevertheless, they all agreed that "Negro inferiority was an unchangeable fact of nature" (Fredrickson, 1971, p. 83). The belief in the inferiority of Native Indians and Black Americans extended into the North and was used as the rationale for denying people of color civil rights. Fredrickson (1971) points out:

> [A] substantial segment of Northern opinion was prepared to welcome the biological theory that the Negro [and other people of color] belonged to a separate and inferior species . . . [some] went out of their way to emphasize that democracy was for whites only. (p. 90)

By extension, one could infer that mental health treatment was also for Whites only.

Having established the belief in biological and genetic racial differences, scientists and scholars set out to establish the specific characteristics of these racial differences on scientific grounds. Guthrie (1976) describes the early work of anthropologists who tried to classify races according to skin color, hair texture, and lip thickness. During the 1800s, psychology emerged as a distinct science that studies the mind, based on the well-established sciences of biology and physics, applied anthropology (a branch of anthropology concerned with classifying human races and groups), and ethnology (the anthropological study of cultural heritage and racial studies). Thus, psychology focused primarily on scientific methods to investigate human behavior, and anthropology studied human behavior through observation and interview. Guthrie observes that psychology adopted the racial systems used in anthropology to explain and justify differences among human groups:

> [A] number of racial classifications were made, all of which placed the black man [and woman] at the bottom of the human family hierarchy. The relative question of racial categorization reached such ridiculous proportions in the country that the U.S. Senate commissioned Daniel and Elnora Folkmar to prepare for the Immigration Commission, *A Dictionary of Races or Peoples*. (p. 32)

The Black person in *A Dictionary of Races or Peoples* was described as "belonging to the lowest division of mankind" (Guthrie, 1976, p. 32). This racial designation was given without regard to a person's national origin. One was classified as Black if his or her appearance showed evidence of Black blood, and ethnic variation was ignored. So, if a person was European, Caribbean, African, or South American and Black, in any visible or documented way, he or she was classified as Black and treated accordingly. Similar practices were used for classifying individuals belonging to other visible racial/ethnic groups.

Most European and American scientists embraced the doctrine of biological determinism. According to Gould (1981), the biological determinist doctrine "holds that shared behavioral norms, and the social and economic differences between human groups—primarily races, classes, and sexes—arise from inherited, inborn distinctions and that society, in this sense, is an accurate reflection of biology" (p. 20). Gould observes that two primary approaches were used to support the contention of biological determinism. One approach—to measure intelligence solely by cognitive ability—dominated the intellectual discourse about human worth. The second, which predated measures of human intelligence, was the study of human skulls. Believing this approach to be both scientific and objective, its proponents relied on craniometry (the study of measuring human skulls) during the 19th century and intelligence testing during the 20th century.

A leading contributor to craniometry was Samuel George Morton, who published three volumes on the various measurements of human skulls. The first volume, published in 1839, focused on American Indian skulls; the second, in 1844, focused on Egyptian skulls; and the third, in 1849, included his entire collection of skulls. Morton's work was guided by his belief that races could be ranked "objectively by physical characterization of the brain, particularly by its size" (Gould, 1981, p. 51). Morton's work received considerable recognition and acclaim as "good" and credible science. These findings were

> reprinted repeatedly during the nineteenth century as irrefutable "hard" data on the mental worth of human races. . . . Needless to say, they matched every good Yankee's prejudice—whites on top, Indians in the middle, and blacks on the bottom; and, among whites, Teutons and Anglo-Saxons on top, Jews in the middle, and Hindus on the bottom. (Gould, 1981, pp. 53–54)

In examining Morton's data, Gould (1981) reports several calculation errors and omissions that make Morton's findings questionable. Nevertheless, the belief in racial inferiority had taken hold. Many scientists, following the sociopolitical climate, continued to hold similar beliefs while engaged in their scientific pursuits.

The belief in racial inferiority, which was strengthened by Morton's work in the 19th century, continues to flourish in the psychological literature of the 20th century. G. Stanley Hall, the first president of the American Psychological Association, stated in his book, *Adolescence* (1904), that visible racial/ethnic Americans were members of races that had not reached maturity or were not yet civilized. Louis Terman, a Stanford University professor and eminent psychologist who adapted the Binet intelligence test, observed that visible racial/ethnic group Americans had low levels of intelligence. He noted that their "dullness seems to be racial . . . [and they] are uneducable beyond the merest rudiments of training. No amount of school instruction will ever make them intelligent voters or capable citizens . . . they cannot be considered normal" (cited in Thomas & Sillen, 1972, p. 7). Guthrie (1976) documents the work of other researchers who verified in their minds the inferiority of American Indians and Mexican Americans by using I.Q. test. Arthur Jensen's (1969) analysis of research on intelligence furthered the inferiority paradigm in educational circles and led many to conclude that Blacks were less intelligent on average than Whites.

More recently a number of scholars have continued to argue that people of color are basically inferior to Whites. Rushton (1995a, 1995b) contends that "Zoologists have identified two or more races in many mammalian species. In humans the three major races of Mongoloid, Caucasoid, and Negroid can be distinguished on the basis of obvious differences in skeletal morphology, hair and facial features, and molecular genetic information" (p. 40). He argues that the races are genetically distinct and implies a comparative standard of better and worse. In his comparisons Whites are portrayed as superior to Blacks. Also Jensen (1995) has stated "We [Jensen & Johnson, 1994] have found that, with a large sample, that Blacks and Whites differ in head size and that head size is significantly correlated with IQ." Lastly, the authors of *The Bell Curve* (Murry & Hernstein, 1994) have echoed the same theme, using intelligence tests, that Whites are superior to Blacks and other people of color. These ideas seem to resurface and are widely spread through media and news reports regardless of the chorus of voices and empirical research that challenges and rejects such thinking.

Thus, through research, "the social sciences [have] provided intellectual support for the elite's cultural hegemony" (Stanfield, 1985, p. 406) and have discounted the experience of Blacks and other visible racial/ethnic group members (Cross, Long, & Ziafka, 1978). Social scientists have also been "detached from the reality of a history of racism in the United States and tend to view minorities as inferior, troublesome, and a blemish to the notion of national excellence" (Cross et al., 1978, p. 263).

Allport (1954) stated that race was and continues to be "an immediate and visible mark . . . by which to designate victims of dislike. And the fiction of racial inferiority became, so it seemed, an irrefutable justification for prejudice" (p. xvii). Once the ideas of racial inferiority fell into disrepute (they nevertheless re-emerge every 10 to 20 years, e.g., *The Bell Curve*) racial factors in treatment were often explained by using psychodynamic constructs such as transference, countertransference, and resistance.

Historically, the inferiority perspective led many social scientists to see people of color as mentally unsophisticated and incapable of suffering from mental disorders.

There was also the common opinion that the "uncivilized races" (for example, Indians and Africans/Blacks) had much less or almost no mental illness. Psychological theorists asserted that the constitution of the civilized was initially more sensitive, more liable to creativity and, unfortunately, to insanity. The lower races, the uncivilized, were less emotionally sensitive and were thereby protected from the strains of progress. Therefore, the American Indian, the Black slave, and various other apparently sluggard groups gave evidence of their retardation through an almost embarrassing lack of insanity, the presence of which thus became considered as a sign of progress. (Prudhomme & Musto, 1973, pp. 29–30)

During most of America's early years, when psychological distress and symptoms of dysfunction did emerge in visible racial/ethnic group people, their mental health needs were met with one of three responses: people of color were ignored, jailed, or placed in segregated mental hospitals. In the post-colonial era, when hospitals were used to treat the mentally ill, people of color were segregated from Whites.

The establishment of mental hospitals in the late 18th and early 19th centuries in the United States was the occasion for some of the earliest decisions we find concerning mentally ill Blacks. "At the Worcester State Hospital in Massachusetts, a landmark social institution established in 1833 by the state and sponsored by leading reformers, it was quickly decided that separate quarters would have to be provided for the races" (Willie, Kramer, & Brown, 1973, p. 27).

Historically, psychologists, psychiatrists, and other scientists embraced the doctrine of biological determinism. Belief in this doctrine led to the notion that biological limitations naturally resulted in pathological personalities and limited social and psychological functioning. Moreover, social scientists became preoccupied with rank-ordering racial groups to justify colonization, slavery, and economic exploitation. For example, Black slaves were seen as psychologically adjusted if they were content with their subservient lot; protest was a sign of mental disorder. As another example, Dr. Cartwright of Louisiana developed a race-based diagnostic category, drapetomania, which was defined as the flight-from-home madness. According to Dr. Cartwright, psychologically normal Blacks were "faithful" and "happy-go-lucky," and mentally afflicted ones raised disturbances with their overseers. Thus, the seeds of racism entered the psychiatric and psychological nomenclature. The use of mental health processes to evaluate racial groups became a preoccupation among scientists.

Epidemiology, a branch of medicine that studies the frequency and distribution of diseases in a population, was manipulated to support one of the main arguments of mental inferiority. As noted earlier, freed Blacks were thought to be mentally disturbed, and acceptance of slavery was a sign of mental health. Evidence for this claim seemed to be supported by the 1840 census, which documented the rate of mental disturbance and defect for Blacks as eleven times higher in the North than in the South. For slaves in the South, "only 1 in 1,158 were insane compared to 1 in 162.4 in the free states" (Thomas & Sillen, 1972, p. 17). Based on these figures, John Calhoun, then Secretary of State, argued that the Africans could not care for themselves when freed. Blacks must be protected from mental disturbance.

Edward Jarvis, in 1844, found that these statistics were part of "a fallacious and self-condemning document" (p. 17). It turned out that many of the Northern towns credited with mentally deranged Negroes had no Black inhabitants at all! Lily-white Scarsboro, Maine, had been assigned six insane Negro inhabitants; Worcester, Massachusetts, was alleged to have 133 Negro lunatics and idiots, but this figure actually reflected the number of White patients at the Worcester State Hospital.

The first issue of *The Psychoanalytic Review,* published in 1913, contained three articles involving mental illness of Blacks. The editor observed that

> the existence side by side of the white and colored races in the U.S. offers a unique opportunity not only to study the psychology of a race at a relatively low cultural level, but to study their mutual effects on one another. . . . This article sets forth something of the anthropology of the Negro. (Evarts, 1913, p. 388)

An example of the unchanging nature of psychosocial characteristics for visible racial/ethnic group people is seen in the idea that Blacks, although protected from mental illness, because they lacked psychological complexity when enslaved, were psychologically impaired after they were freed. Evarts (1913), in an article reporting on the "Dementia Praecox in Negroes," described what he called the racial history of Africans by recounting Theodore Roosevelt's account of his trips to the "dark continent." As Evarts noted:

> During its years of savagery, the race has learned no lessons in emotional control and what they attained during the few generations of slavery left them unstable. For this reason we find deterioration in the emotional sphere most often an early and a persistent manifestation. (p. 396)

Evarts also explained that insanity among Blacks was rare during slavery but became more prevalent after emancipation. He stated: "Because the colored patient already lives upon a plane much lower than his white neighbors, actual deterioration in the individual must be differentiated from the supposed loss of a racial period he has not yet attained" (p. 394).

Another contributor to the first volume of *The Psychoanalytic Review* was Dr. John E. Lind (1913), who was a member of the clinical staff at the Gouverneur Hospital for the Insane. In his article, "The Dream as a Simple Wish-Fulfillment in the Negro," Lind stated that "access to a people the average level of whose development is lower than the white race and which furnishes numerous individuals showing psychological aspects quite similar to those of the savage" (p. 295). Lind argued that the Negro's primitive state and simple mind were similar to those of a White child, and, therefore, Negroes were good subjects for studying Freud's theory that dreams were simple wish fulfillments.

In the same vein, in 1914, E. M. Green, a psychiatrist and Clinical Director at the Georgia State Sanitarium, wrote about the types of psychotic disturbances that differed along racial lines. He noted that the ratio of Blacks to Whites committed to sanitaria had increased from 1870 to 1913. Green (1914) grouped psychoses into three categories. The first group, where the incidence of illness was equal between the races, seemed to be associated with organically based disturbances such as a brain tumor and epileptic psychosis. Organic disturbances, senile psychoses, general paralysis, dementia praecox, and manic-depressive psychoses represented the second category; depression and paranoia represented the third. Overall, these illnesses were low in frequency and were equally prevalent among Blacks and Whites. Instead, Whites were seen more frequently to be victims of mental illnesses that were drug-related and organic such as versions of brain disease, depression, and paranoid conditions. Essentially, Green reasoned that Blacks were too poor to abuse drugs and alcohol. The Negro is less prone to depression and paranoia because, according to Green (1914), "the Negro mind does not dwell upon unpleasant subjects; he is irresponsible, unthinking, easily aroused to happiness, and his unhappiness is transitory, disappearing as a child when other interests attract his attention. He is happy-go-lucky, not philosophical" (p. 703). With respect to paranoia, Green stated:

[T]he Negro is a creature of impulse, logical reasoning is not one of his qualities nor is his behavior usually determined by a thoughtful consideration of its consequences. If the ability to reason from premises and to form conclusions as a result of such reasoning is characteristic of paranoid conditions, it should not be surprising to find that such conditions are more than twice as common in the White as in the Negro race. (p. 703)

According to Green, Blacks were subject to senile psychoses, general paralysis, dementia praecox, and manic-depressive psychoses more often than Whites. Senile psychosis was due to an inability to care for the elderly; general paralysis was due to venereal infections such as syphilis. But why dementia praecox? Green admitted that he did not know, but he felt free to speculate. He described Blacks as suspicious, fearful, and prone to superstitious beliefs. Thus, "the fear of the supernatural, the suspicions of his fellows and the necessity of guarding at all times against bad luck and machinations of enemies, each of these factors may play a part in bringing about a psychosis" (Green, 1914, p. 707).

W. M. Bevis, a psychiatrist at St. Elizabeth's Hospital in Washington, DC, published a paper in 1921 on the psychological traits and psychiatric tendencies of Negroes. He wrote that the low level of evolutionary development characteristic of the Negro leads to particular types of mental disturbances.

[T]he Negro race evinces certain phylogenic traits of character, habit, and behavior that seem sufficiently important to make considerations of these peculiarities worthwhile; especially as these psychic characteristics have their effect upon and are reflected in the psychoses most frequently seen in the Negro. . . . Citizenship with its novel privilege (possibly a greater transition than the first) was thrust upon the race finding it poorly prepared, intellectually, for adjustment to this new social order. Instinctively the Negro turned to the ways of the White man, under whose tutelage he has been, and made an effort to compensate for psychic inferiority by imitating the superior race. (Bevis, 1921, p. 69)

Bevis also described Black traits that are precursors to mental illness, such as laziness, impulsivity, lack of reasoning ability, and suspiciousness. Additionally, he said that Blacks "show no sympathy for each other when in trouble; [are] jolly, careless, and easily amused, but sadness and depression have little part in his psychic make-up" (p.71).

RACE AND PSYCHOLOGICAL TREATMENT

As noted earlier, changes in the sociopolitical environment also affect mental health treatment. The social, economic, and political events from the early 1900s through the 1950s resulted in increased physical and social mobility for people of color, and greater access to treatment. Consequently, more clinical literature described the various issues that visible racial/ethnic group patients or therapists, primarily Black, brought to therapy. Essentially, it was recognized that race stimulated a myriad of issues, mostly associated with the Black or visible racial/ethnic group person.

Adams (1950), Heine (1950), St. Clair (1951), and Kennedy (1952) reported on racial concerns associated with the treatment of Black patients. All clinical scholars acknowledge that Blacks and other people of color were and continue to be subjected to racially based discrimination and social oppression. Nevertheless, the psychological and behavioral patterns they experienced were, and to some degree continue to be, attributed to poor or aberrant ego functioning, uncontrollable id impulses, or an unrestrained superego, rather than to the racial oppression that created their poverty. The dysfunctional personality organization associated with race is thought to produce particularly distinct and difficult transference phenomena. Also, countertransference is thought to be stimulated by the unique problems posed by a patient of color. For the most part, therapists have been instructed to guard against such influences.

The White therapist is instructed to respond to the patient as an individual, rather than a racial being or stereotypic image. But many clinicians and scholars believe that a client of color may use his or her racial experience as a shield against revealing his or her true inner conflicts.

> A therapist may have a patient who rationalizes that death is more desirable than life as a Negro, but this excessive feeling has its origin in other sources. If the therapist gets past his patient's resistance and establishes a positive transference situation, he may discover that it is not inferior status as a Negro that is disturbing; it may be the patient's wounded pride because of his inability to repress his passive feminine wishes, and his lack of masculine attributes. The fantasized castrating agent is probably not altogether the White race, . . . but rather his dominant castrating Negro father, or his dominant and seductive Negro mother, or a weak construction, or more commonly a combination of these factors. (Adams, 1950, p. 308)

According to Adams (1950), this therapeutic approach can create problems or "dangers" in the transference situation for the White therapist: the therapist may be insecure because he or she lacks knowledge about a patient of color's experiences, particularly as it relates to physical appearance or poverty. These circumstances may result in a therapist being indulgent and overly sympathetic toward a client of color.

Heine (1950) argued that while Blacks may experience economic hardships, these disadvantages do not extend to interpersonal experiences except as they produce frustration and hostility. Heine believes that race or concern with one's racial status is a symptom rather than a problem that is appropriate for psychotherapy. Thus, he instructed clinicians:

> As with any other symptom the psychotherapist accepts the patient's account of the discomforts arising out of the symptom but as soon as possible ignores the symptom and leads the patient to explore his feelings and attitudes concerning himself and his relationship with the persons who have had the most significant role in shaping his life. (p. 376)

Kennedy (1952), noting that "the transference phenomenon in Negro and White patients is marked" (p. 313), observed that, for Whites, regardless of ethnic, religious, or regional characteristics, the presentation of his or her individual history is not hampered in the same way as the Blacks' skin color stigmatizes them. He suggested that a White person has more room for "elaboration" and "perception of experience." He added:

> The Negro patient reflects in a unique way the fate he shares with every member of his in-group. Hence his specific life experiences are only

secondarily elaborated, and the development of the individualized ego
is blurred by the phenomenon of color. (p. 313)

Kennedy was emphasizing how the weight and focus of race are borne
by people of color but not by Whites. However, like other clinical scholars, after describing two cases with Black women, Kennedy concluded
that the patients' psychological troubles or neuroses were caused by conflicts associated with "a hostile White ego ideal. The self-hatred generated by the fact of not being White started in earliest infancy"
(p. 325).

In contrast to Kennedy's analysis of the transference issues for Black
clients, Bernard (1953) and Schachter and Butts (1968) focused specifically on interracial transference and countertransference. Bernard suggested that White analysts must be conscious about their own unconscious
needs and prejudices. Also, she noted that a therapist can safeguard
against these unconscious expressions by participating in personal analysis. When the personal analysis fails to uncover or explore unconscious
material associated with one's own and the patient's racial group membership, then a client may not be "protected from the interference of a variety of positive and negative countertransference reactions stimulated by
the ethnic, religious, and racial elements that are present in the analytic
situation" (Bernard, 1953, p. 259).

Bernard pointed out that race (and its significance) may vary for Black
patients, depending on their conscious awareness of its role in their lives.
She felt that both the patient and the White therapist can deny race, and
suggested that White therapists who think they are free of racial prejudice
are particularly prone to denial. "While some White analysts seem compelled to oversympathize the effects of being a Negro . . . others have an
apparent need to deny and sidestep any such effects altogether" (Bernard,
1953, p. 262).

Schachter and Butts (1968) reported on several effects associated with
interracial analysis. They suggested that race may have no effect or influence, or it may be central in the therapy. Racial differences and stereotypes can impede both a therapist and a client in the psychotherapeutic
process (e.g., accepted race-specific cultural behaviors may be misinter-
preted, and important racial material, like racial stereotypes, may be
overlooked by the clinician).

Schachter and Butts (1968) contended that racial differences in therapy have meaning that resides in the subconscious. These differences
must be acknowledged and used, but do not necessarily impede the process of therapy. When racial stereotypes are similar to the client's intrapsychic issues, positive transference can occur. Such transference is
not a true projection of unconscious material pertaining to significant

others in the patient's early life but rather operates as the basis of his or her intrapsychic material.

According to Schachter and Butts (1968), "If the stereotype and the developing transference are both reflections of the analysand's personal difficulties, this confluence of transference and stereotype can facilitate the analysis" (p. 808). The therapist may also use aspects of racial resistance in the course of treatment. In interracial therapy, a White therapist may misread the Black client's pathological character traits as defenses, particularly when they coincide with the therapist's racial stereotypes. Thus, a therapist's lack of racial and cultural knowledge can cause countertransference reactions that hamper and prolong treatment.

More recently Comas-Diaz and Jacobsen (1991) have described ethnocultural transference and countertransference phenomena from interethnic and intra-ethnic perspectives. These authors acknowledge that in the past racial and ethnic issues have been interpreted as underlying "conflicts, defenses, and resistance" (p. 392). They offer and describe a list of reactions that they contend arise from ethnocultural sources. These are basically updated versions of the same issues described by other authors in the past. For instance, ethnocultural issues that occur between groups may be "overcompliant," "mistrust," or "ambivalent." These were alluded to by previous authors. An important contribution that Comas-Diaz and Jacobsen make however is the recognition of within ethnic group issues. They describe several types of transference issues that clients may engage in such as seeing the therapists as the "all knowing therapist" or the "traitor," and so forth. Similarly with countertransference they list possible reactions that are consistent with previous writers. However, these authors do not distinguish race from ethnicity and culture. Thus, even with there elaboration not much emerges about racial effects in psychotherapy.

CULTURAL AND SOCIAL DEPRIVATION PARADIGM

The social activism of the 1950s and 1960s brought about a shift from the inferiority paradigm to the oppression or cultural and social deprivation paradigm. According to Ornstein (1982), concern about social class disparities and the caste structure of the United States captured the interest of scholars well before the political and social movements of the 1960s. Ornstein noted:

[S]ince then educators have become increasingly concerned with the need to study the problems of the poor, in order to remedy their plight. The term "disadvantaged" and its derivative terms "deprived" and "under-privileged" began to appear with reference to the children and youth of lower-class and minority groups. (p. 197)

The cultural and social deprivation or oppression paradigm combines the social and biological meanings of race, creating a criterion whereby visible racial/ethnic group members are compared to a White normative standard to demonstrate the various ways in which visible racial/ethnic group people are socially oppressed, deprived, or deviant. In part, the notion of deprivation began with the works of scholars who wrote about the poverty many Americans experienced during the 1950s and 1960s (Conant, 1961; Harrington, 1963; Riessman, 1962).

The deficit or cultural deprivation view attributes psychological differences between Whites and visible racial/ethnic group members to social oppression or cultural deprivation; by inference, therefore, these differences become the underlying causes for maladaptive behaviors and personalities. Proponents of this perspective assert than uneven economic, social, and cultural experiences are responsible for the apparent psychosocial differences among the "races."

The scholars' focus on the characteristics of social oppression led to studies that catalog the abnormal aspects or effects of poverty and racial discrimination. Consequently, most studies typically report on topics such as discrimination, juvenile delinquency, crime, and poverty. The focus on these negative aspects of a group's sociopolitical and psychosocial life has created a distortion that is ubiquitous in the social and behavioral sciences. As many Black scholars have noted, the literature on Black families displays a "selected focus on the negative aspects" (Thomas & Sillen, 1972, p. 46).

A life of poverty, discrimination, and exclusion from many social institutions (e.g., schools) can have adverse effects on people. Yet, many mental health professionals incorrectly assume that all visible racial/ethnic group members have experienced the destructive influences of racism in society and have been psychologically crippled or destroyed by them. Although it is important to identify the social obstacles that obstruct and hamper an individual's potential, it should not be assumed that these obstacles result in only negative outcomes.

Thus, since the 1960s, the "cultural deprivation" studies have served a useful purpose by highlighting the obstacles facing Black and other visible racial/ethnic group families and children, but these studies often assume that the child is inevitably and permanently damaged by his or her surroundings. For example, Kardiner and Ovesey (1951) published an influential book called *The Mark of Oppression,* which defines the "basic personality" of Blacks in terms of the stigma of their condition in America. These authors believe that racial discrimination produces an unerasable mark that damages the Black person's psyche, suggesting that "there is not one personality trait of the Negro the source of which cannot be traced to the difficult living conditions. There is no exception to this rule. The final result is a wretched internal life" (p. 3). This oppression is presumed to deny Blacks the possibility of developing a positive self-esteem: "The Negro has no possible basis for a healthy self-esteem and every incentive for self-hatred" (p. 3). They deny genetic inferiority and instead offer the idea that discrimination creates a sense of inferiority: "The basic Negro personality is a caricature of the corresponding White personality, because the Negro must adapt to the same culture and must accept the same social goals, but without the ability to achieve them" (p. 317).

These conclusions and generalizations are based on 25 psychoanalytic interviews, where all but one interviewee had a psychological disturbance. Kardiner and Ovesey (1951) stated that their control group is the White American man, and that they

> require no other control. Both he and the Negro live under similar cultural conditions with the exception of a few easily identifiable variables existing for the Negro only. This means we can plot the personality differences of the Negro in terms of these variables against the known personality of the White. (p. 11)

What scholars find disturbing about this work is the liberty taken to offer a psychosocial analysis of a people. Kardiner and Ovesey ignored healthy Blacks or assumed that no psychologically healthy Blacks existed. According to these authors, oppression negatively impacts every Black person, making social relations with other Blacks difficult because of their projected self-contempt.

Kardiner and Ovesey's work was roundly criticized for not acknowledging the variety of individual responses to oppression and stress. For example, Kenneth Clark (1965) noted, in *The Dark Ghetto,*

> Human beings who are forced to live under ghetto conditions and whose daily experience tells them that almost nowhere in society are they respected and granted the ordinary dignity and courtesy accorded others will, as a matter of course, begin to doubt their worth. But the threat to self-esteem does not have uniform consequences. Some individuals may be overwhelmed. Others become aware of the source of the threat, develop appropriate anger at the injustices they suffer and focus their energies on the struggle against oppression. Still others may show a mixture of healthy and unhealthy responses which manifest differently in different situations. (pp. 63–64)

THE PSYCHOLOGICAL INFLUENCE OF RACE IN SOCIETY

Given the social, political, and historical salience of race in our society, it seems reasonable to conclude that it is impossible to be socialized in this society without being presented with several opportunities to internalize beliefs and attitudes about one's racial group. In the sciences and popular culture, the message is that anything other than White cultural norms (e.g., strict familial roles, a future time orientation) is unacceptable in America. African Americans and American Indians, as well as members of other racial groups, have for centuries been the repository for negative projections, distortions, and destructive myths about their race and cultures (Allen, 1994; Franklin, Carter, & Grace, 1993; Frankenberg, 1993).

Such myths and beliefs have been internalized by most Americans, leading to many existing boundaries. No person or professional group, including psychotherapists, is immune to the infectious influence of racism. Nonetheless, few training programs adequately equip their trainees with the knowledge, attitudes, and skills that will allow them to work across racial boundaries that exist in our society. Consequently, much of what is known about race is overwhelmingly negative and focused on visible racial/ethnic group people.

In this chapter, the inferiority and cultural and social deprivation paradigms have been presented and discussed in terms of each model's principal tenets, research studies, and influences on clinical work. In the following chapter, the work of the cultural difference advocates, who use ethnicity and/or culture to explain differences between racial groups, is reviewed.

CHAPTER 3

Psychotherapy with Visible Racial/Ethnic Groups: The Cultural Difference Paradigm

During the past 20 years, social scientists have argued that cultural difference is not synonymous with deviance or deprivation, a view that formed the basis for the cultural and social difference paradigm. The cultural difference (or cultural diversity) paradigm holds that psychological and behavioral differences between Whites and visible racial/ethnic groups are best explained by various influences related to racial and cultural background. Such approaches reject race as a criterion for explaining deprivation or difference and favor criteria such as ethnicity and/or culture. Thus, difference is generally assumed to be determined by social group (ubiquitous), or country (traditional). However, ethnicity and culture are used in ways that in reality refer to racial groups. For instance, *Hispanic,* as noted in Chapter 1, is not a racial group designation based strictly on skin color, because Hispanics cut across all racial lines. Nevertheless, the category functions as a racial marker in that language, physical features, and shared cultural heritage operate as added variables; also, skin color variation among Hispanics influences social inclusion, a point discussed in more detail below. Therefore, although cultural difference adherents argue for cultural and ethnic considerations, they have and continue to use racial categories to characterize visible racial/ethnic group people (i.e., Indians, Asians, Blacks, and Hispanics). In recognition of the cultural difference proponents' use of racial categories when discussing cultural and ethnic factors, these variables will be labeled as such.

Social scientists who have helped establish the cultural difference paradigm have focused their efforts on describing the cultures of various visible racial/ethnic groups and studying the psychological and social variables associated with these specific experiences. Little attention has been given to issues that may surface in therapy. When clinical scholars address the needs of Asian, American Indian, and Hispanic clients, considerable attention has been given, instead, to descriptions of these clients' readiness for therapy or cultural styles that might conflict with traditional treatment (Comas-Diaz & Griffith, 1988). In contrast, much more has been written about the therapeutic process with Black clients. Accordingly, this chapter will reflect this disparity in the literature.

The cultural difference paradigm, currently the most widely endorsed perspective, represents an important advance in our thinking about racial difference. Cultural diversity proponents have helped us acknowledge that racial, class-, and language-bound differences have a profound impact on cross-racial interaction (Sue & Sue, 1990). In terms of mental health practice, advocates of the cultural difference paradigm have slowly begun to develop interventions and instructional guidelines that reflect the racial and cultural experiences of visible racial/ethnic group people. Nevertheless, this paradigm, like the previous perspectives, inflicts the burden of change on those who are racially or culturally different, rather than on the individuals or systems that provide mental health services.

Interest in cross-cultural issues has increased and intensified in many spheres of American life, as evidenced by the proliferation of books and research activities in this area. Authors, scholars, and researchers have offered and continue to offer guidelines, suggestions, research findings, and clinical observations about the status, circumstances, and neglected needs of racial group members, i.e., American Indians, Hispanic, Asian, and African Americans (Pedersen, 1987; Ponterotto, Casas, Suzuki, & Alexander, 1995). Much of the cross-cultural literature suggests that therapists build awareness, increase knowledge with respect to racial groups' cultures, and develop a level of sensitivity to enhance cross-racial effectiveness (Sue, 1981). However, it is unclear from a theoretical position which strategies a cross-racial-cultural therapist should use to be competent.

The literature reviewed in Chapter 2 portrays the White counselor who works with Black clients or clients of color as guilt-ridden, aggressive, inhibited, or ineffective. These presentations have suggested that a White therapist must know himself or herself and his or her culture, as well as the cultures of people of color. Proponents of the cultural difference paradigm contend that understanding variation and difference in cultural patterns is a more salient and useful perspective. Consequently, the focus for many of its proponents has been on describing and comparing racial groups in terms of cultural values. The approach shows the types of influences that cultural values have on therapeutic interactions, and identifies sources of cultural conflict. The term *cultural* will be used during this review, but I maintain that race organizes culture in the United States.

PSYCHOTHERAPY AND CULTURAL VALUES

Many scholars have suggested that, in the psychotherapeutic relationship, cultural values are influential and conflicts may arise from the participants' different cultural values. Writers have argued that therapists must understand their patients' cultural values if they are going to provide effective services. Specifically, Carter (1991) identifies four aspects of the psychotherapy process that may be affected by cultural values: (a) the therapist's racial/cultural background; (b) the patient's racial/cultural background; (c) the assumptions that each participant makes about helping relationships, the nature of the illness, and the locus of problems; and (d) the role of cultural values in the environment where therapy takes place. These aspects of the therapeutic relationship are influenced by racial/cultural socialization and professional training. When mental health professionals refer to cultural encapsulation, they are referring to the therapist's tendency to see the world through his or her own racial/cultural worldview without conscious awareness of this practice. The family provides the primary source of racial/cultural transmissions. A person's expectations, perceptions, feelings, thoughts, behaviors, and way of organizing information are representations of the family's racial and cultural teachings. Because most therapists are White, it seems appropriate to begin with a description of Whites' racial/cultural patterns.

WHITE AMERICAN CULTURAL PATTERNS

Some social scientists argue that there is no distinct White American cultural pattern. However, Katz (1985) and Stewart and Bennett (1991) believe that White Americans share a common set of racial and cultural values and beliefs. Katz suggests that White American culture is the integration of ideas, values, and beliefs from descendants of White European ethnic groups in the United States. Thus, she contends that White cultural patterns are superordinate to ethnic background. Some of the dimensions that characterize White culture are: individualism or excessive self-centered worldview and a tendency to focus on one's personal preferences; an action orientation measured by external accomplishments and a strong need to conform to social rules; a majority rule decision-making system when Whites are in power—otherwise, a hierarchical structure is used; a communication system that relies on written and "standard" English forms; a view of time as a commodity; a religious system primarily based on Judeo-Christian ideals; social customs (e.g., holidays) founded on celebrations of the Christian religion, White American history, and male leaders; a patriarchal and nuclear family structure as the ideal social unit; and aesthetic qualities that emphasize music and art and a philosophical system and existential notions of life and reality based on European cultures. Katz (1985) also suggests that these White American cultural values form the basis of psychotherapeutic theory and practice.

The similarities between White culture and the cultural values that form the foundations of traditional counseling theory and practice exist and are interchangeable. Because counseling theory and practice developed out of the experience of White therapists and researchers working almost exclusively with White client systems, it comes as no surprise that the profession reflects White cultural values. The continued use of this theory base predicated on one world view, one set of assumptions concerning human behavior, and one set of values concerning mental health limits our abilities to be effective cross-culturally. (p. 619)

COMPARING CULTURAL VALUES USING THE KLUCKHOHN AND STRODTBECK MODEL

Kluckhohn and Strodtbeck (1961) offered a value-orientations model for comparing racial groups' cultural styles (Table 3.1). In the model, participants are asked to solve five common problems with three possible solutions. The five problems are:

1. What is the innate character of human nature (Evil, Mixed, or Good)?
2. What is the relationship between people and nature (Subjugation, Harmony, or Mastery)?
3. What is the temporal focus of the culture (Past, Present, or Future)?
4. What is the appropriate form of self-expression (Being, Being-in-Becoming, or Doing)?
5. What are the proper social relations (Lineal, Collateral, or Individual)?

Researchers (e.g., Carter, 1990a; Kluckhohn & Strodtbeck, 1961; Papajohn & Spiegel, 1975) have found that dominant White American cultural values can be characterized by preferences for an Evil or Mixed human nature, Mastery over Nature, a Future time sense, a Doing activity orientation, and Individual social relations.

LEARNING ABOUT CULTURAL VALUES

People seldom question their racial/cultural learning except when they encounter others who are different and have divergent worldviews. Consequently, only Whites who have experienced themselves in racially/culturally different relationships have the opportunity to develop knowledge and awareness of themselves as racial/cultural beings.

TABLE 3.1   Kluckhohn and Strodtbeck Value-Orientations Model with Alternative Solutions

Orientation		Alternatives	
Mode of Human Nature	*Evil:* People are born with evil inclinations.	*Mixed:* Humans are born both good and evil.	*Good:* Humans are born basically good.
Mode of Person/Nature	*Subjugation to Nature:* Nature guides one's life.	*Harmony with Nature:* Nature is one's partner in life.	*Mastery over Nature:* Nature is used for one's own purpose.
Time Sense Mode	*Past:* Traditional customs are paramount.	*Present:* Here-and-now events are most important.	*Future:* Planning for events that are to occur receives primary attention.
Activity Mode	*Being:* Activity is spontaneous self-expression.	*Being-in-Becoming:* Activity is integrated in the personality.	*Doing:* Externally goals are the source of action-oriented self-expression.
Social Relations Mode	*Lineal:* Lines of authority are clearly established based on kinship or heredity.	*Collateral:* Group-oriented goals are most important.	*Individual:* Individual goals are most important.

From "Cultural Value Differences between African Americans and White Americans" by R. T. Carter (1990), *Journal of College Student Development, 31*, pp. 71–79. Copyright 1990 by Journal of College Student Development, American Counseling and Personnel Association. Adapted by permission.

White Americans' worldview influences the way they live and develop. For example, the Future temporal preference is expressed in the manner in which White Americans plan their families, educations, and occupations. The Doing preference for self-expression is seen in how Whites compete for upward mobility and control their feelings in most human interactions. From childhood, White Americans are taught to be independent, and to express their own needs and desires. The dominant American choices in each cultural value dimension fit together nicely.

> Thus, if the personal achievement implied by Doing is to be facilitated, then it is good to be able to plan for the Future, as an Individual not too constrained by family or group ties, with optimism supplied by the Mastery-over-Nature orientation, and the pragmatic morality, with which such self-interest is justified, afforded by the Neutral [mixed alternative] view of the Basic Nature of Man. (Spiegel, 1982, p. 42)

Because White Americans' racial/cultural values are transmitted from an early age and the five domains are so interconnected, it is usually accepted that cultural values play an important role in how participants respond and behave in cross-racial psychotherapy.

THERAPY PROCESS INVOLVING BLACK/AFRICAN AMERICANS

The literature reviewed in Chapter 2 suggests that the White counselor's racial attitudes are an important variable that influences his or her response to racially different clients. That is, White therapists' strategies, interventions, affect, and effectiveness with racially different clients appear to be related to their racial attitudes and cultural background.

The role and influence of race have been debated in the counseling literature for many decades. The debate has been guided by the inferiority and cultural and social deprivation paradigms. Particularly during the early 20th century, the debate primarily focused on Black and White therapeutic dyads. Some authors, theorists, and researchers have argued that Blacks are not suitable for psychotherapy because of their inherent personality characteristics (e.g., resistance, suspiciousness), their inability to comprehend the nature of psychotherapy (e.g., the verbal self-exploratory process), and the effects of their oppressed status in American society.

In addition, White middle-class mental health professionals have typically treated Blacks and other visible racial/ethnic group people as if they were devoid of specific cultures and have assumed that they should adapt themselves to traditional psychotherapeutic practices. The manner in which people of color should adapt themselves to traditional counseling approaches has been less a question of how racial and cultural issues influence the psychotherapy process and more a matter of how visible racial/ethnic people can be taught and prepared to benefit from traditional treatment approaches (Garfield, 1978).

Nevertheless, the preceding review of the psychotherapy literature and other independent reviews (e.g., Highlen & Hill, 1984; Orlinsky & Howard, 1978; Parloff, Waskow, & Wolfe, 1978) suggest that race influences the therapeutic process for the therapist, the patient, and their interactions. This chapter describes a body of literature that attempts to consider the effects of race and/or culture from the cultural difference perspective, keeping in mind that these terms are often used interchangeably in much of the mental health literature.

Numerous scholars have written about cross-racial dyads in therapy (Adams, 1970; Berman, 1979; Cooper, 1973; Franklin et al., 1993; Gardner, 1971; Green, 1985, 1993; Grier & Cobbs, 1968; Griffith, 1977; Jackson, 1973; Jackson, 1983; Jones & Seagull, 1977; Mays, 1985; Sager, Brayboy, & Waxenberg, 1972; St. Clair, 1951; Samuels, 1972; Seward, 1972; Szasz, 1971; Thomas & Dansby, 1985; Thomas & Sillen, 1972; Thompson & Jenal, 1994; Turner & Armstrong, 1981; Vontress, 1969, 1970, 1971). Many writers who have discussed cross-racial therapy have focused primarily on the historical, political, and sociocultural experience of Black and White relationships in American society. Only later were other racial groups (e.g., Asians, Hispanics) included in these discussions. Most authors have suggested that racial stereotypes and cultural biases that exist in American society are also generally present in cross-racial therapy relationships.

Brown (1950) surveyed social work agencies in different states to determine whether race was a salient variable in the therapeutic practice of social workers. In general, the replies she received from caseworkers and social work agency personnel suggested that race was a complex and emotionally laden issue in social work treatment. She found that Black clients had different reactions, depending on the caseworker's race. Some Blacks welcomed a Black caseworker; others felt that a Black professional, because of a shared inferior social status in American society, was unable to assist them. Other Black clients, who identified with Whites, completely rejected Black caseworkers, believing that they were inferior. In addition, Brown found that Black caseworkers experienced more difficulty with an all-Black caseload than did their White counterparts. Caseworkers and agency personnel believed that Black caseworkers were more punitive with Black clients than with White clients. This finding suggests that the Black caseworkers may have identified with Whites and/or internalized society's negative stereotypes of Blacks.

Green (1985), Gardner (1971), Mays (1985), and Jones and Seagull (1977) suggest that the therapist and client each have personal biases regarding race and racism and that a White therapist's cultural background may create racial distortions. These same authors comment that much of the intra- and intergroup relations literature is based on observation, opinion, and conjecture rather than on established scientific data. They propose, therefore, that the observer's or therapist's descriptions of interracial interactions may be distorted and misrepresented; yet, these descriptions form the basis for White and Black psychotherapists to explore and come to terms with their feelings about racial issues. Furthermore, Gardner notes that although psychoanalytic and psychodynamic writings have contributed to the understanding of Black personality development and adaptations, this literature contains a curious "admixture of objective reporting, ethnocentric distortions, updated racial mythology, and paternalistic exhortations" (p. 79).

Given the range of racial attitudes and beliefs held by White therapists, one might ask how these beliefs affect White therapist/Black client interactions in treatment. Gardner (1971) believes that each participant in an interracial interaction approaches the other cautiously while attempting to discover his or her racial attitudes. When a White therapist who has avoided racial issues is confronted with a Black client who stirs up these issues, this therapist may reject the client either by referring him or her to another therapist or agency, or by providing impersonal treatment (i.e., medication). Additionally, a White therapist may use reaction formation as a defense mechanism when confronted with a racially different client, causing him or her to overidentify with the client. The White therapist's effort to cope with his or her racial hostility often results in oversympathizing or attributing all of the client's difficulties to matters of racial difference (Green, 1985) (see Chapter 2). A therapist may view the Black client as emotionally and cognitively damaged by racism and oppression (Kardiner & Ovesey, 1951). For example, the therapist may view the Black client as a victim of racism and consequently may feel guilty. A guilt-ridden therapist could affect the client's treatment in various ways (e.g., overindulging the client, misperceiving the Black client's anger, or becoming defensive) (Adams, 1950; Cooper, 1973; Gardner, 1971; Green, 1985, 1993; Grier & Cobbs, 1968; Mays, 1985; Turner & Armstrong, 1981; Thompson & Jenal, 1994; Vontress, 1971). Additionally, when a White therapist communicates, either overtly or covertly, his or her own race-related anxieties, a Black client may become defensive (Jones & Seagull, 1977).

So far, the discussion about White clinicians involved in cross-racial therapy has involved conscious awareness of the client's race. However, it is also possible for a White therapist to deny the client's color and to react to the client as though he or she were colorless (Sager et al., 1972). A therapist who operates from this perspective is more likely to exert his or her power in the therapeutic relationship (i.e., have the client accommodate the therapist). Unfortunately, a therapist who does not allow the client to define himself or herself in the relationship typically behaves in a paternalistic, patronizing fashion (Jackson, 1973; Jones & Seagull, 1977; Seward, 1972; Vontress, 1971).

Furthermore, a White therapist may display to a Black client a variety of reactions, including: inhibiting his or her own aggressiveness and assertiveness to avoid feeling or acting bossy; apologizing for being White by denying White abilities, privilege, and power; avoiding issues that may be painful to the client; and hindering spontaneity for fear that he or she might say or do something that would expose his or her prejudice.

In those instances in which therapists inhibit themselves, their verbal behavior may involve more efforts to seek information than to build the relationship (Jackson, 1973; Samuels, 1972; Sattler, 1977). In Berman's (1979) study, Black and White trainees viewed videotapes of a White, Black, or Hispanic client and indicated how they would counsel each client. When Berman compared White and Black counseling styles with the different racial groups, he found that White counselors primarily used attending skills 84% of the time, that is, they used open- and closed-ended questions, paraphrased, and reflected feelings. Fry, Kropf, and Coe (1980) found that White and Black counselor trainees used fewer attending skills (asking open- and closed-ended questions, paraphrasing, and reflecting feelings) and more expressive or active counseling skills (e.g., being directive and offering interpretations) with Black clients than with White clients.

Most studies that have examined the White therapist and Black client dyad have discussed barriers White counselors may experience when working with Black clients (e.g., Parker & McDavis, 1983; Vontress, 1971). Few studies have examined a Black client's perspective when working with a White therapist. Therefore, it is necessary to examine the existing literature on the effects of race in psychotherapy to hypothesize about how a Black client might experience the counseling relationship with a White therapist. This examination will be guided by two central questions: (a) Do the Black client's racial attitudes affect the way he or she reacts to a White therapist? and (b) What emotional responses characterize the Black client/White therapist dyad? But, before exploring these questions, a description of Black/African American cultural values is in order.

Black Cultural Values

Black cultural values are characterized by beliefs in Collateral group relations, or sharing, Present time, and Harmony with Nature or Spirituality

(Carter & Helms, 1987). The major strengths of Black families, as described by Hines and Boyd-Franklin (1982) and Boyd-Franklin (1989), have been and continue to be their role adaptations. Hill (1972) suggested that although slavery and socioeconomic oppression attempted to destroy Black families, they have survived because of strong kinship bonds, flexible family roles, and the high value placed on religion, education, and work (Thomas & Dansby, 1985). According to Boyd-Franklin (1989), Black families are organized around extended kinship networks that may include blood- and non-blood-related persons. Family roles, responsibilities, and jobs are often interchanged among family members. Family functions are shared across generation lines and gender. Blacks also participate in social equalizer roles and activities in the community or churches. These roles and activities are used by many Blacks and other visible racial/ethnic group people to reinforce their self-worth (Carter & Cook, 1992).

It is important for counselors to understand the Black family's strong emphasis on work and education. As Pinderhughes (1982) points out, the efforts of Black parents to instill the value of education and work are continually undermined by the realities of a racist American society. Black parents expect their children to take advantage of opportunities and to strive for a better life than their own (Boyd-Franklin, 1989). Children who earn a living and maintain themselves are as likely to receive parental approval as those who pursue professional careers. The cultural values of Blacks and their families may lead them to mental health professionals who have a Present orientation or a Collateral worldview.

Black Clients and Psychotherapy

It appears that Black clients pay close attention to signals that reveal White counselors' racial attitudes (Grier & Cobbs, 1968; Griffith, 1977; Mays, 1985; Sager et al., 1972; St. Clair, 1951; Vontress, 1969) and thereby influence the way Black clients behave in therapy. For instance, a Black client may be sensitive to a White therapist's efforts to avoid racial issues, which may further reinforce barriers to the therapeutic process (Beaton, 1974). If a White therapist behaves in a paternalistic and patronizing fashion, a Black client may experience the therapist as condescending (Seward, 1972; Vontress, 1971) and become enraged. Additionally, if a Black client is sensitive to a White therapist's race-related anxiety, he or she may become defensive and cease self-exploration (Jones & Seagull, 1977).

It is also possible that a Black client may enter the relationship with a number of defenses related to race. He or she may have anxieties about a White therapist that are rooted in a culturally conditioned "paranoia" around the White race. This race-related paranoia probably will compound any anxieties related to merely entering a therapeutic relationship (Carter, 1991; Pinderhughes, 1973).

Majors and Nikelly (1983) note that lower-class Blacks in treatment view White middle-class therapists as representatives of mainstream American society. When these Black clients enter therapeutic situations with White therapists, they do so with a cultural perspective of maintaining their "cool." Thus, lower-class Black clients may be less verbal and less likely to self-disclose, and may be anxious that they will be rejected or punished for their skin color. They often perceive White therapists as being distant and unable to relate to Black experiences. More importantly, many Black clients may simply desire a therapy relationship in which they can self-disclose without having to educate the White therapist about Black culture and being Black in America (Ridley, 1995; Thompson & Janel, 1994).

The studies previously cited (e.g., Majors & Nikelly, 1983), in which Black clients' therapy experiences were described, have suggested that the Black client who enters counseling with a White therapist may be preoccupied with discovering the therapist's level of racial awareness and may be beset with anxieties associated with his or her Blackness and status in American society. Consequently, the client may be less actively involved in the process and may react negatively to the White therapist's counseling interventions. Beyond anxiety, the Black client may exhibit feelings of guilt, resentment, and hostility either toward himself or herself or the therapist. In such instances, one would expect the client to either terminate prematurely or leave with little symptom relief. It may be concluded that client/counselor same-race pairs would reduce the range of possible issues encountered in cross-racial therapy. The counseling process literature involving White therapists and Black clients may lead one to believe that Black clients should be seen by Black therapists, a view supported by some discussants (e.g., Banks, 1977; Calnek, 1970; Vontress, 1971). This view is based on the premise that Black therapists and Black clients have similar racial issues, and, therefore, racial issues will not impede the therapeutic process (Banks, 1972; Calnek, 1970; Jones, 1991).

Some authors have argued that Black therapists, because of their presumed experience of oppression and discrimination as a Black person, are better suited to treat Black clients than White therapists. However, this may not be so. A general criticism of mental health training programs is that they do not train mental health professionals to be racially or culturally aware or competent, nor do they provide trainees with theoretical or practical knowledge that will facilitate their work with culturally different clients. Bell (1971) notes that Black therapists, like White therapists, are usually trained to work with White clients. Cultural differences and issues specific to people of color are seldom included in the theories presented and practice provided in training programs. When working with Black clients, Black therapists, therefore, are subject to many of the same pitfalls as White therapists.

Calnek (1970) believes that the Black therapist must cope with his or her own feelings regarding racism and discrimination, and suggests that Black therapists must examine the extent to which they see themselves in other Blacks and monitor their racial stereotypes about Blacks. In effect, Calnek suggests that a Black therapist working with a Black client must monitor possible countertransferential reactions.

On the other hand, Banks (1972) notes that many Black therapists who have attained middle- and upper-class status may adopt White middle- and upper-class customs, behaviors, and values and choose not to identify with Black clients and Black culture. This rise in status, he suggests, may lead a Black therapist to deny any identification with a Black client or to acknowledge the client's Blackness and its influence on his or her life. Calnek (1970) suggests that both the therapist and client may become angry and hostile when examining Blacks' disparaged position in society. Therefore, he argues, "one way to forestall the possibility of loss of emotional control is to avoid the entire matter of race" (p. 41). However, the other side of denial is overidentification. That is, a Black therapist working with a Black client may overemphasize racial issues or may presume that race is important when the client may not hold such a view.

It is possible for a Black therapist to react to a Black client in a manner similar to that of his or her White colleagues. Banks (1975) cautions Black and White therapists to be aware of their racial attitudes while working with Black clients, and other writers have supported this view (e.g., Cohen, 1974; Harper, 1973; Helms & Carter, 1991; Jackson, 1973; McDavis & Parker, 1977; Vontress, 1971). However, Turner and Armstrong (1981), in a study of Black and White counselors, found that Black and White therapists differ in their reactions and attitudes toward cross-racial experiences. These authors conclude that "Black therapists treating Black clients emphasize, make salient, and bring forth the psychological significance of the client's race more often than White therapists with Black clients" (p. 377).

It is interesting how little has been written about the counseling process involving Black therapists and White clients. There are two ways to explain the paucity of literature concerning Black therapist/White client dyads: (a) there are relatively few of these dyads and many more White therapist/Black client dyads, and (b) perhaps scholars do not view this dyad as problematic or interesting.

Fooks (1973) observes that a Black therapist working with a White client can be either productive or unproductive. One view is that the therapist's skin color elicits fear and anxiety in a White client, creating resistance toward the therapist (Curry, 1964). A White client may become preoccupied with a therapist's race, which can hamper the treatment process. In some instances, the therapist must not allow his or her own race to be a barrier to treatment. As some writers (e.g., Grier, 1967) have suggested, transference and countertransference issues may be used to facilitate rather than hinder treatment.

In summary, some writers have assumed that one way to cope with the influence of race in psychotherapy is to have members of the same racial groups treat one another (e.g., Blacks treating Blacks). However, the notion that same-race dyads will be devoid of racial issues appears to be unsupported by the literature, which suggests that racial issues still may be present in Black therapist/Black client dyads.

The counseling process literature involving Asians, Native (Indian) Americans, and Hispanics is seldom presented in terms of dyadic interactions. For the most part, scholars and researchers discuss process issues in therapy from the perspective of the counselor or the client separately. Therefore, the following section will deviate from the previous one in that the psychotherapeutic process will be discussed in terms of separate counselor and client issues and concerns. Moreover, for these groups, most writers have avoided race, in spite of the fact that members of the Asian, American Indian, and Hispanic groups, particularly those group members who tend to be historically disenfranchised, are identifiable based on skin color, physical features, or language. Those who are less visible or who are racially White may experience greater social acceptance. Nevertheless, most writers have chosen to emphasize cultural traits or adaptations rather than racial issues. In the literature, one finds discussions of conflicts in cultural values and descriptions of within-group cultural preferences so that mental health providers can learn how to provide effective treatment. Assimilation, acculturation, communication styles, gender roles, and group-specific meaning systems are delineated and explained. In the hope of guiding the therapist, less is said about what might occur in the therapy interaction. Thus, the information presented in the following sections will be quite different from that of the previous section.

NATIVE (INDIAN) AMERICAN CULTURAL VALUES

American Indian and Alaska Native families and cultures have been described, using the Kluckhohn and Strodtbeck (1961) values model, as indicating preferences for a Present time, Harmony with Nature, Collateral social relations, Being-in-Becoming activity, and a Good human nature (Atteneave, 1982; Dufrene & Coleman, 1994; Garrett & Garrett, 1994; Herring, 1994; Peregory, 1993). Time for Native Americans is cyclical and rhythmic, and events that are important "are geared to personal and seasonal rhythms rather than ordered and organized by external and me-chanical clocks or calendars" (Atteneave, 1982, p. 62). Native Ameri-cans' cultural patterns are geared toward natural forces as a way of maintaining their sense of harmony with nature. However, when this is not possible, generational and intrapsychic conflicts may arise and be-come obstacles for Native American families to overcome. The group orientation is for individuals to subordinate their wishes and wills to the decisions and consensus of the group. Atteneave (1982) offers the fol-lowing description of a Native American cultural orientation:

> Emphasis on group collaterality and identity, including the shared pos-sessions and rapid redistribution of excess, is again a source of ambiva-lence and tension for the urbanized Indian. This problem becomes more marked when an urban Indian family establishes itself with employment or when a student receives a stipend or fellowship. . . . Other Indian rel-atives see it as something to be shared. They cannot be Indian and at the same time be self-centered. . . . This tradition hinders more promising careers than perhaps any other obstacle to adaptation into full participa-tion in the life of contemporary urban American society. (p. 69)

American Indian Clients and Psychotherapy

Devereux (1951), Trimble (1976), LaFromboise, Trimble, and Mohatt (1990), Thomason (1991), and Garrett and Garrett (1994) have written about mental health treatment for American Indians. Much of this liter-ature serves to educate a therapist about the cultural characteristics of In-dians that will enhance treatment. Devereux (1951), writing about Plains Indians, describes cultural issues that surfaced in his analytic treatment of three Indians who were "extensively acculturated . . . their Indian her-itage—which they themselves sometimes believed to be peripheral to their personality structure—played an important role in their neuroses, and materially influenced the course of their treatment" (p. 411).

Devereux illustrates that a lack of knowledge regarding Indian customs and traditions inhibits a therapist's ability to understand and interpret transference reactions and dreams. He shows that a patient's projections, attitudes, and behaviors toward a therapist were "echoes of earlier signif-icant interpersonal relationships" (p. 412). He offers examples from his cases to illustrate how racial/cultural knowledge of Indians is critical for interpreting transference material. Devereux argues that psychotherapists must be aware that, in Plains Indian culture, dreams play an important social role and are integral to many activities in the population. He sug-gests that the manifest content (i.e., the actual content of the dream) lim-its the latent or symbolic content that requires interpretation. Thus, dreams, for Plains Indians, do not require symbolic interpretation because the meaning is apparent even to the dreamer. For Devereux, assimilated Indians still have access to simple, uncomplicated, unconscious dream material.

When working with people from visible racial/ethnic groups, Devereux believes that a therapist must avoid his or her tendency to see the "patient's illness in [terms] of the therapist's own concept of 'health'" (p. 420). Rather, treatment objectives should help people to live well within their sociopolitical context. He warns therapists not to "attempt to transfer a Plains Indian into a go-getting, rugged individualist . . . because to do so would create a patient with high aspirations that would be incompatible with external restrictions" (p. 420) imposed on American Indians by a racist White society.

Trimble (1976) emphasizes the importance of cultural value differences between Indian clients and White counselors. He describes the values of Indian culture, contrasts them with those of Euro-American culture, and delineates the counseling process. According to the Kluckhohn and Strodtbeck (1961) cultural values model, American Indians have a Present time orientation; time is less often present in the language system or consciousness of many Indians than it is for White Americans. Respect for elders, in contrast to the glorification of youths, is characteristic of many Native American people, as is harmony with nature and social cooperation. Thus, according to Trimble (1976), "understanding of salient and specific value differences is the key to successful counseling and psychiatric interviewing" (p. 77), particularly when participants in the therapeutic dyad are from distinctly different cultures and, therefore, "look at the other's behavior from a different frame of reference" (p. 77). Communication and mutual understanding and respect between the therapist and client are core problems when cultures are different (LaFromboise et al., 1990). Moreover, counselors overwhelmed by cultural differences are likely to ignore these problems and be prone to the countertransferential errors described in Chapter 2.

Thomason (1991) offers a model for treating Native Americans that he contends is derived from aspects of their cultures. He cautions that American Indians are culturally diverse and notes that the legal requirement for American Indian classification is "a person who is an enrolled/registered member of a tribe or someone who has at least one-fourth or more Native American blood" (p. 321).

With respect to psychotherapy, Thomason and others (e.g., Dufrene & Coleman, 1994; Garrett & Garrett, 1994; Herring, 1994) suggest that a counselor should not ask direct questions, should expect family members to be present, and should be problem-focused. Additionally, he recommends that a counselor should learn about the client's tribal culture, with respect to beliefs, customs, history, tribal organization, family structures, generational, gender, and power roles, and the meanings associated with different types of nonverbal and paralinguistic behaviors. He also suggests that a counselor understand the preferred modes of healing and know how tribal members might address the types of problems presented in counseling sessions.

In summary, a counselor must consider the Native American Indian client's acculturative status, physical appearance, and lifestyle preferences (Dufrene & Coleman, 1994; Garrett & Garrett, 1994; Herring, 1994; LaFromboise et al., 1990). A client who is characterized as traditional may not maintain eye contact, talk about his or her problems in a personal way, or self-disclose, and may act passively (Trimble & Fleming, 1989). In contrast, a client who is characterized as assimilated or acculturated will have a general understanding of the counseling process and his or her role in this process (Garrett & Garrett, 1994). Trimble and Fleming (1989) suggest that a counselor can be effective with an Indian client if the counselor can communicate and exhibit behaviors that characterize traditional helpers such as shamans, spirit healers, and medicine people. They describe a traditional healer's qualities as exemplifying "empathy, genuineness, availability, respect, worth, congruence, and concreteness. . . . Effective counseling with Indians begins when a counselor carefully attends to these basic characteristics" (p. 185). These characteristics, however, must be expressed with an understanding of Indian culture and its variations. A mental health professional needs concrete and specific cultural knowledge to be effective in therapy with Native American Indians because they may present with psychological orientations unfamiliar to the clinician.

ASIAN AMERICAN CULTURAL VALUES

During the past two decades, America's Asian population has become increasingly ethnically diverse (Leong, 1986; Sue & Sue, 1990). Prior to 1960, Chinese, Japanese, and Filipinos were the dominant groups. Now, Koreans, Asian Indians, Vietnamese, Cambodian, and other groups are also significant within America's Asian population (Axelson, 1993; Lin, 1994; Solberg, Ristma, Davis, Tata, & Jolly, 1994; Sue, 1994; Sue & Sue, 1971, 1990; Tata & Leong, 1994).

Since the beginning of Asian civilizations, their cultural systems have been guided by many philosophies. Two of the most influential were the ideas of Confucius and Buddha. Shon and Ja (1982) describe Asian cultural systems as follows:

Those systems do not stress independence and autonomy of the individual but rather that the individual is superseded by the family.

Furthermore, the family adheres to the Confucianistic tradition of specific hierarchical roles established for all members. Rules of behavior and conduct are formalized in members' roles to a greater extent than in most other cultures. An individual's response and adherence to this code of conduct becomes a reflection not of the individual but of the family and kinship network to which he or she belongs. (p. 209)

In Asian family culture, the individual is viewed as a product of his or her ancestry line. According to Shon and Ja (1982), this belief is reflected in "rituals and customs such as ancestor worship and family record books which trace family members back over many centuries" (p. 211). Other influences on Asian cultures come from other religious and philosophical thoughts such as Hinduism, Taoism, Shintoism, and Christianity (Axelson, 1993). Sue and Sue note that "[A]lthough the Asian immigrants and refugees form very diverse groups, there are certain areas of commonality such as deference to authority, emotional restraint, specified roles and hierarchical family structure and family and extended family orientation" (p. 197).

The socialization processes used in many Asian families usually employ shame and loss of face to reinforce prescribed sets of obligations (Shon & Ja, 1982). Obligation is central in Asian cultures and families and is acquired through relationships of ascribed roles or status, such as parent and child, and employer and employee. The strongest obligation is to one's parents. Because an individual always seeks to maintain harmonious interpersonal relationships, family obligations are communicated indirectly and without confrontation.

Asian American Clients and Psychotherapy

Kitano (1989) offers a model for treating Asian Americans that he believes can be used with a variety of Asian groups. He contends that "two variables . . . appear most critical when dealing with Asian Americans . . . assimilation and ethnic identity" (p. 142). Assimilation refers to how Americanized or acculturated the person has become, and ethnic identity "refers to the retention of customs, attitudes, and beliefs of the culture of origin" (Kitano, 1989, p. 142). According to Kitano's model, assimilation includes such things as social integration and acculturation, and is correlated with ethnic identity (Atkinson & Gim, 1989; Axelson, 1993; Solberg et al., 1994; Sue & Sue, 1990; Tusi & Schultz, 1985). Therapists should attempt to understand where a client is in the model and discover where he or she might want to be in the future. The interaction of these two variables gives rise to four categories:

Type A—high assimilation and low ethnic identity;
Type B—high assimilation and high ethnic identity;
Type C—high ethnic identity and low assimilation;
Type D—low ethnic identity and low assimilation.

An Asian who has a low ethnic identity and a high level of assimilation (i.e., Type A) is described as basically "American" in culture, values, and language, and the person's ethnic origin is barely evident in his or her lifestyle (e.g., clothes). Kitano (1989) states that "generation and length of time in America are the most important factors influencing this category . . . a counselor is dealing with an 'American' but one with an Asian face" (p. 144). Nevertheless, a counselor should be mindful that "the reality of looking different in a society in which role models are primarily Caucasian, . . . precludes complete absorption into the mainstream. Counseling that ignores this factor may foster unrealistic expectations and a barrier to credibility" (p. 144). Consequently, a counselor should cautiously use his or her knowledge about Asian cultures when working with a Type A client (Tata & Leong, 1994).

An Asian client who is highly assimilated and has a high ethnic identity (i.e., Type B) is bicultural: he or she is psychologically and emotionally comfortable with both cultures. This individual will have social networks in both cultures and will possibly belong to organizations oriented to each culture. Kitano (1989) believes that "few people at present fall in this category" (p. 145). However, Lin (1994) found that more Chinese Americans will stay in psychotherapy if they are matched with an ethnic and language-similar therapist. These findings are supportive of previous research with other Asian ethnic groups (Kim, Lee, Chu, & Cho, 1989; Sue, Fujino, Hu, Takeuchi, & Zane, 1991).

An Asian client who has a high ethnic identity and low level of assimilation (i.e., Type C) is someone who retains traditional ways and avoids assimilation. People in the Type C category usually remain in ethnic enclaves or are at an age when change is undesirable. A client in this category is more likely to express emotions, such as anger, indirectly than directly. Many clients will be reluctant to share specific details about themselves and may be modest and self-deprecating. These cultural styles should not be mistaken for signs of poor self-image. Also, clients may be less willing to share information about familial and sexual matters than to discuss physical symptoms and bodily discomforts. Thus, with these clients, therapists should explore symptoms for their cultural significance. Talking about emotions, increasing introspection, and sharing feelings are not common in Asian cultures. Instead, in most Asian cultures, "disturbed behavior is often viewed as a result of a lack of will, supernatural causes, or physical illness" (Kitano, 1989, p. 146). Based on these cultural styles, some researchers and clinicians have advised counselors to use short sessions and short-term, directive treatment strategies in treating Types A through C Asians.

An individual with a low ethnic identity and a low assimilation level (i.e., Type D) is described as a dropout because he or she feels alienated from both Asians and Americans. A person in this category may have severe psychological and social problems.

In summary, Asian Americans' levels of acculturation and ethnic identity will in part determine how a therapist might provide effective mental health services. It should also be pointed out that the model minority notion often applied to Asian Americans may operate to blind therapists from important psychological and several stresses experienced by members of the group (Crystal, 1989). Sue (1994) warns that the model minority notion detracts from the history of racism and discrimination experienced by many Asian groups, ignores within group differences, pits Asians against other visible racial/ethnic groups, and minimizes their mental health needs. "A closer analysis of the status and treatment of Asians in the United States does not support the myth of their success. The historical treatment of Asian Americans has been filled with examples of prejudice and discrimination. . . ." (p. 292). He goes on to observe that the economic success story of Asians does not account for the number of family members working, the experience of poverty among Asians, low wages given their educational attainment and so on. More importantly, Sue argues that Asian cultural values influence their use of mental health services and symptom formation and expression. He states "Asians are more likely to express psychological conflicts somatically and to present their problems in a much more symbolic and circuitous manner than their counterparts" (p. 293). Sue notes that race influences one's personality and one's level of investment in his or her race or culture will affect the manner and form of symptom expression.

HISPANIC AMERICANS' (LATINOS') CULTURAL VALUES

Like Asian Americans, Hispanic Americans are ethnically diverse (Axelson, 1993). The term *Hispanic* was created by Americans to group people who share a language and a cultural heritage derived from Spanish colonialism. Unlike other groups, Latinos are racially diverse, with race and skin color ranging from White to Black. Mexicans, Puerto Ricans, Cubans, and Central and South Americans represent the largest Hispanic groups in America (Marger, 1994).

The skin-color variation that characterizes Hispanics is due to the mixing of Indian, African, and European people. Marger (1991) suggests that

Mexicans in the United States are mostly mestizos (meaning that their ancestors were Spaniards and Native Americans) but are physically distinct from most White Americans. According to Marger, "Puerto Ricans inherit a racial background that is a combination primarily of European and African with some Indian elements" (p. 282). Thus, despite a wide color range among Puerto Ricans, many "are racially intermediate" (p. 282). As Marger points out:

> On the island, racial distinctions are not so acute, and one's color is seen along a scale, or continuum. . . . But problems arise in the United States, where there is a racial dichotomy, allowing for no intermediate categories. Many who are "White" on the island may find themselves classified as "Black" when they come to the mainland. (p. 282)

On the other hand, Cubans in the United States have less racial variation than Puerto Ricans, and most would be classified as White. Marger (1991) notes:

> An entire range of attitudes and actions has characterized the relations between Anglos and the several Hispanic groups. Variations have turned on the group's historical context, its geographic location, and its racial make-up. Those closer to the dominant Anglo group, like Cubans, have experienced only minimal prejudice and discrimination; at the other extreme, dark-skinned Puerto Ricans have suffered ethnic antagonism equal in form and degree to that suffered by African Americans. (p. 304)

There is ethnic variability among Latino Americans (e.g., Puerto Rican, Cuban, and Mexican) and there are class differences. Value systems are greatly influenced by socioeconomic status. Some Latinos who emigrate to America have an economic status that favorably influences their entrée; others enter with a less favorable economic status. Even though Hispanics of many social and economic classes have entered the United States, there are some similarities in the traditional value systems of Latino groups.

Traditional cultural values such as fatalism, dignity, respect, spirituality, and personalism are reflected in Latino lifestyles (Dillard, 1983). From a mental health perspective, these values are most consistent with the humanistic approach to interpersonal interactions, i.e., sensitivity to the feelings of others, interdependence, and a cooperative therapeutic stance rather than a confrontational one. Thus, extended family affiliations might display a high need for affiliation and collaboration. Additionally, in Latin culture, emphasis is placed on status and role definitions within the family and community, leading people to be aware of their responsibilities to others, others' expectations of them, and their expectations of others (Dillard, 1983).

Hispanic Americans (Latinos) and Psychotherapy

To be effective with a Hispanic client, Casas and Vasquez (1989) argue that a therapist must be conscious of countertransferential influences, assumptions, and biases that result from their personal and professional experiences. They posit that a mental health provider's lack of awareness of core cultural values can influence his or her behavior. For example, Casas and Vasquez point out:

> Cultural differences also pertain to evaluating acceptable patterns of client behavior during counseling sessions. A premise prevalent among professional counselors equates cooperativeness in counseling with the client's willingness to be verbally open and direct. In fact, many if not most of the world's cultures view revelations to a stranger of intimate personal and family details as highly unacceptable. The acceptable pattern for the traditional Hispanic is to handle one's problems discreetly, from within the family or other natural support systems. Once again, cultural expectations conflict with the counselor's professional expectations. (p. 160)

A Latino client brings to treatment historical, sociocultural, familial, and personal experiences and issues that can influence the therapeutic process. A Hispanic client may be primarily concerned with the present, may believe that external forces (e.g., spirits, nature) control his or her life, and may look for specific and concrete solutions to problems. Additionally, many Hispanics have extended family systems and show deference to authority figures. Unlike other immigrant groups, Hispanics are likely to retain their language, in part because of the close proximity of their countries of origin. Thus, many Hispanics may only speak Spanish, and others may speak Spanglish, a blend of Spanish and English (Axelson, 1993; Marger, 1994; Sue & Sue, 1990).

In summary, counselors who work with Hispanic clients may need to learn about the Hispanic cultures and to explore their own feelings about these cultures.

IMPLICATIONS OF THE CULTURAL DIFFERENCE PARADIGM: WHAT DO WE KNOW?

The proponents of the cultural difference paradigm have effectively described the cultural patterns of American racial groups and delineated issues that each group might bring to therapy. Clinicians now know more about the pitfalls that may arise from their lack of cultural knowledge and their failure to examine their own racial background and professional limitations. However, most mental health professionals are still ill-equipped to handle race in psychotherapy. In fact, many clinical scholars have explained that cultural values, patterns, and behaviors are as important as transference and countertransference, but these cultural factors do not exclusively constitute transference or countertransference issues. Rather, the treatment situation characterizes the salience of cultural patterns. According to Abel, Metraux, and Roll (1987):

> It is important to note that cultural patterns do not themselves create transference and countertransference—the conditions of treatment do that. Rather, any issue from the patient's past (for example, being misunderstood as a child) can be exacerbated by cultural factors (for example, having a therapist from a different culture who does not understand the influence of a particular cultural factor on a patient's life). Cultural factors, then, are persistent issues in transference and countertransference. Language, religion, time orientation, . . . become ways the patient's conflicts surface or disguise themselves to help or hinder the therapeutic work. (pp. 154–155)

Thus, a therapist can misunderstand cultural factors, and transference can be hampered by differences in cultural value-orientations. And, according to Papajohn and Spiegel (1975), cultural value-orientations, as measured by the Kluckhohn and Strodtbeck (1961) model, can contribute to transference and countertransference, too.

Based on their worldview, White American therapists and visible racial/ethnic group therapists who accepts this worldview have certain expectations. They expect patients to self-disclose and be independent from their families. Additionally, they expect that the past, present, and future are appropriately distinguished, and that clients strive for lives in which the future is more important than the present. A client is supposed to see a therapist as a powerful, knowledgeable expert; a therapist sees himself or herself as responsible, able to determine the client's reality, and nonjudgmental. The expectation is that a clinician will help the client to uncover important aspects of the client's past and present, thereby affecting the client's future, without allowing his or her personal values to enter the treatment (Casas & Vasquez, 1989).

Yet, when cultural values conflict, as can be the case in cross-racial dyads, a therapist and patient encounter innumerable problems. Under these circumstances, transferential and countertransferential difficulties introduced by race must be overcome before effective therapeutic work can occur.

The literature suggests that racial and cultural attitudes of both the therapist and the client affect therapy. Nonetheless, it is unclear how race influences interactional dynamics during therapy. The literature indicates that the client's race creates transference problems in treatment and can produce negative countertransference. However, the literature is unclear about patient and therapist characteristics that predict or determine specific types of influences. The following questions remain: How does one determine whether a client is using race or culture in a particular way? In what way does race influence a person's identity or personality? How does race influence interpersonal and familial relationships? How do the therapist's and client's racial attitudes or identities interact to affect therapy?

Despite the vast amount of literature on the topic of race and culture in therapy, little consistent and reliable information is available to mental health professionals. It is my belief that intellectual, emotional, and sociopolitical barriers have limited our understanding of racial influences in therapy and have prevented the articulation of a clear set of theoretically based guidelines for comprehending race's influence in psychotherapy.

Typically, social scientists and mental health professionals explain race-related social and psychological boundaries, divisions, and conflicts by engaging in an intellectual shell game in which racial issues are replaced by other topics, including economics, education, values, and communication styles. The tendency to substitute other issues for racial issues reflects the strength of most Americans' emotional, social, political, and psychosocial resistance to examining and understanding racial issues in their lives and our society. Generally, racial differences and perspectives are often described in emotional terms. And, according to White American cultural traditions, emotionalism is considered irrational and, therefore, renders the topic inaccessible to enlightened discussion. Hence, intellectual boundaries have been created to limit meaningful discussions about race and to hamper our understanding of it.

Another obstacle to understanding racial influences in therapy is the marginal status of race in human development and personality theories. The lack of theoretically based models keeps the discourse about race speculative and emotional, and prevents genuine insight. The tendency to use visible racial/ethnic group categories as the primary units of analysis is another barrier. This practice implies that racial issues are the exclusive province of people of color and not a social or psychological issue for Whites. Therefore, racial issues are generally construed as unimportant or a "minority" concern when differences of opinion arise. For some, racial issues and conflicts exist only when people of color raise them. The assumption seems to be that White Americans do not consider racial issues to be important to them. Yet, if race is one-sided, how do we understand the influence of race in our work as helping professionals? I argue that race has significant psychological meaning for the personal and social development of Blacks, Whites, American Indians, Asians, and Hispanic Americans.

The psychological significance of race varies according to each individual's interpretation of the socialization and psychosocial developmental processes. Psychologically, race affects how one thinks, feels, acts, and perceives the world and others. Because race has a personal meaning for each individual, it follows that it affects interpersonal relationships. Yet, to date, little attention has been given to how one's personal meaning of race affects his or her interactions, roles, and performance as a helping professional.

In American society, specifically in the mental health profession, race and racial issues are complex and multileveled. The complexities of race and racial issues stem from U.S. history and the forms of expression used to weave the topic into the fabric of our society. By focusing on the sociocultural factors surrounding race instead of race itself, mental health professionals continue to approach racial issues ahistorically and atheoretically, which perpetuates racial barriers.

I think the way writers approach the issue of race and its influences in therapy reveals some problem areas. Scholars and clinicians have attempted to understand a psychological phenomenon by using nonpsychological criteria such as racial group membership, acculturation, or social class (Carter & Helms, 1988). Furthermore, social scientists have used these nonpsychological variables as if they were equivalent to personal identity. For example, the psychological literature (e.g., Fleming, 1984) suggests that Blacks, in general, have lower levels of measured self-esteem than Whites, and that their lower self-concepts are related to their Blackness, or reference group orientation (Jaynes & Williams, 1989).

Most studies of Black or visible racial/ethnic group personality characteristics have been primarily comparative, with little consideration of within-group race-specific variations (Carter, 1991). In most of these studies, researchers examined what were considered to be universal constructs (e.g., self-esteem) using measures developed for and normed on White samples. If differences were found between racial groups, the conclusions focused on how Blacks felt about themselves and their racial group. Cross (1991), in his book *Shades of Black,* notes that studies focusing on personal identity usually exclude race-related variables or treat them as subject variables or characteristics of the participants, while studies focusing on racial identity or reference group orientation (RGO) use race-specific stimuli in assessment materials (e.g., doll preferences, Black consciousness, racial identity attitudes). Cross also notes that the debate about the psychological well-being of visible racial/ethnic group members has centered on the relationship between personal identity and reference group orientation. To be mentally healthy, assessed in terms of personal identity scales, one was believed to have a positive reference group orientation. Poor psychological functioning was associated with a low reference group orientation or an out-group orientation as evidenced in low personal identity scores. As Cross demonstrates, the practice in the social sciences was to measure only one dimension—either personal identity or reference group orientation—and then make inferences about the other dimension. In effect, racial group membership and personal identity have been treated as one construct in studies of Blacks and perhaps other racial groups. Little attention has been given to similar psychological and reference group relationships among Whites, and even less attention has been given to racial or culture-specific variation within racial groups. The absence of within-group racial and cultural variables in studies of visible racial/ethnic groups is a serious shortcoming and, perhaps, a barrier to understanding their psychological functioning (Carter, 1991; Fleming, 1984).

Another major flaw in using racial group membership as the primary unit of analysis lies in its atheoretical nature. By using racial group membership or race as the major explanatory construct for psychological health, we are drawn into the sociocultural and historical traditions of viewing racial group members as identical and as people who possess particular characteristics. These characteristics are usually stereotypes in which visible racial/ethnic people are seen in more negative terms than Whites.

Until recently, social scientists and helping professionals have failed to use a consistent theoretical framework for understanding racial issues in mental health relationships. Given the historical, sociocultural, and political barriers associated with race, the mental health literature has been subject to centuries of speculation and debate about race in psychotherapy and other helping relationships. The present work represents a first step toward an integration of theory-based empirical research and clinical insights for understanding the influence of race in the psychotherapeutic process.

In the next part of the book, race in personality and racial identity theory (i.e., the extent to which one identifies with one's socially ascribed racial group) will be presented. I argue that one's cultural group affiliation is a function of one's psychological orientation to his or her racial group.

Where Do We Go?
Theoretical Frameworks

Part Two represents a new direction for clinicians and scholars. This new direction—where to go when we depart from traditional concepts associated with race in psychotherapy—emerges from the elements that comprise the Racially Inclusive Model of Psychotherapy. The model goes beyond traditional constructs associated with race by offering a way to understand race as a psychological construct that is also an important aspect of personality and human development. Chapter 4 argues that, in the United States, race is an important part of personality for all people. Another critical element in the model is the notion that each individual belongs to a racial group and forms some psychological resolution regarding that group membership. Chapter 5 focuses on Black and visible racial/ethnic group identity developmental processes and highlights implications for clinical practice. Chapter 6 presents White racial identity theory and gives clinical examples. Chapter 7 addresses commonly asked questions and concerns regarding racial identity and discusses biracial identity. The final element of the Racially Inclusive Model of Psychotherapy is a discussion of how the racial identity statuses of therapy participants interact to influence psychotherapy process and outcome.

CHAPTER 4

Race and Identity Development

The majority of articles and books about cross-cultural counseling and psychotherapy (e.g., Axelson, 1993; Locke, 1994; Pedersen, 1987; Sue, 1981; Sue & Sue, 1990) describe how culture influences therapy with visible racial/ethnic group members (i.e., Africans, Asians, Hispanics, Native Americans). Some authors have defined cross-cultural as international (e.g., Triandis & Lambert, 1980); others have used the term cross-cultural to mean cross-racial. For instance, many authors of texts with cross-cultural titles (e.g., Comas-Diaz & Griffith, 1988; Pedersen, 1987; Sue & Sue, 1990) either outline mental health issues from an international perspective or describe various cultures or racial groups and discuss treatment for members of these groups. In addition, some authors discuss ethnic differences within a racial group (e.g., McGoldrick, Pearce, & Giordano, 1982). Although much has been written about the therapeutic needs of these groups, less is known about how race, as a psychological construct, influences the therapeutic process for members of various racial/ethnic groups and for White people. Typically, racial issues in the therapeutic process have been seen from the counselor-as-problem perspective: clinicians in training are taught what they do not know or understand about cross-racial interactions and visible racial/ethnic group members' cultures (Helms, 1990). Few theorists or researchers have discussed or studied behavioral and cognitive issues in the development of racial identity. There are a few racial identity theories, but, to the author's knowledge, only one theory (i.e., Helms, 1984) has outlined intrapsychic and interactional process dynamics in racial identity development, and only a few empirical studies (cf. Carter & Helms, 1992) have attempted to explore cross-racial therapy process issues.

Racial identity theories have been constructed to help understand how White and visible racial group members identify with their racial group membership. As outlined in Part One, the cultural difference perspective that currently characterizes the psychological literature presumes that the client's racial group membership or race per se is the primary determinant of influences in psychotherapy. Clinical scholars have emphasized that ethnic identity, acculturation, and social class also may influence treatment. Nevertheless, scholars and clinicians have paid less attention to race, equating it with other constructs such as ethnicity or culture. In other words, race is usually subsumed under discussions of ethnic or cultural differences. A discussion of ethnicity and culture, assuming they are different, may be important, but it does not clarify the meaning of race. Furthermore, when writers address issues of ethnicity and culture in the therapeutic process, they do so without a clear theoretical perspective.

The need for a racial theory that examines intrapsychic dynamics is evident from the literature review presented in Part One. Much of what is known about race in therapy has been derived from the work of psychodynamic writers who simply describe the interplay of transference and countertransference in cross-racial interventions. Although these ideas have been useful, they are unidimensional, demographically oriented, and lacking in empirical support. I advocate an approach to understanding race in psychotherapy that examines behavioral and cognitive issues and is driven by theory and supported by empirical evidence.

LIMITATIONS: TRANSFERENCE AND COUNTERTRANSFERENCE

Transference reactions, be they positive or negative, are the client's *unconscious* projections onto the therapist. These projections are characteristic of significant relationships with others in his or her early life (i.e., usually family members). Although transferential reactions move from patient to therapist without conscious awareness, in a positive therapeutic relationship the client learns about them from the therapist's interpretations and feedback. Therefore, the meaning and significance of these particular thoughts, feelings, attitudes, and behaviors are primarily determined by the therapist (see Figure 4.1). Similarly, positive and negative countertransference responses are a therapist's unconscious thoughts, feelings, behavior, and attitudes that are stimulated by the client.

Thus, a therapist is presumed to have the knowledge and power in this dyad. He or she is thought to be able to understand both the client's and his or her own material even though often expressed in disguised or distorted forms. Moreover, the client may have limited participation in the process of interpreting the meaning of his or her or the therapist's behavior.

In most of the literature concerning race, psychodynamically oriented writers argue that transference and countertransference reactions must be managed to uncover underlying intrapsychic conflicts. Particularly because these reactions are being managed, a therapist who simply focuses on transference and countertransference reactions may miss the centrality of race in an individual's intrapsychic and identity structure.

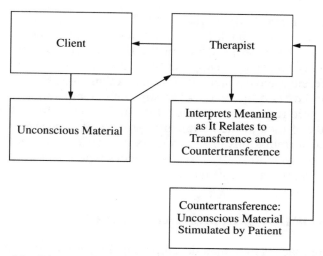

Figure 4.1 Diagram of transference and countertransference processes.

Finally, because racism and discrimination are often the focus of psychological literature on race, victims of racism (visible racial/ethnic group members) receive attention while the creators of racial hierarchies (Whites) are ignored.

Tyler, Brome, and Williams (1991) point out that traditional concepts of transference and countertransference

> . . . refer to aspects of an individual's personal history that become part of the therapeutic relationship and shape client-therapist interactions. However, . . . there is another level of history and experience that enters into and shapes the therapeutic relationship. . . . The sociocultural historical level is ingrained into our . . . existence and binds us to our social and political realities. (p. 25)

Traditional concepts of race in psychotherapy have focused on intrapsychic conflicts and have excluded from treatment approaches the psychosocial and historical aspects of race and White therapists' racial orientation.

The impact of race on countertransference and transference reactions has not been theoretically derived nor empirically supported, and is, therefore, speculative. Moreover, race has not been considered an important aspect of personality theories, from which transference and countertransference are derived. Clinical scholars who have used transference and countertransference were usually trained to think of human psychology in psychodynamic terms. The psychodynamic model was thus used as an approach for understanding race without integrating race into the basic propositions of the theory. Also, no empirical evidence, to my knowledge, supports these constructs.

Transference and countertransference explanations for cross-racial interactions have considered racial group membership a sociodemographic characteristic rather than a psychological attribute. To understand the complexity of race in the therapeutic process, it is necessary to extend traditional formulations of race and its influence in psychotherapy and construct a psychologically grounded theory where race is an important aspect of identity and worldview.

LIMITS OF DEVELOPMENTAL THEORY

Recent approaches to human development and personality models in the social sciences have equated race with culture, suggesting that familial and social influences will vary, depending on one's culture. Moreover, scholars typically use culture broadly to define differences in geography, language, physical features, customs, and cultural values. As a result, Americans who have been segregated from the White mainstream on the basis of skin color, language, and/or customs are also considered to be members of cultural groups. They are usually discussed with respect to special needs and deprived social conditions (such as prejudice, discrimination, and underrepresentation in most institutions) (Henderson, 1986).

Miller (1993) has summarized Erikson's belief about cultural influences in human development:

> Psychosocial development is culturally relative in two ways. First, although children in all cultures go through the same sequence of stages, each culture has its own idiosyncratic way of directing and enhancing the child's behavior at each stage. . . . Second, there is cultural relativity within a culture as it changes over time. Institutions that meet the needs of one generation may prove inadequate for the next. (p. 158)

The thrust of Erikson's model of development is identity; although he acknowledged culture and its differential effect on development, he held that the acquisition of "a conscious sense of individual identity [involved] a maintenance of an inner solidarity with a group's ideals and identity" (Erikson, 1959, p. 102). Thus, for Erikson, having an identity that was consistent with one's society was central to healthy identity development. Yet, the structural and sociohistorical influences of racial segregation and the racially based identity processes for different racial groups were overlooked in his initial work, *Childhood and Society*. Erikson tended to focus on culture broadly defined and did not deal with the issue of race for all people. Erikson (1968) did discuss race in his book *Identity: Youth and Crisis;* in the final chapter, he noted that racial categories have effects on all members of society wherein those who are denigrated are used by those who denigrate to project negative aspects of themselves. He argued that members of all racial groups need to evolve wider identity structures that include positive and negative elements of all groups. It should be pointed out that Erikson was at that time attempting to reconcile the identity metamorphosis of Black people. He was, in part, explaining the civil rights and Black Power movements, not necessarily altering in any fundamental way the basic ideas presented in his classic book *Childhood and Society*. None of his observations was incorporated in subsequent editions of his classic work. Nevertheless, his stages of psychosocial development were thought to be universal, with a differential emphasis for individuals from different cultures.

In criticizing the limitations of most theories of development, Miller (1993) points out that few, if any, address sociohistorical or ecological factors and influences on human development. These omissions might account for why race has been overlooked. Riegel (1976) argues that personality development or identity occurs as a result of a sequence of interacting events and episodes that take place within the context of a social history. Miller chides developmental theorists for treating human development as if it occurs in a historical vacuum. She observes:

> Bandura emphasizes that an individual's behavior alone can change his environment. . . . Like Piaget, however, Bandura ignores sociohistorical changes. In fact, Freud, Gibson, ethnologists, and information-processing psychologists also ignore the role of sociohistorical change. . . . Erikson comes closest to dealing adequately with sociohistorical changes. He points out that these changes lead to changes in social institutions, which in turn lead to changes in society's expectations of the child at each point in development. For this reason he found it necessary to compare development in different cultures. (p. 434)

Because the effects of social history and customs on personality and identity development have been absent in the psychological literature, one might infer that race, as a central feature of social and historical life in the United States, has also been ignored or minimized, or thought about from the perspective of visible racial/ethnic group inferiority or cultural deprivation.

In fact, race is not mentioned in psychological models of personality development. Traditional psychology has emphasized the role of intrapsychic forces in human development and treated race as a social factor that only has relevance for visible racial/ethnic group members. Generally, race is used to describe differences in economic and social conditions that may explain people of color's personality "deficits." Many writers in psychology believed that people who were structurally constrained and disenfranchised from mainstream society were likely to internalize negative and demeaning social perceptions and myths and develop personalities that were primarily pathological (Kardiner & Ovesey, 1951). Thus, for people of color, race was considered to be a source of dysfunction in their self-concepts, personalities, and worldviews.

For Kardiner and Ovesey (1951), the basic personality of a Black person was inherently pathological. They stated:

Though he lives in American culture, the Negro lives under special conditions which give this personality a distinctive configuration. Taking as our base line the white middle class, the conditions of life for the Negro are so distinctive that there is an actual alteration of the pressures to which he must adapt. Hence, he develops a distinctive personality. This basic Negro personality is, however, a caricature of the corresponding white personality, because the Negro must adapt to the same culture, must accept the same social goals, but without the ability to achieve them. This limitation in social opportunities accounts for the difference in personality configuration. (p. 317)

The omission of the influence of race in human development theories is quite curious, particularly when studies (e.g., Phinney & Rotheram, 1987) consistently show that race and its social meaning are aspects of identity development during the formative years of human development, particularly in the United States. Studies have demonstrated that American children begin to identify themselves as racial beings by age three or four (Clark, 1988).

To understand racial influences in psychotherapy, one must first understand how race is integrated into personality. The manner in which race is incorporated into our personalities has received little attention from most theorists of human behavior and development. When social scientists have attempted to discuss racial factors in personality, they have applied anthropological and sociological concepts to psychological phenomena. Consequently, psychological theories describing how race is interwoven with personality have been slow to evolve, despite the fact that an understanding of race in psychotherapy is impossible to discuss without an understanding of its influences on the psychological structure.

RACE AND IDENTITY

Developmental Processes

Human development begins with male and female genetic material that determines a child's gender, physical characteristics and attributes, as well as some emotional and psychological predispositions. The primary markers for racial categories are a person's skin color and physical features, which are in part genetically determined. They have considerable import in a racially segregated society that maintains social taboos about interracial unions and injects racial concerns at the point of human conception. A child's skin color, eye color, hair texture, and physical features will also be determined by genetic factors. Thus, to the extent that it is biologically based, race as a visible characteristic enters human development at the point of conception.

A child matures physically, emotionally, psychologically, and socially in the context of a family, community, and society. The physical, emotional, and psychological development of a child occurs within the context of the family and the community, which are usually racially homogeneous in America. However, most families and communities operate within a racially divisive and fragmented society. Physical development is affected by the family's economic resources; likewise, the external environs impinging on a family affect the emotional and psychological interplay between parent and child. A child's awakening self-awareness, recognition of others, and parental modeling are thought to begin during the first few months of life. As a child's motor and sensory skills develop, so do his or her cognitive and social skills (Miller, 1993).

Jean Piaget's (1952/1968) model of cognitive development suggests that intellectual development is a gradual process. According to his model, ideas or schema, which might be thought of as models for interacting with the environment, are essential for cognitive development. Piaget's model describes assimilation, the way in which new information is added to a schema; accommodation is the mechanism used to take in new knowledge and information. He suggests that cognitive maturation requires a balance between these processes. At varying stages of maturity, a child learns from different vantage points. The perceptual stages begin with sensorimotor perception, when a child learns that objects have permanence, and continue through preoperational perception, when a child develops symbolic thinking and is able to classify objects into categories (preschool years). These perceptual stages are followed by concrete operations (ages 5–7 years), when a child begins to perform simple transformations. In the final stage, formal operations, an adolescent develops abstract and hypothetical thought. While cognitive and physical maturation are proceeding, so does social and identity development. But, as noted earlier, these human processes occur in a racial context that is not described in theoretical models.

Nevertheless, a racial group's physical-social environment and worldview are guided by different basic assumptions and propositions about the nature of the universe and humankind. These basic cultural assumptions guide how a person processes sensory information into precepts and how a person thinks and behaves. Thus, as described in Chapter 3, for most racial groups, these basic worldviews determine how a member of that group experiences self, others, and the world. As a child develops intellectually and socially, he or she creates schemata consistent with those held in his or her racial group, comprised of his or her family, community, and society.

Because race is an aspect of American culture, it is reasonable to conclude that, in early intellectual and social development, a child will internalize the respective psychosocial meanings assigned to his or her racial group. For instance, racial groups vary in terms of family structures and the values attached to particular activities (e.g., cognitive versus interpersonal skills) and to forms of language (e.g., standard English, Black English, traditional Native American Indian, Korean, Chinese, and Japanese languages, Spanish, and Spanglish). These variations are also influenced by social customs and stereotypes regarding members of each racial/ethnic group.

As noted in Part One, visible racial/ethnic group people have been, and continue to be, portrayed as socially and culturally inferior, deficient, and different from White Americans. White Americans are seen as competent, hard-working, clean, and good, and opposite terms or images are often associated with, or projected on, visible racial/ethnic group people. Much of this societal information is communicated and received in subtle and indirect ways (e.g., images, traditions, selective attention). Prior to the civil rights movement in the 1950s and 1960s, these same messages were explicit and often unquestioned.

Personality Development

There are a number of viewpoints on personality development. Early personality theories claimed that biology determined many aspects of one's personality, a perspective used to buttress the inferiority paradigm and to explain temperament. There is some agreement that nature and nurture interact to affect biologically determined tendencies.

Freud's theory of personality development is divided into psychosexual stages and is derived from a biological viewpoint, suggesting that our biological drives for pleasure are the basic sources of psychic energy. The demands of pleasure seeking (id) are controlled by reality (ego) and by the demands of social acceptance and morality (superego). This developmental process occurs via five hierarchical stages (oral, anal, phallic, latency, and genital). According to Freud, personality is a function of an individual's ability to manage numerous conflicts among the id, ego, and superego during the course of development.

Behavior theorists explain personality development in terms of the principles of conditioning and learning. These theorists suggest that one's personality is shaped by the patterns of behavior that have been acquired through imitation and reinforcement. In contrast to the biological viewpoint, behavior and social learning theorists emphasize the role of the environment in personality development. The environment is considered to have an important impact on the development of social-emotional interactions.

Erikson describes identity development as a lifelong process and focuses on specific ego developmental tasks at different stages of an individual's life. Erikson's model consists of eight stages:

Stage One—Trust vs. Mistrust

Stage Two—Autonomy vs. Shame and Doubt

Stage Three—Initiative vs. Guilt

Stage Four—Industry vs. Inferiority

Stage Five—Identity vs. Role Confusion

Stage Six—Intimacy vs. Isolation

Stage Seven—Generativity vs. Stagnation

Stage Eight—Ego Integrity vs. Despair.

In each stage, there is a "critical period" for the development of a specific ego capability. For example, during Stages Four through Six, from about age 6 to adolescence and young adulthood, an individual must develop a sense of mastery and competence, or else he or she will feel inferior.

Moral and social behavior is transmitted through socialization processes. The primary aim of socialization is to teach a child the values of his or her society, and the goal is for the child to internalize these values such that violations of social norms and standards produce psychological distress (i.e., guilt, anxiety, etc.).

The effect of socialization on personality development has primarily focused on gender identity or sex-typed behavior. From the moment a child is born, he or she is distinguished by behavior deemed appropriate to his or her gender and typically learned through identification with a same-sex parent. In the same way that gender identity is modeled, shaped, learned, or identified with, I contend that race-appropriate roles and behavior are also communicated through socialization.

Therefore, social and personality development is intertwined with prevailing assumptions about race that are learned through imitation, and internalized and reinforced by a need to conform to cultural norms and be accepted by society at large. As an individual matures, he or she develops a personality that is informed by social and moral attitudes, behaviors, and feelings. In general, personality is thought to be a constellation of attributes and characteristics of a person that are internally enduring and guide his or her interpersonal behavior.

As personality and developmental theories tell us, an individual's personality is an outgrowth of the dynamic interplay of his or her genes and the surrounding environment, particularly family, community, and society. It is well established that the family is a primary socializing agent in the social and psychological development of the child.

There is substantial empirical evidence (e.g., Phinney & Rotheram, 1987) that describes the development of racial awareness and attitudes in children as young as 3 years old (for a comprehensive review of the literature, see Katz, 1982, and Phinney & Rotheram, 1987). This literature has examined children's responses to race and racial cues (particularly in terms of Black/White differences) with respect to cognitive, affective, and behavioral dimensions (Ramsey, Vold, & Williams, 1989). For instance, Clark (1988) reports that 75% of Black and White children, by age 4 are able to identify themselves and distinguish between their racial group and other racial groups. He states:

> There is no doubt that children learn the prevailing social ideas about racial differences early in their lives. Not only are they aware of race in terms of physical characteristics such as skin color, but also they are generally able to identify themselves in terms of race. (pp. 22–23)

In addition, Aboud (1987) reports that racial differences are recognized by children at the ages of 3 and 4, whereas ethnic differences are not recognized until age 7. Aboud states that "presumably, the features salient to children such as skin color and hair type allow them to distinguish these [racial] groups" (p. 37). In examining children's racial attitudes, Aboud reports that "White children consistently expressed favorable attitudes toward their own group at 4 years of age" (p. 42). In numerous studies (e.g., Aboud, 1987; Ramsey, 1987; Vaughn, 1987), White children's attitudes toward other racial/ethnic groups were found to be primarily negative through age 12. Yet, visible racial/ethnic children generally viewed other racial groups in more positive terms, and immigrant children were less likely to think of themselves in racial terms. Ramsey (1987) and Vaughn (1987) report that children are capable of emotional and social judgments associated with race and that these social and emotional responses generally come from a child's environment. Ramsey (1987) explains one White child's declaration about race:

"I'm gonna kick the Black people out of the workplace!" Although it is doubtful that he knew what a workplace was, his comments reflected some economic bases of expressing negative cross-group attitudes. One could argue that he was expressing an association he learned from adults. However, he did elaborate with some vehemence by describing how he would "kick them" and "punch them." He also generalized from this statement by saying that he would not let Black children into his school. He was assimilating the adult attitudes and beginning to apply them to his more immediate situation. (p. 64)

Branch and Newcombe's (1986) longitudinal study of racial attitude development found that the racial attitudes of Black children changed as they grew older. In addition, these researchers reported that children's racial attitudes did not always coincide with their parents' views. However, parents were found to play a complex, yet critical, role in shaping their children's racial attitudes. Branch and Newcombe (1988) point out that the parents' views and teachings about race have a clear but not direct effect on a child's racial learning. Parents who avoid or deny race communicate less positive feelings about race, whereas parents who confront racial issues in the child's early years may initially upset the child, but as the child matures, the early learning becomes a source of strength.

Clark, Hocevar, and Dembo (1980) found that children between the ages of 2½ and 10½ years conceptualize race according to a developmental hierarchy consisting of six levels, beginning with a lack of comprehension and culminating in genetic explanations for racial differences. Katz (1982) posits a "developmental sequence of racial attitude acquisition, which span[s] approximately ten years of the child's life" (p. 46). This sequence consists of eight "overlapping but separable steps that begin in the first year of life with the 'early observation of racial cues' and progresses through to 'attitude crystallization' in the upper elementary years by which time cultural conditioning [is] apparent" (p. 46). Although Katz reveals contradictions and inconsistencies in her review of this literature, one consistent finding is that young preschool children are aware of, have reactions to, and display an ability to recognize racial differences (Goodman, 1952; Katz & Zalk, 1978; Porter,

1971; Proshansky, 1966). Thus, children's attitudes about race are well formed before they enter school (Clark, 1988).

SUMMARY

As an individual grows up as a citizen of the United States, he or she also learns that each citizen belongs to a racial group. The challenge for each individual is to incorporate race into his or her personal identity. As children develop ideas and feelings about race, their race-appropriate roles become stable and integral to their personality. Researchers, when investigating child and adolescent racial awareness, have not considered how this awareness influences identity or personality formation, and developmental theorists have denied race as an aspect of a child's socialization process and personal identity development.

Personal identity is presumed to be made up of the dynamic interaction among self-image, attitudes, beliefs, and feelings that occurs within an intrapsychic domain. That is, "a person's identity is a complex integration of each person's psychosocial context, physical characteristics, personality attributes, unique experiences, and personal choices" (Babad, Birnbaum, & Benne, 1983, p. 37). Within the context of family, an individual is believed to develop a constellation of characteristics that make up his or her personality. Our personalities are also products of social identities; religious and political affiliations are chosen social identities, and race, gender, and ethnicity are inherited.

When considering the socialization associated with social identities like race, family influences may be equally differential. For example, one family may consider race to be significant; another may consider race to be insignificant. Children are taught about race through the family network and primary caretaker, and racial identity and personality are by-products of the interaction of various social, familial, and intrapsychic systems. One's identity as it relates to race is affected by the manner in which race is denied, avoided, or discussed in the family or other socializing institutions (e.g., schools). All of these factors influence an individual's understanding of the implications of race.

For example, a White male raised in a predominantly White environment with no mention of race is implicitly taught that he is superior to visible racial/ethnic people. A Black person whose family minimizes or denies the significance of race may hold similar beliefs. Consider the situation of a light-skinned Latino, living in a racially mixed community, whose family teaches only about ethnicity (e.g., Mexican, Cuban, or Puerto Rican) and not race, even though this person might be the object of envy and hostility for his or her distinctive physical features and might be confronted with racial remarks. These examples show how the context of one's family influences the development of characteristics—racial and nonracial—that constitute personal identity.

It is simplistic to assume that all Blacks, Whites, Asians, or Latinos are similar psychologically or culturally simply because they appear to share a common racial category. Instead, each individual's sociocultural environment and socialization experiences with respect to race will influence him or her differently. Racial group membership, based on skin color alone, is not a sufficient indicator of cultural group membership.

The components of personal and racial identity may have distinct sources of influence and reinforcement, and each component's significance may vary from situation to situation; nevertheless, they interact with each other. As Helms (1990) notes to the extent that society stereotypes one racial group as dirty, shiftless, and ignorant and another as clean, industrious, and intelligent and can enforce such stereotypes, then it is likely that the individual will find it easier to use the second rather than the first as a reference group. However, this type of identification may become problematic if it requires denial and distortions of oneself and/or the racial group(s) from which one descends.

Given the dearth of theories about race and identity development, the influence of race on individual and interpersonal interactions in a therapeutic setting and in society is unclear. Moreover, theoretical approaches to understanding race in psychotherapy have allowed mental health professionals to remain ignorant about themselves as members of a racial group and about how an individual incorporates race into identity.

Furthermore, the legacy of race in our society shapes individuals' psychosocial and racial identity development (Helms, 1990). Many people in America are subject to similar racial norms and racial attitudes, yet members of racial groups vary with respect to their psychological response to racial information. Therefore, to consider members of a racial group to be culturally homogeneous is erroneous. The most promising models for examining psychological differences within racial groups are the racial identity models (cf. Atkinson, Morten, & Sue, 1993; Cross, 1980; Helms, 1990).

Racial identity theories describe psychological development from the perspective of racial, rather than ethnic, identity. Therefore, racial identity theories describe multidimensional and multifaceted aspects of identification. Helms (1990) puts it this way:

> Black racial identity theories attempt to explain the various ways in which Blacks can identify (or not identify) with other Blacks and/or adopt or abandon identities resulting from racial victimization; White racial identity theories attempt to explain the various ways in which Whites can identify (or not identify) with other Whites and/or evolve or avoid a nonoppressive White identity. (p. 5)

Because one's personality is formed in the context of racial group membership, the relationships between racial identity and personality are quite complex and interrelated, particularly as one considers the psychosocial environment in which they evolve. Thus, personality includes race and racial identity in extremely dynamic and complex ways and, taken together, explains individual development.

CHAPTER 5

Visible Racial/Ethnic Identity Theories

Identity development is a central feature of personality theories. Theories of personality offer different explanations for personality development. Psychodynamic theories hold that one's personality is shaped through a process of intrapsychic conflict resolutions. Erikson (1963), a neo-Freudian, believed that psychosocial development occurred throughout the life span, and each life stage had its own developmental task. According to Erikson, in early stages of development, a child must learn to *trust,* become *autonomous,* take *initiative,* and develop *industry,* to feel confident and productive. For Erikson, during adolescence, individuals must "synthesize their past, their present, and their future possibilities into a clear sense of self." Erikson called this attempt to establish a sense of self the adolescent's "search for identity" (Myers, 1989, p. 95).

The process of identity development involves asking and answering questions like "Who am I?" "What do I want to do with my life?" and "What do I believe in?" Furthermore, the questions must be answered in such a way as to provide a "stable and consistent identity . . . essential to finding a meaningful place in society" (Myers, 1989, p. 95). Although Erikson acknowledged that cultural norms learned through family socialization were critical to identity formation, culture was used in the broader anthropological sense of the word. Therefore, race, as a distinct aspect of culture, was and continues to be excluded from his theory of identity development.

From the 1950s through the 1970s, during the civil rights/Black Power movement, social scientists observed and were compelled to describe a psychosocial conversion process among Black Americans. In the span of two decades, scholars recognized that people belonging to a historically denigrated group were struggling for their basic rights as American citizens and, in the process, redefining themselves, individually and collectively, from colored or Negro (each imposed group identities) to a self-designated identity as Black(s).

During the 1970s, numerous scholars, working independently, began to describe this phenomenon and to apply these descriptions to individuals rather than to the social movement. Some observers developed theories that described individuals as static; others designed more dynamic stage models (Cross, 1991; Helms, 1990).

The development of racial identity among individuals of various racial groups probably began to emerge some time during the 15th century, when the relationship between races shifted from one of equality to inequality. For instance, racial group membership probably became more salient when the relationship between Europeans and Africans, Asians, and Native American Indians changed from trader, statesman, and partner to civilized and savage, and finally slave and master (Allen, 1994; Fredrickson, 1989; Smedley, 1993; Sue, 1994). Little has been written about how individuals adapted psychologically to these new relationships, but I suspect that members of one racial group who interacted with members of another group had to consciously or subconsciously orient themselves to that other group's new role (e.g., a White person who used to view Blacks or Indians as partners had to adapt to the new, subordinate role of Indians or Blacks).

Skin color is a characteristic used to classify one into a racial group. This classification system has little to do with one's personal identification with that group and more to do with visible physical traits. Cook and Helms (1988) describe people who are so classified as *visible racial/ethnic group members.* Visible racial/ethnic group members with more ambiguous characteristics are often pressured to select a group to identify with, or they are thrust into a group against their will. As a consequence, they experience ambivalence and frustration surrounding their group identity. For example, a light-skinned American Indian, Hispanic or Black person, who can "pass" as White, is likely to be in situations where he or she hears Whites honestly express their opinions and beliefs about people of color. According to societal customs, traditions, and norms, these individuals are often forced to choose one racial group or develop a psychological defense to explain why they have chosen another group. More about this later.

Theories of the psychological development of racial identity for visible racial/ethnic and non-White immigrant populations have existed in the psychological literature for some time (Cross, 1978, 1980, 1991; Helms, 1984, 1990, 1994; Thomas, 1971). These models have offered a way to comprehend the psychosocial complexity associated with racial identity issues. But these models have provided little insight into how racial identity attitudes may be applied to the psychotherapeutic process. Existing racial identity models must be examined in depth to understand how racial attitudes may be useful for understanding racial issues in therapy. Racial identity proponents argue that an individual's sense of connection to a particular racial group varies with respect to his or her psychological identification with that group.

It is important to explain the various derivations and advances in racial identity theories since their introduction in the 1970s. The clarification is needed because of the changes in terminology and theoretical emphasis. The first models of racial identity were proposed to explain Black American racial identity. Many scholars have proposed Black identity models. Some of the initial models proposed that there were different types of Blacks whose personalities varied according to how they understood who they were racially. One such early model was proposed by Vontress (1971), who suggested that three invariant types of Black people existed: (a) Colored, (b) Negro, and (c) Black. Each type displayed a distinct form of "race" identity. Colored people had race identities that were consistent with societal stereotypes. Negro racial views were grounded in efforts to integrate, and Blacks were people who valued their Blackness and would work against racism in the society. According to scholars who proposed typologies, it was not possible to alter one's type. Stage theorists, however, argued that one could progress from one stage of racial identity to a more advanced one. Thomas (1971), for instance, proposed a stage model that has been the precursor for later models. In the typical stage model of racial identity, a person would move in a linear progression from the least developed stage to the most advanced stage. Each stage had associated emotional, psychological, and behavioral elements.

In the late 1970s and 1980s, scholars began to extend Black racial identity stage theories to other groups. Atkinson, Morten, and Sue (1979) introduced a minority identity development model that was supposed to be applicable to all people of color. Later, Sue and Sue (1990) extended the minority identity model and referred to their model as the racial/cultural identity development. In the mid-1980s, Helms (1984) first introduced White racial identity (see Chapter 6) and, in subsequent writing, extended and expanded Black racial identity theory.

Racial identity was initially thought to be a personality type, and later models proposed that racial identity was a stagewise process. The stagewise perspective is apparent in the work of Thomas and Cross. The stages in Thomas and Cross's work were presented as linear and invariant. In latter extensions of the model, influenced by measurement and empirical investigation, Helms and Carter (1990) suggested that the racial identity for all groups should be thought of as attitudes or levels and discussed in terms of the influence of the most predominant level or attitude. These changes were made primarily to deemphasize the linear stage notions of previous models and to make theory consistent with racial identity measures.

More recently, racial identity theory has been expanded further (e.g., Helms & Piper, 1994; Carter, in press) and now contends that:

1. Racial identity development is applicable to all racial groups, even though separate models are presented for Blacks, Whites, and members of other racial groups. The different models reflect distinct sociopolitical histories of the groups, because each group's history and sociopolitical interactions in the society have some impact on how racial issues are understood and dealt with. Each racial group, given its social status in the society, experiences race from a distinct vantage point. One might think of race and racial groups on a continuum, with Whites at one pole, Asians, Indians, and Hispanics in the middle, and Blacks at the other pole.

2. Racial identity involves two sets of perspectives, one about self which influences how one views and understands members of the dominant or nondominant group and the second involves one's view of his or her own group.

3. Racial identity represents ego differentiation or statuses, where one's racial worldview is more or less mature. Less mature ego statuses derive definition from external sources (peers, media, family, institutions, and so on), and more mature and differentiated racial identity ego statuses are internally derived through a personal process of exploration, discovery, integration, and maturation. Race at more mature levels of racial identity is seen in complex and dynamic ways based on accurate information and examined personal and group experience. Less mature racial identity statuses are simplistic, inaccurate, and unexamined personal and group notions about race and race relations.

Helms and Piper (1994) describe the most recent extension of racial identity this way:

> Because of the differential racial-group reward structure, one's racial-group membership becomes a critical aspect of one's psychosocial identity; . . . healthy identity development occurs by means of a maturation process in which the person learns to substitute internal definitions and standards of racial-group identity for external or societally imposed definitions; and . . . the maturation process potentially involves increasingly sophisticated differentiations of the ego, called "ego statuses." . . . Although it is possible for each of the racial-group appropriate statuses to develop in a person and govern her or his race-related behavior, whether or not they do depends on a combination of life experiences, especially intrapsychic dissonance and race-related environmental pressures, as well as cognitive readiness . . . the statuses are hypothesized to develop or mature sequentially. (pp. 127–128)

To represent the ego, one might think of a circle in which the racial identity statuses that occupy more space also have more influence on ego functioning. Also, it is possible for each status to exist in a person's ego structure. It is also possible for someone to express blends of statuses or to express a particular status in one situation and another status in another situation. Thus, in the chapters to follow, I will describe the development of racial identity from the initial work of Thomas and Cross to the extensions of the racial identity models offered by Helms. Remember, the changes in terminology stages were first discussed, then attitudes, and then ego statuses or what I call *levels*. The levels or statuses are more fluid, whereas stages were proposed as linear. I will begin in this chapter to describe Black and visible racial/ethnic identity models and continue in Chapter 6 to describe White racial identity, and biracial identity in Chapter 7.

In these models, racial identity (initially referred to as *stages,* now *ego statuses*) is comprised of attitudes, thoughts, feelings, and behaviors toward oneself, as a member of a racial group, and toward members of the dominant or non-dominant racial group(s). The manner in which one's own racial identity is integrated into his or her personality depends on several factors, such as family, community, society, one's interpretive style, and the manner in which important peers validate, deny, or ignore this aspect of one's identity (cf. Cross, 1978, 1991; Helms, 1990). Visible racial/ethnic identity (formerly minority identity), as derived from the work of Atkinson, Morten, and Sue (1979), is used here to describe racial identity development for American Indians, Asians, and Hispanic Americans. In accordance with these models, the names originally given to each stage or status will be used.

BLACK RACIAL IDENTITY

Thomas (1971) has written revealing descriptions of the Negro-to-Black conversion process, a five-stage process that began with what he called *Negromachy*. As defined by Thomas, *Negromachy* is:

> . . . that which is ruled by confusion of self-worth and shows dependency upon white society for definition of self. Inherent in this concept of approval is the need to be accepted as something other than what one is. Gratification is based upon denial of self and a rejection of group goals and activities. The driving force behind this need requires Afro-Americans to seek approval from whites in all activities, to use white expectations as the yardstick for determining what is good, desirable or necessary. Any indication of reflection by or hostility from whites

results in these Afro-Americans changing their pattern of actions, even when the individual hurts himself and others of his people. (p. 104)

Thomas describes this identity as characterized by repressed rage, compliance, subservience, and a high sensitivity to racial issues. He adds that an individual in this stage will often blame Whites for his or her personal and social plight.

According to Thomas (1971), in the second stage, a person becomes aware of the pain and suffering he or she has endured as a result of being Black, while continuing to deny his or her Black identity. This awareness is associated with anxiety and confusion about becoming Black. Thomas suggests that, in an effort to alleviate this confusion and anxiety, a person begins gathering information about his or her cultural heritage, which provides a broader context for living in and more fully understanding the Black experience in America. For Thomas, the final stage of identity development is racial transcendence, when race is not the primary indicator of identity.

Cross (1978, 1980, 1991), working independently of Thomas and other scholars proposing Black identity models, suggests that Black racial identity is a developmental process that consists of five stages: (a) *Pre-encounter,* (b) *Encounter,* (c) *Immersion–Emersion,* (d) *Internalization,* and (e) *Internalization–Commitment.* According to Cross, in the Pre-encounter stage, one depends on White society for definition and approval. Racial identity attitudes toward one's Blackness are negative, and White culture and society are idealized. Cross, Parham, and Helms's (1991) description of Pre-encounter follows:

At the core of Pre-encounter is an aggressive assimilation–integration agenda. An individual in Pre-encounter is simultaneously searching for a secure place in the socioeconomic mainstream and attempting to flee from the implications of being a "Negro." A Negro in Pre-encounter is depicted as a deracinated person who views Black as an obstacle, problem, or stigma rather than a symbol of culture, tradition, or struggle. A Negro in this stage is preoccupied with thoughts of how to overcome his stigma, or how he or she can assist Whites in discovering that he or she is "just another human being" who wants to assimilate. (p. 322)

Cross suggests that the next stage of racial identity, Encounter, is triggered by a personal and challenging experience with Black or White society. This stage is marked by feelings of confusion about the meaning and significance of race and by an increasing desire to become more connected to a Black identity. He suggests that an individual attempts to reinterpret the world and his or her experiences in light of the Encounter experience. Following Encounter is Immersion–Emersion. In this stage, an individual idealizes Black culture and denigrates Whites and White culture. An individual is absorbed in the Black experience and completely rejects the White world. As this emotional intensity subsides, and psychological defensiveness is replaced with open-mindedness, a person moves into the fourth stage of Black racial identity, Internalization. An individual in Internalization recognizes that both Blacks and Whites have strengths and weaknesses. In this stage, a person has a Black worldview and experiences his or her Black identity as positive, important, and to be valued, while tolerating and respecting differences in Whites. Internalization–Commitment is the final stage of Black racial identity, according to Cross. In this stage, one turns his or her positive and internalized personal identity toward activities that are meaningful to the group and to oneself. Thus, a person recognizes that lasting change must come for the self and others who share similar problems.

Helms (1984, 1986, 1990, 1994) and Helms and Piper (1994), using the same names for identity stages as Cross, expanded Black racial identity theory. Helms and Piper suggest that racial identity is best understood in terms of statuses rather than developmental stages. At any one point, an individual has many levels of identity but only one dominant level. According to Helms, the predominant racial identity level operates psychologically as a worldview or ego state, and each level has its own constellation of emotions, beliefs, motives, and behaviors, which influences its expression. Helms proposes that each level of racial identity might have more than one phase.

Helms (1990) suggests that Pre-encounter might be expressed in two distinct ways, passively or actively. Pre-encounter is characterized by a psychological or ego identity status where race has little or no personal or social meaning and one's personal and social status is determined by personality, ability, and effort. An individual in passive Pre-encounter has staunch individualistic views that are characteristic of American cultural beliefs; an individual in active Pre-encounter may consciously idealize Whiteness and White culture and denigrate Blackness and Black people, as Thomas described. In an effort to be accepted into White society and culture, an individual in this status attempts to assimilate.

Helms suggests that the passive phase of Pre-encounter is internalized and subconscious, reflecting American cultural values that are accepted without question or awareness by many Black people and society at large. A Black person in this status views other Blacks in stereotypic ways and invests considerable psychic energy in maintaining distance between himself or herself and other Blacks. Passive expressions of Pre-encounter are difficult to recognize "because their world view so clearly mirrors that which is dominant in White society" (Helms, 1990, p. 14). Yet, an individual in this phase of Pre-encounter has little or no conscious awareness that his or her worldview might be difficult for other Blacks who are at higher levels of racial identity. Thus, an individual characterized by Pre-encounter attitudes might consider himself or herself to be a good American, emulate Euro-American leaders and institutions, and adopt the Protestant Work Ethic.

Behaviorally, an individual whose racial identity ego status is characterized by Pre-encounter may choose or learn to not use "Black English" and may feel embarrassed by those who do. Instead, he or she may use standard English exclusively, eschew distinctive Black clothing styles or fashions, associate primarily with Whites, and avoid contact with Blacks. If he or she resides in a Black community and has few contacts with Whites, his or her worldview will nevertheless be White-oriented, and he or she will denigrate Black lifestyles and people. When avoidance is not possible, this person may just feel and act superior. Also, he or she might embrace negative racial stereotypes because of limited accurate knowledge and information about Black American culture and history. He or she may be aware of discrimination but believe that Blacks, not Whites, are at the core of this problem. An individual at this level of racial identity views himself or herself as an individual, not as a Black person, and resents Black or White people who interact with him or her as such.

Encounter is the level of racial identity that is the most tumultuous and disconcerting for the Black person. At this level, an individual has an experience or a series of experiences that challenge his or her previously held beliefs and often lead to a search for a new African identity. Encounter ego identity status reflects a state of psychological confusion and emotional turmoil. This level of development is characterized by two phases: phase one is a jolt to one's old identity resolution, and phase two is an energized decision to discover the meaning and significance of one's Blackness.

During phase one of Encounter, an event or series of events shatters one's feelings about himself or herself with respect to race and his or her interpretation of the condition of Blacks in America. These feelings can be a result of positive experiences with Blacks or negative experiences with Whites, or a combination thereof. In brief, the "encounter event has the effect of 'pulling the rug' from under the feet of the person operating with the Negro identity" (Cross, Parham, & Helms, 1991, p. 324). Encounter is like a series of emotional blows that are so powerful that they begin to weaken and break down the person's previous defenses. Initially, as is true when one's defenses are not effective, these experiences are wrought with anxiety, confusion, and emotional turmoil, which can be either acute or chronic.

In phase two of Encounter, one begins to consciously experience conflict and confusion about who he or she is as a person and as a racial being. In the later half of the phase, an individual begins to view his or her racial identity more positively and works to become deeply involved in learning and experiencing the meaning and value of his or her race and culture.

Because these experiences challenge an individual's prior identity, he or she may feel disoriented, believing that he or she fits in neither a Black nor a White world. Therefore, in Encounter, little behavioral change occurs. As an example, an individual in Encounter may maintain a primarily White social support system, although he or she may begin spending time with Blacks. One's knowledge about Black and White relationships may be in a state of flux and confusion. Confusion may also surround one's knowledge about how he or she sees himself or herself as a Black person and whether Whites see him or her as a Black person or as a person. The primary motivation is to attempt to resolve the conflict regarding the old view of self and the encounter experience that has led to reevaluation of the view of Blacks and Whites. The energy used to search for a new identity or resolve the conflict between the abandoned identity and the newly emerging identity leads to the next level of racial identity.

In Immersion–Emersion, an individual becomes deeply involved in discovering his or her Black or African American cultural heritage. The result may be idealized images and intense emotions about his or her Black identity. This individual is likely to feel anxious about his or her new identity and hostile or angry toward Whites.

Immersion–Emersion has two distinct phases. The first phase, Immersion, is characterized by an all-consuming and obsessive involvement in Black culture. This individual immerses himself or herself in Black experiences (e.g., clubs, groups, political organizations) and withdraws— physically when possible, or at least psychologically—from White society as a way to discover and affirm his or her Black identity. This individual may express anger and feel anxious as a result of immersing himself or herself into Black life. In general, a person at this level of Black identity development idealizes everything Black, has an abundance of Black pride, and devalues everything that is White. Tremendous energy is invested in discovering a new, and more decidedly Black, identity. The obsession during this level of development is fueled by the fact that the person is actually more familiar with his or her old identity than with the one to be acquired. An individual in Immersion may view Blacks who attempt to assimilate into White society and culture with the same hostility previously held toward Whites. Although the person's knowledge of Black history and culture is extensive, the perspective is distorted, in that a decidedly positive or idealized view of Blackness is juxtaposed with a negative and hostile view of Whiteness. An individual at this level of racial identity development embraces the culture and history once denied or withheld, in order to gain self-esteem and racial pride. In time, the intensity of Immersion subsides, and a person begins to enter Emersion.

In the Emersion phase of Black racial identity, a person begins to integrate this new identity into his or her personality. During this period, the psychological intensity of Immersion subsides, and the person begins to acknowledge and accept the strengths and weaknesses of Black people as well as their role in American society. When an individual begins to internalize and integrate the new Black identity into his or her personality, this person is moving toward the next level of Black racial identity, Internalization.

During the first phase of Internalization, the individual achieves a sense of inner pride regarding his or her Black identity and develops a sense of security with respect to his or her cultural heritage. Cross et al. (1991) describe a person in the fourth level of racial identity in the following manner:

> This person has resolved conflicts between the "old" and "new" world view, and tension, emotionality, and defensiveness are replaced by a calm, secure demeanor. Ideological flexibility, psychological openness, and self-confidence about one's Blackness are evident in interpersonal transactions. Anti-White feelings decline to the point that friendships with White associates can be renegotiated. While still using Blacks as a primary reference group, the person moves toward a pluralistic and non-racist perspective, although relationships are negotiated from a position of strength rather than weakness. (p. 32)

Thus, this individual, motivated by personal preferences rather than a denial of his or her racial group or racial identity, may associate with Whites and even date interracially. This person becomes socially flexible and able to move comfortably in varied racial contexts. He or she can adapt to and function in a White environment, even though the closest social support system may still consist of a few, if any, Whites, unlike a Pre-encounter Black person. The integration of racial and cultural knowledge into the personality of an individual who reaches this level of racial identity is extensive. Such an individual is aware of racism and social norms regarding race relations in the United States, but maintains a positive identity that stems from pride in his or her racial-cultural heritage.

The second phase of Internalization is equivalent to Cross's original fifth stage, Internalization–Commitment. In Commitment, an individual adopts a behavioral style that is characterized by social and political activism.

> Moreover, in the Internalization stage one will find a variety of individuals expressing themselves in a variety of ways. Internalization frees the person to be. Persons no longer need judge people by their cultural group

memberships. . . . Rather they are concerned with common peoplehood. (Helms, 1990, p. 31)

The reader should keep in mind that each ego identity status can be expressed by the same person. What will matter most is the prevailing theme in one's racial identity expressions.

VISIBLE RACIAL/ETHNIC IDENTITY

Atkinson, Morten, and Sue (1979) proposed the Minority Identity Development (MID) model, which is intended to describe the issues of identity development common to members of all groups in the United States who are politically and/or socially oppressed.

In their model, Atkinson et al. proposed that the search for a positive racial-cultural identity involves progression through five stages:

1. Conformity.
2. Dissonance.
3. Resistance.
4. Introspection.
5. Awareness.

In content, the stages are similar to those of racial identity development, as addressed in the previous section, and to Asian identity models (Sue & Sue, 1971). The dimensions described by Atkinson et al. (1979) are: (a) feelings of self, (b) attitudes toward other members of one's own racial/cultural group, (c) feelings and attitudes toward other minorities, and (d) attitudes toward members of the majority culture. The Visible Racial-Ethnic Identity Model, as modified by Helms and Carter (1986), includes statuses with attitudes toward the self and members of the majority racial group.

It should be noted that Helms (1994) has proposed that the names for visible racial/ethnic identity be used for all people of color. Nevertheless, these levels or statuses will be used for Native American, Hispanic, and Asian Americans. In Helms and Carter's (1986) model of visible racial-ethnic identity, adapted from Atkinson et al.'s (1979) model, the first level, Conformity, is characterized by attitudes that reflect preferences for the dominant race, and negative attitudes toward one's own race and culture. The second level, Dissonance, is associated with feelings and attitudes that reflect racial-cultural confusion and conflict. Knowledge of, and experience with, the dominant race challenge prior values and beliefs held during the conformity period. In the Resistance status, the dominant society and race are rejected and a person immerses himself or herself into his or her race and culture of origin. During this period, negative feelings and attitudes are held toward the dominant race, and positive attitudes and feelings are held toward one's race of origin. The final status, Awareness, is characterized by a sense of self-fulfillment, as the confusion and conflict from the previous stages are resolved. The visible racial/ethnic person becomes capable of accepting and functioning within the dominant society while valuing and taking pride in his or her own racial-cultural heritage.

Clinical Implications

The following examples of racial identity levels for both patients and therapists are presented to enhance one's grasp of racial issues in psychotherapy. However, the reader should keep in mind that, in psychotherapy, a power differential mirrors the power dynamic of race relations in this country. Just as White Americans are in power in this country, so, too does a therapist hold the power in the therapeutic interaction. A therapist is the presumed expert with respect to mental health, and the patient, by virtue of seeking help, is less powerful. Moreover, a patient is presumed to be equipped with only his or her life experiences, concerns, or problems; a therapist is presumed to have his or her life experiences *and* mental health training. Many therapists have acquired credentials, such as an advanced degree, official certification, or a license, to support this presumption.

The power and authority differential in the therapeutic relationship can influence the expression of one's racial identity and encourage the counselor and client to behave consistently in their respective roles as therapist and patient.

To illustrate how racial identity status influences therapists and patients, I will give examples of how each level of racial identity might be expressed by a therapist or client. The following clinical example from Atwell and Azibo (1991) provides a glimpse of Pre-encounter racial identity ego status in patients and a more advanced racial identity status in the therapists.

The case describes "Erica," a 29-year-old Black woman who is energetic, attractive, and motivated. Initially, she sought treatment from an emergency room physician because she was experiencing chest pain, shortness of breath, and other physical symptoms. Her visit to the emergency room led to a concern that she was having heart failure, although tests showed no basis for that diagnosis. She was later referred to a mental health clinic and was diagnosed as having panic attacks. During the early phase of treatment, relevant personal history was uncovered, including the fact that Erica was the daughter of an interracial marriage (a Black father and a White mother who divorced when she was 6 years old). After the divorce, Erica and her younger sister were reared by the father's mother.

Atwell and Azibo (1991) also found that:

> Erica experienced significant loss with the sudden absence of her mother. Her grandmother alluded to the idea that the reason why Erica's mother left was due to the fact that she didn't want Black children. This created a sense of guilt, low self-esteem, and no sense of worth. Then there would be times . . . that her grandmother told them to take pride in their Black heritage but not to be ashamed of being partly White. Again, this enhanced guilt and shame. It also caused significant conflict around which culture to identify with as each one . . . did not want to accept her. (p. 7)

When Erica's father established another family and left her and her sister to be reared by the grandmother, she became convinced that she was "unwanted."

At age 16, her relationship with her grandmother became strained and she was asked to leave because she became pregnant by a White man. However, after some moving around, she eventually returned home. Atwell and Azibo (1991) point out that:

> Racial harmony became more difficult and racial strife was exacerbated as Erica could not align to a Black/White culture. Instead, she fluctuated between the two cultures. . . . Erica confided that she didn't understand why her family identified with the Black culture, since identification with Blackness was associated with shame, poverty, and discrimination.
>
> The panic attacks seemed to be triggered by her confrontation with her being Black. Her conflict around race, culture, etc. created extreme anxiety that was discharged through her symptoms and led to the attacks of panic. (pp. 7–8)

The therapist who worked with Erica was operating at a higher racial identity ego status than Erica. This allowed him or her to recognize Erica's core racial issues. However, a therapist who is characterized by passively or actively held negative or distancing attitudes about his or her racial group is likely to "share the dominant society's racial stereotypes of Blacks and to behave in a manner toward the client that confirms these stereotypes. Due to his or her professional training, the Pre-encounter counselor might attempt unsuccessfully to empathize with his or her Black client" (Helms, 1990, p. 136).

A Dissonance or Encounter client is likely to seek a therapist from his or her own racial group, believing that their shared racial group membership will increase understanding. However, because a person at this level of identity feels ambivalent about his or her race, he or she is likely to approach racial issues in therapy with considerable anxiety. The anxiety may manifest itself as a reluctance or assertiveness about racial beliefs. For instance, the client may assume that a Latino, Asian, or Black therapist will be able to identify with his or her problems and to offer clear and quick solutions. On the other hand, because this client is self-conscious about the therapist's reaction to his or her race, he or she may address race cautiously, if at all. Thus, the Dissonance or Encounter client is likely to be slow in engaging in the therapeutic process with a same-race therapist. This depends on the phase of Encounter or Dissonance. In phase one, discovery of race, one would not seek a same race therapist.

Similarly, an Encounter therapist may have mixed feelings when working with a same-race client. A therapist, similar to a client, wants to be seen positively but will be concerned about meeting the litmus test of his or her own racial group membership. A therapist with these ambivalent feelings may alter his or her usual therapeutic style to measure up to a client's assumed and/or unstated racial standards.

A Dissonance or Encounter therapist may express his or her confusion about race in this way. The therapist has to visit homes of clients in the course of the clinic's follow-up activities. The therapist describes an overpowering sense of fear and apprehension.

> I am now feeling afraid to go on home visits . . . I always took a cab with the same driver . . . Yesterday, they sent a new cab driver and I was suspicious of who he was. When he didn't take the same route. I was panic-stricken until I saw the house. (Pinderhughes, 1989, p. 106)

An Asian therapist in a training workshop shares the following.

> I have always rejected my race. It seemed that people held negative views of Asians so to fit in I rejected being Asian. Now I realize how that might have been harmful to me and my view of other Asians and people of color. I am not sure anymore what being Asian means but I think I need to understand and accept that part of myself. Because I am uncomfortable around other Asians and people of color. I am not sure how I would respond to an Asian client. (Pinderhughes, 1989, p. 109)

An Immersion client is likely to share his or her psychological distress only with a Black therapist. If unable to work with a Black therapist, an Immersion client may be in a continual state of psychological withdrawal, sharing only his or her anger and sense of disconnection with the non-Black clinician. In working with a Black therapist, an Immersion client will need to be convinced that this therapist meets his or her idealized standards of Blackness. An Immersion client will subject the Black therapist to a "Blackness" test before allowing himself or herself to become psychologically close and to share openly. This client may be concerned that the therapist is not truly Black because his or her status, authority, education, and training require participation in the White world. Moreover, an Immersion client might believe that these accomplishments are an indication that the therapist is psychologically invested in the world that he or she is rejecting.

A therapist whose racial identity is characterized by Immersion attitudes will typically use psychoeducational techniques with clients of his or her own race. This therapist will want to teach his or her patient the meaning of his or her racial heritage and view the patient's psychological distress in terms of race and racism. A patient who is unwilling to be educated in this manner may experience anger and hostility from the counselor.

SUMMARY

Racial identity models have aided mental health professionals tremendously in understanding the psychological aspects of visible racial/ethnic group identity development and have helped others grasp the wide diversity among Blacks, Hispanics, and other visible racial-ethnic group people. In addressing issues of racial difference and cultural diversity, the thinking has been that if we can understand them, we can help them adapt to mainstream society, that is, the onus to change remains with members of visible racial/ethnic groups.

The multicultural movement's almost exclusive emphasis on visible racial/ethnic people suggests that little effort has been extended to consider the racial identity of Whites. Instead, the assumption has been that White Americans do not belong to a distinct racial group and do not have a culture. In fact, White Americans do belong to a racial group with ethnic subgroups—Italian-American, Irish-American, German-American—and they would benefit from examining their racial backgrounds.

CHAPTER 6

White Racial Identity

If White Americans are to understand race's influence in psychotherapy, they must be able to examine and explore their own racial attitudes and traditions and to develop positive White identities that value and incorporate racial differences into American systems and institutions. Currently, Whites who espouse a positive White identity are seen as racist, perhaps because they are frequently members of race hate groups (e.g., the Ku Klux Klan). Whites can view themselves as either part of the problem or part of the solution. Typically, Whites have not included themselves in the dialogue about race, because they have been taught to explore ethnicity rather than racial group membership. This strategy leads many Whites to assume that their ethnic experiences are equivalent to the racial experiences of visible racial/ethnic group people (Carter & Goodwin, 1994).

Whites are not offered ways to develop a sense of themselves as racial beings, nor are they presented with opportunities to understand the meaning of their race if they choose, to abandon their racist perspectives. Although knowing and appreciating one's ethnic heritage is as important as other social identities (e.g., gender, socioeconomic class, religion), race, as an aspect of identity, is minimized by Whites. As a result, many discussions of cross-racial therapy have excluded Whites and their White racial identity.

Some general factors and difficulties faced by Whites in a multiracial society are offered by Karp (1981):

> The same racist view of history and the world that ignores the contributions of Third World persons also clouds the realities of the White race, which is overwhelmingly made up of people who would never defend racism. It is possible to be fully proud of all the greatness and all of the accomplishments of members of the White race without in any way being oppressive. . . . All Whites are vulnerable to the installation of racist recording. It is important to make a distinction between the . . . good nature of each person and the inappropriate, negative nature of [racist beliefs], for which a person is responsible but not to blame. (p. 93)

I agree with Karp's statement. Race is not solely the province of Blacks or people of color, so it is desirable for Whites to be positive about and proud of their Whiteness without being racist.

In 1984, Helms introduced her White racial identity theory and its five-stage developmental model, in which one moves from a low level to a higher level of identity development. Recently, she revised and expanded her 1984 model to incorporate the relationship between White racial identity, racism, and ego differential. Much of what follows is drawn from her writings in *Black and White Racial Identity* (Helms, 1990), *A Race Is a Nice Thing to Have* (Helms, 1992), and the most recent revisions of her theory (Helms, 1994; Helms & Piper, 1994). The more recent work on racial identity as discussed in Chapter 5 conceptualizes racial identity as ego identity statuses. Thus, lower, less mature statuses are more strongly associated with racism than are the more differentiated internally defined statuses. Recall also that each status may exist in a person's personality structure and be expressed in various ways. Dominant statuses may be expressed as blends of different statuses. The discussion to follow will describe each status.

Helms (1990) states that "the development of White identity in the United States is closely intertwined with the development and progress of racism in this country. The greater the extent that racism exists and is denied, the less possible it is to develop a positive White identity" (p. 49). Frequently, when race or racism is discussed, people refer to individual prejudice and discrimination or individual racism (e.g., personal ideas, attitudes, and behaviors that reinforce the belief in White superiority and visible racial/ethnic group inferiority). Individual racism is just one type of racism that exists. Jones (1972, 1981) identifies two other types: (a) institutional racism and (b) cultural racism. Institutional racism refers to social policies, legal status, and rules and regulations designed to maintain the sociopolitical and economic advantages of Whites over people of color. Cultural racism involves general social beliefs and customs that directly and indirectly communicate the superiority of White cultural ways (e.g., language, behavior, appearance, symbols, art, values) over those of visible racial/ethnic cultures. In the literature, prejudice and discrimination are acknowledged more than institutional racism or cultural racism.

All three forms of racism (i.e., individual, institutional, and cultural) can be aspects of a White person's racial identity, because each type of racism is ingrained in American cultural patterns and institutional practices (education, employment, housing, media, law, and so forth). For a White person to evolve a healthy White identity, one that is mainly nonracist, he or she must relinquish all three types of racism. This means that Whites must accept their Whiteness, understand the cultural implications and meaning of being White, and develop a self-concept devoid of any element associated with racial superiority. Helms (1990) states:

[T]he evolution of a positive White racial identity consists of two processes, the abandonment of racism and the development of a nonracist White identity. Because White racism in the United States seems to have developed as a means of justifying the enslavement of Black Americans during the slavery eras of the 1700s and 1800s (cf. Comer, 1980; Cross et al., in press; Giddings, 1984), Blacks and/or Black culture have been the primary "outgroup" or reference group around which White racial identity development issues revolve. . . . White racial identity contains parallel beliefs and attitudes about Whites as well as Blacks. (pp. 49–50)

Before the introduction of the White racial identity theory, the examination of White identity focused on explaining prejudice or individual racism. Carter and Helms (1990) observe that when White racial attitudes, defined as Whites' prejudice toward other racial groups, are explored, they are considered from the point of view of Blacks or people of color rather than Whites. That is, people of color are often the focus of racial exploration communicating the idea that race is something Blacks or Asians have, not Whites. Usually, investigators study what Whites believe, feel, or think about Blacks, Hispanics, Asians, or American Indians, and not about themselves as Whites. Helms (1984) observes that the "[investigation of] prejudice provides no information about how Whites feel about themselves as racial beings" (p. 155). The assumption that Whites' attitudes toward the outgroup(s) should be studied exclusively stems from the belief that racism was and continues to be harmful only to the oppressed and that race is associated only with Blacks or other people of color. Seldom are the harmful effects of racism on Whites discussed or studied.

Several authors argue that Whites need to understand the effects of racism on their psychosocial development. These authors describe different ways Whites avoid or do not acknowledge their racial group membership. For example, Katz and Ivey (1977) write that "when a White person [is asked] what he or she is racially, you may get the answer 'Italian,' 'English,' 'Catholic,' or 'Jewish.' White people do not see themselves as White" (p. 486). Helms (1990) believes that most Whites have no concept of what it means to have a White identity that is not supremacist. With this in mind, it is possible that many White people feel threatened by people of color who appear to have developed racial identity. However, Helms (1990) observes that "in spite of the pervasive socialization toward racism, some White people do appear not only to develop a White identity but one that is not predominated by racial distortions" (p. 53).

Two basic assumptions underlie Helms's (1990) White racial identity development theory. One assumption is that Whites are socialized to feel superior to visible racial/ethnic people by virtue of their White skin alone.

This sense of White superiority is so prevalent that it operates as a racial norm in our society, on an individual, institutional, and cultural level. The second assumption is that Whites can avoid, deny, or ignore dealing with their Whiteness. Most Whites do not recognize their race until, or unless, they have to confront the "idea" or the physical reality of Blacks and other visible/ethnic groups in their life space. Even when this happens, the emphasis is on the person of color. Helms (1990) suggests that when a White person cannot control or ignore the presence of people of color, he or she is forced to deal with White identity issues "in some way." That is, one can choose to be oblivious to race and the differential effects of race on how one is perceived and treated by society at large, or one can decide to remain fixated at one of the identity [levels] (p. 54).

Awareness of Blacks or Native American Indians comes about through indirect and direct experiences. Whites can become aware of and think about Blacks from people in their environment (e.g., parents, peers) and from societal images and messages (e.g., media). It is true that an individual's interactions with Blacks or people of color can be enjoyable and devoid of racist undertones, but eventually a White person will learn about the social norms governing cross-racial relationships. According to Helms (1990), "Significant White persons in one's environment may use the socialization pressure available to them to ensure that the White person learns the rules of being a socially accepted White person" (p. 54). Smith (1961, as cited in Dennis, 1981) describes the socialization process this way:

> From the time little . . . white children take their first step they learn their ritual, for the . . . tradition leads them through its intricate movements . . . [and] these ceremonials in honor of white supremacy, performed from babyhood, slip from conscious down deep into muscles and glands and become difficult to tear out. (pp. 72–73)

WHITE RACIAL IDENTITY

Helms's (1990, 1992, 1994) and Helms and Piper's (1994) revised White identity development theory proposes a six-status process:

1. Contact.
2. Disintegration.
3. Reintegration.
4. Pseudo-Independence.
5. Immersion–Emersion.
6. Autonomy.

In the revised model, the statuses are divided into two phases: (a) the abandonment of a racist identity (Contact–Reintegration); and (b) the establishment of a nonracist White identity (Immersion–Autonomy).

Contact

The Contact status, the first level of White identity development, is characterized by a lack of racial awareness about the self and others. A person's family environment influences him or her to be naive, curious, or timid about Blacks and other people of color. A person with a Contact racial identity status will have attitudes and beliefs that lead him or her to engage in unsophisticated behaviors reflecting individual racism. Because the person is only minimally aware of race and racial issues, he or she unknowingly benefits from institutional and cultural racism. Generally, a person at this level of development will unconsciously judge people of color by using White society's standards (e.g., White cultural values, standardized tests) and can be unaware of other criteria (e.g., interpersonal skills, ability to read nonverbal messages). More importantly, the individual is unaware that he or she might be judged according to other racial/cultural group criteria (e.g., communication styles, spiritual emphasis; see Kochman, 1989).

Usually, people with a Contact ego identity status have limited social or occupational interactions with Blacks or people of color, unless people of color initiate the interactions and "seem" White (i.e., have Preencounter attitudes). Statements such as "I don't notice what race a person is" and "I just treat people as people" illustrate attitudes associated with people in the Contact status. An individual is likely to remain in Contact, especially if his or her interactions with Blacks are indirect. Usually, a lack of direct involvement leaves a person fearful and cautious of Blacks. Since much of what a person can learn about people of color, especially Blacks, is negative,

> the person [in Contact] is likely to continue to engage in minimal cross-racial interaction, is unlikely to be forced to rethink her or his racial perspective, [and his or her behavior and views are] . . . tolerated by his or her racial peers. (Helms, 1990, p. 57)

If a person has had and continues to have cross-racial interactions, eventually his or her peers will make it known that such behavior is unacceptable, especially if the person wants to maintain his or her good standing within the "White" group. Through these cross-racial interactions, a White individual will begin to understand the norms governing these interactions and the different treatment of Blacks and Whites in the United States.

Disintegration

Awareness of racial differences leads to the development of the second status, Disintegration. This level of White racial identity is characterized by conscious awareness of one's Whiteness and conflictual feelings regarding this awareness. Disintegration is associated with emotional conflicts, psychological confusion, and moral dilemmas that arise as a person confronts his or her sense of human decency and the racial norms in the society. People become conflicted about their beliefs in life, liberty, and happiness, and the reality of racial inequalities. While believing in equality, they discover that people of color and Whites, as groups and as individuals, are not equal, regardless of statements to the contrary. A particularly difficult dilemma occurs when an individual is cognizant that negative social consequences can befall a White person who does not respect racial inequalities. As a result, people feel caught between racial groups and realize that maintaining their position among Whites depends on how well they can split their personality (Helms, 1990). However, a person may selectively attend to information that supports his or her new beliefs and limit interactions to those individuals who support the new beliefs.

Associated with the moral and psychological discoveries and dilemmas are intense feelings of discovery and excitement, as well as guilt, depression, helplessness, shame, and anxiety. To resolve his or her confusion and conflict, a White person may (a) avoid people of color or Blacks altogether, thus fixating at this level, (b) try to convince people that Blacks or Native Americans are not inferior, or (c) decide and then support the view that racism really does not exist, or, if it does, that Whites have little to do with it. The option chosen depends on the degree to which cross-racial interactions are voluntary. The most expedient option for alleviating these conflictual feelings would be to remove oneself physically if possible or psychologically from interracial contact. This option is only possible when contact is voluntary. If it is not voluntary, then other options must be considered. However, if people can avoid contact with Hispanics or Blacks, given the support they are likely to receive from an exclusively White environment for the development of their individual racism and the maintenance of cultural and institutional racism (Helms, 1990), this is a likely choice.

Given the pressure to be accepted by one's own racial group and the sociocultural depth of the beliefs in White superiority, one is likely to believe that racism does not exist, or, if it does, that it is a remnant of the past. These types of ideas lead the person to enter the next level, Reintegration.

Reintegration

Reintegration, the third level of White identity development, becomes more prominent when a person acknowledges that he or she is White and adopts a belief in White racial superiority and visible racial/ethnic group inferiority. An individual believes that: White cultural and institutional racism is a White person's right because he or she has earned the privileges and preferences. "Negative race-related conditions are assumed to result from Black people's inferior social, moral, and intellectual qualities" (Helms, 1990). Thus, people at this status selectively attend and reinterpret information to conform to societal stereotypes. Affectively, people may feel afraid and angry; however, these feelings are usually unconscious and seldom overtly expressed.

In the Reintegration level of White identity development, people tend to express their beliefs and feelings either passively or actively. Each form of expression reflects the extent to which these racial views are held as part of a conscious ideology (i.e., active expression) or as facts (i.e., passive expression). People who hold these views passively may stay as far away as possible from Blacks; individuals who hold these views actively may be involved in organized efforts to protect White privilege, traditions, and heritage by deliberately promoting measures that treat Blacks as inferior, engaging in acts of violence, or maintaining racial exclusion.

American society's racial and cultural norms enable many Whites to remain fixated in the Reintegration status. A personally significant and powerful event with either Blacks or Whites may be necessary for an individual to begin questioning and to abandon this racist identity. For example, events occurring during certain social or political movements (e.g., the civil rights movement, the multicultural movement) may trigger a person to examine long-held beliefs about race and culture. This type of questioning facilitates the person's movement into the Pseudo-Independent White racial identity status.

Pseudo-Independence

The process of defining a positive White identity begins in the Pseudo-Independence status, when an individual reexamines ideas and knowledge about Blacks and other people of color. In the Pseudo-Independence status, a White person begins to question whether Blacks are innately inferior to Whites and to realize that Whites have a responsibility for racism. Additionally, Whites at this level begin to comprehend how intentionally or unintentionally he or she has supported and participated in all forms of racism. Consequently, these individuals are uncomfortable with themselves as White people and start to alter their outlook. These changes, however, are primarily intellectual.

Discomfort with a White identity and increased awareness of Blacks (and other visible racial/ethnic group people) may lead a person to feel more identified with Blacks and less comfortable with Whites when racial issues are discussed. In Pseudo-Independence, a person's interactions with Blacks may take the form of helping them to meet the prevailing White societal standards. Applying these mainstream standards to people from other racial groups demonstrates minimal awareness on the part of the White person, particularly when the goal is to understand a person from his or her own racial-cultural perspective.

People in the Pseudo-Independence level interpret racial differences from a White perspective, usually ethnically derived, and promote the use of their successful strategies for members of other racial groups. At this level of development, Whites ask Blacks exclusively to explain the history and effects of racism and to provide solutions to racial issues.

At this point, an individual is in the process of rejecting externally defined racial views and is transitioning to a positive, nonracist White identity. Helms (1990) points out that the paucity of White models of positive Whiteness means that the person usually has no visible standards against which to compare and/or modify himself or herself. During this developmental transition, a White person can feel marginal, as if he or she does not belong to either racial group. During this transition, an individual discovers that both Blacks and Whites question his or her motives and react to him or her with some distrust. According to Helms (1990):

> Whites may respond as if the person has violated racial norms and Blacks will wonder about their motives, since a White individual focuses his or her energy on changing Blacks, not Whites. The person at this level of White identity begins to feel marginal regarding race and racial issues. However, if they have incentives to persevere, these people will continue their quest for positive aspects of being White that are unrelated to racism and a better understanding of one's Whiteness. These activities lead individuals into Immersion–Emersion, the fifth [level] of White racial identity development. (p. 62)

Immersion–Emersion

For Whites, the Immersion–Emersion status is distinct from the corresponding level for Blacks in that Whites do not reject Blacks, but embrace Whites. In this level of racial identity development, Whites revise myths about Blacks and Whites by incorporating accurate information about the present with the historical significance and meaning of racial group memberships.

In Immersion, a person starts a process of self-exploration and discovery fueled by questions such as "Who am I racially?," "Who do I want to be?" (Helms, 1990, p. 62), and "How can I feel proud of my race without being a racist?" These types of questions lead an individual onto a path of learning and soul searching. During the self-exploration and discovery process, an individual may seek out other Whites for answers to specific questions. An individual may read biographies and autobiographies of people who have had similar identity journeys or may join a White consciousness-raising group. During this status, the focus has shifted from changing Blacks to changing themselves and other Whites. According to Helms (1990):

> Emotional as well as cognitive restructuring can happen during this stage [status]. Successful resolution of this stage [status] apparently requires emotional catharsis [or release] in which the person reexperiences previous emotions that were denied or distorted (cf. Lipsky, 1978). Once these negative feelings are expressed, the person may begin to feel a euphoria perhaps akin to a religious rebirth. These positive feelings not only help to buttress the newly developing White identity, but provide the fuel by which the person can truly begin to tackle racism and oppression in its various forms. (p. 62)

Autonomy

The final level of White racial identity, Autonomy, occurs when an individual internalizes, nurtures, and applies the new meaning of Whiteness to his or her interactions and does not oppress, idealize, or denigrate people of color based on racial group membership. Because race is no longer a threat, he or she can abandon cultural, institutional, and personal racist practices and have a more flexible worldview. Helms suggests that a person in Autonomy is open to new information about race and, consequently, can operate effectively across racial groups. Also, a person in this level of White identity values and seeks out cross-racial experiences, and views these interactions as beneficial and worthwhile. It is important to show how White racial identity might be expressed in clients and counselors. The next section describes levels of White identity in terms of clinical expressions.

Clinical Expressions: White Racial Identity Statuses

A counselor should be aware of his or her client's racial identity level, the corresponding value orientations associated with each level, and their impact on the client's personal lifestyle. In addition, many familial characteristics of visible racial/ethnic group members are antithetical to those of White Americans.

The client with predominantly Contact ego identity status believes, at least consciously, that race is irrelevant and does not think in racial terms. Consequently, when confronted, he or she is likely to psychologically deny or avoid a racial issue or a visible racial/ethnic therapist. The person may make an exception and accept the therapist of color as being unlike members of his or her racial group. Additionally, the client may focus on the person's professional role as mental health expert or may emphasize how their personalities are similar or dissimilar.

A person is likely to seek treatment from a therapist because of interpersonal or intrapsyche experience(s) that he or she is unable to comprehend. The experience might come from members of his or her own race or from an interracial experience. But, regardless of a patient's race, a counselor who is at the Contact level essentially approaches race as less important than other intrapsychic or subjective experiences. The clinician's knowledge of race and culture is derived from his or her traditional training, which ignores race except for noting that Blacks, Asians, Latinos, and Native Americans are from different cultures. A therapist who believes that Whites and visible racial/ethnic people are culturally different is likely to think that a client should be treated by a member of his or her own race. When that is impossible, the clinician may approach cross-racial therapy from a paternal or overinvolved stance, which often results in frustration and failure. As taught, the therapist may try to be "sensitive" to those "facts," but his or her belief that all people are basically the same and should be accorded equal treatment will guide the clinician.

On a subconscious level, a client at the Disintegration status does not believe that race is important; however, he or she may be open to discovering its importance. The psychological trauma associated with this discovery process causes considerable pain and discomfort. Spurlock (1973) offers an example of racial discovery involving Susan, a 16-year-old:

> . . . [an] honor student in a suburban high school [who] talked of her "awareness" stemming from her interest in history. She was at a loss to explain why she suddenly felt driven to delve into the history of slavery. At any rate, she did and began to learn much about American history that was not a part of her textbooks and/or was a distortion. At the same time, she was a participant in an exchange-student program and came to know Blacks other than the household help. As she became more exposed to the "real world," she became more aware of the great discrepancies in what she had been taught and "what's for real." Having always been a verbally aggressive and questioning child, she felt no hesitation in questioning instructors about the value of texts selected for use in her school. She raised the same question and related ones with her parents, from

whom she got "double-talk" as a response. The budding cynicism spread like wildfire during her spring-vacation experience of working in a social agency, the clients of which were mostly inner-city Blacks.

Her parents had initially supported her in this venture. Her mother had always been active in several charitable organizations, and she knew her father had frequently made sizable financial contributions to liberal causes. So it seemed as if she was simply carrying on a family tradition. But the more she raised questions about what she saw as institutionalized racism and questioned her parents' support of the same, the less enchanted her parents became about her volunteer services. They expressed concern that she was being wrongly influenced by the kind of people who came to the center and strongly suggested that she abandon her plan to spend a month of her summer vacation working at the agency. Susan angrily exclaimed that she got the same kind of response from their minister, whom she had previously viewed as a "true liberal" who had genuine concern for all people. As Susan's cynicism grew with leaps and bounds, she became increasingly less effective in any undertaking. Susan experienced a disastrous, intense idealization of parental images and/or the good superego, leading to defensive patterns to protect her from archaic superego remnants. The precipitant is clearly racism. (pp. 160–161)

Susan's story shows some of the experiences and emotional conflicts that are characteristic of someone at the Disintegration level of racial identity. Such a person might not present in therapy specifically with race as an issue. Susan's problem was family conflict; nevertheless, race conflict was at the root of the family conflict.

Ordway's (1973) case of a White, male social worker who consulted a White therapist, who appeared to be at a more advanced level of racial identity, illustrates some of the racial issues associated with the Pseudo-Independence level that may arise in treatment. The social worker's cases were in a Black community, and, over time, he became deeply invested in the people and their community. However, he began to gradually recognize signs that he was conflicted. He understood the angry feelings voiced by Whites toward Blacks and vice versa, and he felt torn between the two communities.

In the White community, on the one hand, he learns through the city hall grapevine that the police feel he has "become Black, gone over to the enemy, and is no longer trustworthy." On the other hand, in the ghetto, he feels that he "tells it like it is" to Black acquaintances, but that his words are still greeted with suspicion. (p. 125)

Ordway's (1973) client describes the sense of marginality characteristic of a Pseudo-Independent ego identity status in the following exchange:

CLIENT: I get mad as hell at "them," and as a matter of fact I seem to be mad every time I go over to the Black community. There seems to be no casual liking, agreeableness, affection, trust, charity, or anything positive in some of "those people," and I don't know if there ever will be. There is really no pleasure whatsoever in dealing with some of "these" Black workers. "They" seem more insistent on showing anger or finding loopholes or weaknesses in what I say or do than in working with me.

THERAPIST: Didn't you say that three years ago you and the regional NIMH [National Institute of Mental Health] office purposely picked out the most militant and angriest group with which to work?

CLIENT: Yes, I did. Consciously I did it out of a sense of challenge and some kind of a crazy wish to explore territory that I thought I understood before, but really didn't. But now it seems to me that I did it out of masochism. I'm fed up with the whole damned business. I'm really not. But then again I am. Every time that I get on stable ground or what seems like stable ground with these people, they cut it out from under me and leave me wondering just what the truth is and where I am. I feel impotent and nagged and kind of beaten up.

THERAPIST: Didn't you say that Black–White interface was marked by a struggle to see who is the master and the slave? Isn't everything you describe inevitable?

CLIENT: Yes, I suppose it is. They don't know that they're beating on me sometimes. Other times they do know they're beating on me. Sometimes they enjoy it and know what is going on. Other times I'm not sure that they really know how difficult it is for me to stay motivated to help when their main reaction is negative, critical, and hostile. And in fact they still seem to see me so much as a White master whom they unconsciously expect too much of or want to kill and destroy that I don't really know if we'll ever be able to work together. They say they're not racist, but I dunno. *(Pause)* You know, I hadn't thought of it before, but I think that I'm acting like a suffering slave. I don't really have to take all of this as an attack on me personally. It's an attack on me as a White. . . . Perhaps I can listen to all this anger but not react quite so much—"quite so much"—that was an interesting statement. I shouldn't react at all as a slave; but be myself, to be me, a professional—empathic but objective. I don't have to live out slavery in order to understand it. Perhaps some of the people in my project were right when they said to go back to my White friends for a while and get them together. Perhaps what they meant also was for me to get myself together psychologically. (p. 12)

Summary

In the therapeutic process, an understanding of race, racial identity, and culture as separate constructs is important; however, understanding the interconnections among these three variables is essential as well. As I have indicated, every person belongs to a racial group from which he or she derives a psychological, emotional, and behavioral filter through which the self, others, and the world are seen. Historically and presently, people are assigned cultural characteristics based on their racial group. For example, Asians, Hispanics, or Blacks are likely to have cultural patterns ascribed to them simply and primarily because of their racial group membership (e.g., Asian—submissive, disciplined; Latino(a)—spiritual, with large families; Black—present- and family-oriented).

I have argued that a mediating factor in assessing a person's cultural group membership is equivalent to the psychological state of his or her racial group membership or racial identity. Members of visible racial/ethnic groups who identify psychologically with White American culture reflect low levels of racial identity development. Also, Whites can reach a level of racial identity such that they are no longer invested in American cultural patterns (e.g., belief that people of color are innately inferior; focus on the future). Therefore, race per se does not determine one's cultural orientation; rather, one's overall psychological view of his or her racial group is the primary indicator of culture. For Whites, who rarely think of themselves in racial terms, low levels of racial identity development reflect a tacit acceptance of White American cultural patterns and traditions. For Blacks and other visible racial/ethnic group people, low levels of racial identity usually indicate a belief in White American culture. People from any race who develop or who are raised to attain higher levels of racial identity will probably be active participants in their group's culture. An individual's cultural group membership, which is associated with one's racial identity, will create a filter that one uses for understanding people and the world.

CONCLUSION

The first step to becoming a competent clinician in cross-racial counseling is to assess your level of racial identity. If, based on this assessment, one concludes that he or she has not progressed through these levels of White racial identity, then an individual should engage in a process of raising his or her level of racial identity. One way to facilitate this process is to expand one's knowledge and awareness of racial/ethnic issues and concerns, such as learning about the nature and history of race relations in the United States.

Thus far, I have presented racial identity development theory as it pertains to all racial/ethnic people and have argued that racial identity is an integral aspect of personal identity. In Part Three, I will present research findings which indicate that an individual's level of racial identity development is related to his or her intrapsychic life, interpersonal competence, perceptions of the environment, and worldview or cultural values. Recently, Carter and Helms (1987) have found that Blacks with racial identity attitudes associated with one's Blackness or racial group (Immersion–Emersion and Internalization) are predictive of Afrocentric cultural values. This finding supports the contention that only when people psychologically identify with their racial group do they participate in their group's cultural patterns. On the other hand, Blacks and other visible racial/ethnic group members who have attitudes associated with low levels of racial identity (e.g., Pre-encounter) identify with White American cultural patterns.

Similarly, Carter and Helms (1990) have found that Whites who have attitudes associated with low levels of racial identity development (i.e., Contact, Disintegration, Reintegration, and Pseudo-Independence) have traditional American cultural values. This suggests that ones identification with his or her racial group is related to the person's psychological investment in his or her cultural group.

A person's worldview, through the lens of racial identity, has implications for how he or she processes information, forms perceptions, understands behavior, and selects and understands what is important. Stewart and Bennett (1991) argue that racial and cultural assumptions have powerful influences on how a person interprets himself or herself and others. Additionally, a person from any racial/ethnic group who psychologically identifies with traditional White American cultural values uses this orientation to guide his or her thoughts, behaviors, and feelings. Therefore, one's racial identity operates as a filter for one's thoughts, feelings, and behaviors and shapes his or her worldview. Race, racial identity, personality, and one's worldview are intimately connected and intertwined. If this is the case, then each participant in a therapeutic relationship brings a particular mental framework that originates from his or her racial identity.

CHAPTER 7

Biracial Identity and Questions and Concerns about Racial Identity Status Development

After learning about racial identity theories, people usually have a number of questions. Some inquiries have to do with the process of racial identity development, as outlined in the model, and others have to do with its application. Some confusion also arises around the distinctions among racial, ethnic, and cultural identity, and related terms. Lastly, people ask how the theory addresses biracial individuals. In this chapter, I share my thinking about biracial identity and address some of these questions and concerns.

BIRACIAL IDENTITY

A biracial person is someone who is born to parents from two different racial groups or a person of color who was transracially raised by White parents. Where does a biracial person belong in the context of racial identity theory? One might argue that separate theories of biracial identity are essential, because being biracial involves learning how to embrace two racial groups, which can be difficult when an individual is uncomfortable in one of the two groups (Herring, 1995; Poston, 1990). So, how do we understand biracial identity development and the processes by which a biracial person develops a biracial identity? Many scholars have addressed this issue in the psychology literature (e.g., Gibbs & Moskowitz-Sweet, 1991; Grove, 1991; Johnson, 1992; Njeri, 1991; Overmier, 1990; Tizard & Phoenix, 1993; Winn & Priest, 1993).

Some writers (e.g., Poston, 1990; Herring, 1995) argue that a separate theory is needed to explain how people who are biracial develop a racial identity. Poston proposes that biracial identity has five stages:

1. *Personal identity*—the person has no awareness of himself or herself as a biracial person. Poston suggests that this stage occurs

during childhood, when children are influenced by factors other than race.

2. *Choice of group categorization*—the individual is forced to choose one racial group to identify with. This stage is described as a time of crisis and alienation, where society forces a choice. The person can reject such a choice by declaring a "multicultural" identity, or he or she can identify with one of his or her two racial groups. The choice is influenced by the social status of each group, in conjunction with the community in which the person lives, and parental and peer influences. *Social support* refers to how one's parents participate in or identify with his or her racial group. Lastly, the choice is influenced by physical features, personality, age, and political affiliation.

3. *Enmeshment/Denial*—one becomes confused and guilt-ridden at having to make a choice that is not a true reflection of his or her identity. Poston suggests that this person experiences lack of group acceptance and suffers from low self-esteem. The individual feels disloyal to one of his or her parents, and worries about how his or her peer group will respond if they meet the parents. The child strives to resolve the guilt and confusion by identifying with both racial groups.

4. *Appreciation*—while still invested in one racial group, the person begins to explore and acquire knowledge about the denied group.

5. *Integration*—the person recognizes and values all his or her "ethnic identities" (Poston, 1990, p. 154).

Poston's model is useful but limited: he confuses race, ethnicity, and culture (Herring, 1995). In describing the five stages, he uses *culture* and *ethnicity,* not *race,* and thus does not consider important sociopolitical realities. Johnson (1990) describes the rationale and importance of the term race, rather than ethnicity, when referring to biracial individuals. He suggests that biracial individuals possess a combination of the physical characteristics of different racial ancestries. The use of the term biracial implies this genetic mixture, whereas physical or genetic differences are not inherent within different cultures or ethnicities. However, these realities are alluded to in the choice stage, where Poston acknowledges that physical features, social group status, and parental level of racial identity are factors that influence biracial identity. Furthermore, Poston's model and most mixed race identity development models do not describe the process wherein even if a biracial person chooses a reference group, he or she may not have guaranteed acceptance by that, or any racial group. Root (1990) suggests that the process of looking for acceptance from others keeps the biracial person trying to live by dichotomous racial classification rules which may keep her or him marginal to any group.

Instead, Root suggests that to have a healthy racial identity, a biracial person must do the following: accept both sides of his or her racial heritage, declare how he or she wishes to identify themselves, and develop strategies for coping with social resistance or questions about their racial identity. Her schematic model for understanding the process of identity development for persons with different types of "other" status presumes that the central conflict for the biracial person is the tendency to compartmentalize and separate the racial components of their parents. According to Root, there are four general resolutions of biracial identity when one no longer compartmentalizes the parts of their heritage. The first resolution is *Acceptance of the Identity Society Assigns.* This is a passive resolution where the person has accepted the identity that has been assigned him or her. This resolution can be positive if the individual feels that he or she belongs to the racial group to which they are assigned. However, this resolution is the most tenuous since the individual may be assigned to a different group in different locations. The second resolution is *Identification with both Racial Groups.* This is the most idealistic resolution where an individual identifies with both racial groups they have inherited and feel privileged in both groups. The third resolution is *Identification with a Single Racial Group.* In this resolution a person actively chooses to identify with a particular racial group that may not have been assigned by society. The fourth resolution is *Identification as a new Racial Group.* This person probably feels more connected to other biracial people rather than to any other racial group.

I understand the issues of biracial identity in the following way. Historically, race has been defined in this country in terms of (presumably) biological or genetic criteria. Initially, people used physical features to classify others into racial groups (see Chapter 2), and physical anthropologists actually set out to identify races on the basis of physical characteristics such as hair texture, lip size, and skin color (Tizard & Phoenix, 1993). They developed measures and procedures for utilizing these physiognomic features, but, despite their efforts, people could not be accurately characterized according to these measures, no matter what their standards. Scientists then shifted their search from physical features to genetics; however, classification problems persisted, given the large genetic population pools. The next popular approach to classifying people was the "one-drop" racial standard, by which one quantum of non-White blood classified a person as being a person of color, regardless of his or her actual skin color. Poussaint (1984) notes that any individual with one Black and one non-Black parent is considered Black. This was especially true for classifying people of color. To be White, one had to be pure White, that is, have no non-White blood. Special terms (e.g., *mulatto, quadroon*) (Root, 1990) were created to reflect gradation of Whiteness or portions of White blood that Black–White biracial people were presumed to have. Historically, biracial people were labeled as persons of color or Black because of their non-White blood. When an individual's racial mixture was other than Black and White, the term *half-breed* was usually used to identify the person.

Today, people argue that the one-drop solution is not a useful way to categorize people who are biracial. They propose the creation of a category for biracial people that acknowledges them as separate and distinct from people of color and Whites. Others, however, argue that this new category is designed to distance biracial people from people of color and enable them to avoid the stigma associated with membership in a visible racial group. And yet, the societal practices associated with racial group membership suggest that if a biracial person whose skin color and/or physical features indicate a racial mixture decides to categorize himself or herself as biracial, he or she could so identify internally or psychologically, but this self-designation would be constantly challenged. These challenges are frequently subtle and indirect. This type of person would encounter continual questioning about race because of his or her appearance. (As noted earlier, skin color is a primary criterion for racial categories.) Although people may identify themselves as biracial or as White, society says they are people of color if they are too dark. If one's physical appearance is ambiguous, then one has to explain oneself by answering questions such as: What are you? Where are you from? Root (1990) argues that while biracial people should have the right to declare their racial identity, they must also develop strategies for coping with social resistance or questions about their racial group membership so that they do not begin to question themselves.

If a person wants to be racially neutral (i.e., mixed, or human, or biracial), then in all social settings, he or she has to avoid relatives, especially non-White relatives, because the individual will be identified as a person of color, regardless of what he or she thinks or looks like (Johnson, 1992).

I believe that it is possible to have a biracial identity. The process a person goes through to accomplish a biracial identity involves an acceptance of both aspects of his or her racial heritage (Root, 1990). Let me use the Black–White biracial group as an example. For a biracial person with a Black and a White parent to evolve a positive biracial race identity in which both the Black and White aspects of his or her identity are embraced, I contend that he or she has to (1) evolve a positive internalized Black identity, and (2) embrace and internalize the White side of the biracial identity. (This does not mean that he or she develops a positive White racial identity.)

This process of identification is important for several reasons. First, biracial persons do not have much choice in how they are identified. Any person with non-White features or traceable non-White blood will be considered non-White. Thus it is imperative that biracial (Black/White) person have a positive Black identity since he or she is likely to be assigned to that racial group. Second, given the hierarchy of racial groups in the U.S., a biracial person (Black/White) is likely to experience oppression from the higher status group (White). Root (1990) suggests that biracial people from two minority groups are likely to experience oppression from the higher status group. Thus, it is even more important to be grounded in the devalued racial group.

If a person wants to achieve a biracial identity, he or she has to take in and value both racial parts of himself or herself. Any effort to let go of either part necessarily sabotages the process. If the Black part is rejected and the person looks White, what that person essentially has to do is become White. He or she could not have a biracial identity, but could have a White identity as long as "passing" is possible and no one would ever know that there were any Black people in the person's family history. Passing for White presents some problems, particularly for biracial persons: their heritage may reveal itself if they have children. They cannot develop a positive White identity because they are not White. "A sense of belonging and of historical continuity is a basic psychological need. We may ignore it or cut it off by changing our names and rejecting our families and social backgrounds, but we do so to the detriment of our well-being" (McGoldrick et al., 1982, p. 5).

If, however, the person looks White and chooses to pass for White, thus rejecting the Black half of his or her identity, then the individual has to disown his or her family (i.e., totally divorce himself or herself from anyone in the family who is Black). The biracial person cannot invite his or her parents to social functions because then he or she would be found out and unable to pass for White. So, the process of passing for White requires a person to give up any part of his or her identity and family that is Black.

I believe that one cannot develop a biracial identity if he or she tries to pass for White, because this requires letting go of one's biracial identity. I do not think that it is possible to develop a "mixed-race" or a White and a Black identity at the same time, because I do not see how a dual identity process can occur. One can value both sides, but that means that one cannot focus on one race, so it is not possible to develop a positive "dual race" or "mixed-race" identity by evolving the Black and the White aspects simultaneously. If the goal is to ultimately develop a biracial identity in which one accepts both racial parts, I think a base is needed. In other words, to have an identity, one has to have a psychosocial foundation. I do not think it is possible to have an identity on a psychosocial foundation that is at odds with itself. To the extent that racial groups have been and continue to be separate and to some extent in conflict, they are at odds if they are comprised of parts that do not value one another in sociopolitical or other terms. Psychosocial conflict results. Historically, Whites and Blacks have been at odds with each other. So, a psychosocial basis is needed, a foundation on which one can evolve a positive sense of self. If one evolves a sense of self that is combined racially, then one essentially is psychologically and socially marginal. One may remain forever marginal while not admitting it to anyone. The feeling of marginality may be hard to shake: one may feel uncomfortable around and with Black people and at the same time not feel totally accepted and comfortable with Whites. A psychologically grounded identity has not been formed because of the consistent experience of marginality.

I think a biracial individual needs to have a firm psychosocial foundation in one of his or her racial groups, to enable him or her to develop and embrace the other racial group. For instance, if the person is a Black Asian, he or she has to choose which racial group to be grounded in before he or she can incorporate the other group. Then, in time, he or she can merge the other racial group with the grounded racial identity. But, in the absence of the psychosocial grounding, one is not quite complete; one may feel as if he or she does not have a hold of his or her self.

I contend that it is possible to evolve a biracial identity. Again, take Black and White as an example. When one has first developed a positive Black identity and uses the Black identity as a foundation, it allows incorporation of the White aspect of identity. Only then can a person be truly biracial, identifying with both racial groups. One can be positive, internalized, and biracial, and not have to compromise any part of oneself. The person would also have a psychological home where he or she is accepted—maybe not on all terms and with everyone, but enough to be psychosocially grounded in a biracial identity. Essentially, I am suggesting that a person who is biracial should become grounded in the devalued racial group as a foundation for facilitating the merger of the two racial groups. This is particularly true for racial groups in the United States.

Clinical Implications

Although studies on the psychological well-being of biracial people have produced inconsistent findings, most clinicians and researchers agree that the identity process is particularly challenging for biracial people. Erikson (1959) suggests that a developmental task is to develop a personal identity (sense of uniqueness and self-esteem) among other things.

Several authors have noted that in addition to Erikson's personal identity tasks, adolescents must develop a racial identity in order to form a cohesive total identity (Chestang, 1984). Other authors (e.g., Piskacek & Golubs, 1973; Sommers, 1964) argue that identity formation is even more problematic for biracial adolescents. Gibbs (1990) and Gibbs and

Moskowitz-Sweet, (1991) propose that biracial adolescents may experience conflicts around the following five major psychosocial tasks: the formation of a dual racial/ethnic identity, conflicts around social marginality, conflicts about sexuality and choice of sexual partner, conflicts about separation from their parents, and conflicts about their educational or career aspirations. These conflicts may be expressed in symptoms of anxiety and depression, academic under achievement, substance abuse, or suicidal behaviors (Gibbs, 1990).

Nonetheless, Gibbs (1990) proposes that the biracial adolescent must first resolve his or her underlying attitudes toward their dual racial/ethnic heritage before successfully integrating the developmental tasks in the four related areas of identity achievement (Overmier, 1990).

DISTINCTIONS AMONG CULTURAL, ETHNIC, AND RACIAL IDENTITIES

The distinction among cultural, ethnic, and racial identity will be addressed first. *Cultural identity* refers to the extent to which one learns through socialization to interpret meaning in his or her world. *Meaning* has to do with communication, language, symbols, family systems, and one's understanding of the nature of the universe. Much of this cultural learning is subliminal and often not conscious unless one encounters another worldview. However, a separate and distinct group with unique cultural patterns can function within a larger society or culture. A group's distinctiveness might be due to one factor or a combination of factors, including national origin (different from larger society), geographic distance (isolated from larger society), segregation (forcibly separated from larger society), lifestyle choice (maintaining traditional lifestyle within a developed society), and/or religious beliefs. Ethnic and cultural identity are associated to the extent that both are learned (see Chapter 1), and a person is psychologically invested in his or her ethnic or cultural group. The term *cultural group* is extremely broad and includes ethnicity. *Ethnicity* refers to national or religious origin, which exists in a distinctly different superordinate culture. For instance, for some people, *ethnicity* and *culture* are the same: some White Americans identify with an ethnic group—Italians, Greeks, Jews—and with American culture. The essential idea here is that one's ethnic or cultural identity is flexible and fluid; it can change. A Korean or Navajo or Mexican can choose to identify as primarily American.

Skin color and physical features, which are criteria for defining races in America, have been used to group people whose characteristics were thought to be permanent. Ethnic variation within racial groups exists, but ethnicity is not the same as race, as used in the United States. For instance, all Americans are, to some extent, culturally American, yet persons from Irish, West Indian, Vietnamese, and Hopi origins all have distinct ethnic or cultural beliefs and patterns. Even though ethnic variation exists within racial groups, the differences among racial groups are believed to be unchangeable and more pronounced than those among ethnic groups, and Blacks, Asians, Hispanics, American Indians, and Whites have formed relationships with one another based on racial group membership rather than on ethnic origin.

I believe that ethnic or cultural identity is a salient part of identity for many people and that each person in the United States has a racial and an ethnic identity. These identities may interact, but they are not equally potent in society and they cannot be substituted for one another. Few models of cultural identity have been proposed. Banks (1988) proposes an ethnic identity development typology that can be thought of as describing both cultural and ethnic identity. I present this model in recognition of the importance of ethnic and cultural identity and also to note the similarities and differences between racial and ethnic identity. Banks states that this typology "attempts to outline the basic stages of development of ethnicity among individual members of ethnic groups" (p. 194) and consists of six developmental stages:

1. Ethnic psychological captivity.
2. Ethnic encapsulation.
3. Ethnic identity clarification.
4. Biethnicity.
5. Multiethnicity and reflective nationalism.
6. Globalism and global competency.

Stage one, ethnic psychological captivity, is analogous to the Pre-encounter level of the Black racial identity model and the Disintegration phase of White racial identity theory. An individual at this stage of ethnic development "absorbs the negative ideologies and beliefs about his or her ethnic group that are institutionalized within society" (Banks, 1988, p. 194) and seeks to assimilate into the social mainstream.

During stage two, ethnic encapsulation, the individual defines his or her ethnic group as superior to others. According to Banks, this may be a consequence of several factors: the internalization of social misconceptions about certain other ethnic groups; the emergence of a "new ethnic consciousness" or "revitalization" (p. 195) where one's ethnic group is idealized; or the consideration that one's ethnicity and way of life must be protected against "out groups." Ethnic encapsulation is analogous to the Reintegration phase of White racial identity development and to the Immersion phase of Black racial identity development.

Ethnic identity clarification, stage three, is characterized by self-acceptance and the ability to "respond more positively to outside ethnic groups . . . to accept and understand both the positive and negative attributes of his or her ethnic group" (p. 196). These characteristics reflect those of individuals at the Emersion level of Black racial identity development or the Immersion–Emersion stage of White racial identity development.

Stage four is termed biethnicity. Individuals at this stage have "a healthy sense of ethnic identity" (p. 196) and are able to function effectively in two ethnic cultures. This ability to participate in ethnic contexts different from one's own is extended and further developed in stage five, multiethnicity and reflective nationalism, where one is "able to function, at least beyond superficial levels, within several cultures within his or her nation and to understand, appreciate and share the values, symbols and institutions" (p. 196) of these ethnic cultures. Individuals at stages four and five are comparable to those who have reached the Autonomy level of White racial identity development and the Internalization status of the Black racial identity model.

Finally, in Bank's stage six, globalism and global competency, the individual is able to function comfortably in ethnic cultures and contexts globally, having achieved "the ideal delicate balance of ethnic, national and global identifications, commitments, literacy, and behaviors" (p. 197).

Banks's typology remains primarily hypothetical and uses ethnicity or culture rather than race as a primary construct, but there are clear similarities and conceptual connections between his work and that of the racial identity theorists. Nevertheless, ethnic or cultural identity is dynamic, and race is thought of and treated as if it is static. The confusion regarding these forms of identity arises because the terms race, culture, and ethnicity are often used interchangeably in social scientific writing. However, consider the fact that although Black, Indian, and White Americans are in many ways culturally similar and ethnically variable, they remain separate and distinct groups in North American society primarily on the basis of race.

I maintain that it is one thing to work through the meaning of being Nigerian, Italian, Jewish, Korean, Jamaican, Hopi, Seneca, Vietnamese, Mexican, Dominican, or American, and quite another to integrate the meaning of being an Asian, Hispanic, Native American, Black, or White American.

Does ethnicity have the same valence on personality as race? No, primarily because one's ethnicity is less visible than one's race. This does not mean that ethnicity is irrelevant. It depends on how societal institutions reward and punish on the basis of ethnic group membership. Ethnic discrimination usually occurs within racial groups. In the United States, race outweighs ethnicity in between-group relationships and interactions.

Most people seem to prefer to address ethnic or cultural issues rather than racial issues, but in the daily workings of American society, racial group and racial identity matter greatly, and I believe race has the greater psychological cost and benefit, particularly between groups.

Racial identity theory helps lift the deadening silence surrounding the meaning and significance of race in our society. The model allows for each person to have race and to accept its value. But confusion about how members of racial groups evolve, mature, and differentiate racial identity ego states often arises.

THE PROCESS OF RACIAL IDENTITY DEVELOPMENT

Most questions regarding racial identity tend to be related to process issues. Typical questions are: Do all members of a racial group go through the same identity development process? Is it possible to begin one's identity development at a higher level? Does one's racial identity differ from situation to situation? Are all the stages linear? Is it possible to skip levels? Does racial identity only apply to adults?

I believe that racial identity is a lifelong process that begins in childhood and must be resolved by every person who is born in or immigrates to the United States. However, as children approach puberty and social and peer relationships take on increasing importance, race and racial identity become particularly salient. The lessons of childhood are enacted and played out in these relationships. Young people apply cross-racial interaction rules with little conscious thought.

What matters in the development of a person's racial identity is how he or she interprets the messages received about racial groups (e.g., what his or her family teaches, denies, avoids, or confronts about race). How the issues are addressed in his or her family, community, and peer group will determine when one begins the process of developing a racial identity. Just as one's knowledge and sophistication about his or her gender matures, depending on the individual's willingness to learn and grow, one's racial identity also matures from an externally defined identity to an internally and personally meaningful identity. It is currently unclear what specific events or experiences move a person to work toward racial identity development. A person's values, experiences, and personal resolve seem to be relevant factors. Strong social movements and general shifts in societal values may also facilitate movement.

Are the stages or statuses linear? Original theories (Cross, 1978) suggested a linear developmental process. Other writers thought of racial identity as invariant types, as noted in Chapter 5. However, more recent revisions and extensions (e.g., Helms, in press) of racial identity theory argue for nonlinear processes. Parham (1989), in particular, argues that

Black racial identity may be expressed by adults in distinct age-related ways. That is, racial identity interacts with and is expressed through a Black person's particular developmental tasks within three age periods: (a) young adulthood; (b) middle adulthood, and (c) late adulthood.

Parham (1989) also suggests three possible resolution alternatives: (a) stagnation, (b) recycling, and (c) stagewise or sequential progression. The stagnation resolution alternative is defined as the adherence to one specific racial identity level throughout life. The recycling option is the reinitiation of racial identity struggles that had been experienced at an earlier life stage. Thus, recycling could occur for all racial identity levels except Pre-encounter. For instance, one could achieve Internalization in young adulthood and, during middle adulthood, have new encounters that trigger the recycling back to Encounter and Internalization. Parham suggests that recycling is possible because of two dimensions of Internalization. He calls these dimensions "ethnocentric," which is a blend of Immersion–Emersion and Internalization, where one remains distrustful and suspicious of Whites, and "humanistic," where one has de-emphasized race and identifies with all oppressed people, including Whites. According to Parham, a person with a strong humanistic dimension is more prone to recycling because one or more racist or oppressive incidents are likely to occur and shatter his or her belief in idealistic relationships and social experiences (Parham, 1989, p. 214). Lastly, one may move through racial identity in a stagewise or sequential progression, with movement triggered by personal growth and self-actualization.

Helms (1994) and Helms and Piper (1994) propose extensions to visible racial-ethnic group and White racial identity models that shift the development process from a stage approach to a growth-and-maturation approach in which one's "race-ego" becomes more differential as one's racial identity becomes more complex. One may begin with an externally derived identity and mature to an internally and personally meaningful racial identity. In more recent versions of racial identity theory, it is possible to have blends of racial identity statuses. Each status may exist in a person's psyche with varying degrees of influence.

Situations are likely to influence the expression or level of one's racial identity because the importance of race varies from one situation to the next. For example, in racially homogeneous situations, race is less salient than in racially heterogeneous ones.

CHAPTER 8

Race and Psychotherapy: A Process Model

Racial influences in the therapeutic process can occur in a number of ways. Clients may present racial issues by discussing work settings, career paths, personal issues, family relations, or interpersonal relationships. As discussed in the previous chapters on racial identity theory, race's influence on the psychotherapeutic process comes from a person's race as expressed by his or her racial identity, which also reflects his or her cultural affiliation. With this in mind, knowing a patient's racial identity level provides an initial step toward understanding how race-related issues may affect him or her and how race may be manifested in his or her intrapsychic and interpersonal relations. However, focusing solely on the client's racial identity level is insufficient when trying to fully grasp the process of psychotherapy; the therapist's level of racial identity must also be considered. Thus, a critical element in the Racially Inclusive Model of Psychotherapy involves the racial identity interactions that influence the process and outcome of therapeutic encounters.

Other research and theories that have addressed how racial attitudes may affect the therapeutic relationship have focused on the client who, more often than not, was a visible racial/ethnic group person. As was described, a focus on visible racial/ethnic clients ignores the therapists, their race, and its influence on the therapeutic process. Scholars and clinicians agree that transference (a client's subconscious internal projections onto the therapist) and countertransference (a clinician's subconscious internal triggers stimulated by the client) issues might arise when the client and therapist are from different racial groups. An analysis of race as a type of transference provides a simplistic understanding of how racial group membership functions as a stimulus. The three main problems with this approach to understanding race are: (a) it ignores the race of many participants, namely, Whites; (b) it implies that race is only a superficial factor in cross-racial dyads; and (c) it does not emphasize interactional dynamics, that is, how a therapist and patient affect each other.

Helms (1986) suggests that a person's level of racial identity—given its intricate relationship with one's worldview, personality, and race—should have a direct influence on the psychotherapeutic process. Her contention is supported by the findings of traditional psychotherapy research as presented in Chapters 2 and 3, as well as race-specific studies suggesting that race, racial attitudes, acculturation, and cultural variables are associated with the use of mental health services, duration of therapy, determination of diagnoses, development of treatment plans, depth of exploration, formation of relationships, and therapeutic outcomes. However, what is unanswered and often not addressed in the psychotherapy literature is how specifically race or race-related variables operate to affect the psychotherapeutic process.

What is needed in the psychotherapy literature is a framework that guides mental health professionals in their effort to understand how race and racial identity influence the therapeutic process. Helms's (1984) interactional model attempts to satisfy this need. Her framework considers within-group variation in psychotherapeutic interactions through the use of the racial identity construct. Moreover, she hypothesizes about the interactional dynamics that may occur in dyads as a result of the various combinations of racial identity attitudes held by the participants. The inclusion of interactional dynamics is important, yet many scholars have failed to speculate about how each participant's racial variable may interact (e.g., Jones, 1978). All too often, scholars and clinicians suggest that nonpsychological factors such as social class either do or do not have some effect on therapeutic relationships. While ignoring a psychological factor such as race altogether, only a few scholars have investigated how a patient's racial issues influence not only his or her behaviors, feelings, and thoughts in therapy, but also a therapist's behaviors, feelings, and thoughts. Typically, transference and countertransference issues are addressed when the therapeutic dyad is cross-racial (usually, White therapists with visible racial/ethnic group patients). Helms's interactional therapy process model goes beyond the cross-racial dyad to consider how racial issues may influence same-race dyads as well as therapeutic relationships with a visible racial/ethnic therapist and a White client. Before Helms's White racial identity theory, no existing models posited that a White American could develop a positive nonracist White identity. I believe that the White racial identity theory can be used to unravel the complexities associated with race, racial identity, and the psychotherapeutic relationship.

In addition, Helms (1984) suggests that a client and a counselor exhibit differential self-presentation styles commensurate with their roles (i.e., helpee in distress and a helper as expert and authority) and levels of racial identity, and engage in appropriate role behavior during psychotherapy. The different roles might be understood as each participant holding differential power. A patient, for example, seeks, is referred, or is mandated to participate in psychotherapy because of a life-related distress, and may be less powerful in the therapeutic relationship than the clinician, who has chosen his or her role. Unlike a client, a therapist is not distressed and is vested with the knowledge, skill, and ability to help the patient through treatment. Because of the therapist's powerful role in the interaction, his or her racial identity has the potential to exert more influence on the therapeutic process than the client's. The basis of the interactive psychotherapeutic relationship is the interaction of these self-presentation styles.

Four types of relationship—(a) parallel, (b) crossed, (c) progressive, and (d) regressive—are created by the interaction of the patients' and therapists' racial identity statuses, and each relationship type produces specific client behaviors and counselor strategies during the psychotherapeutic process. Additionally, a client's and a therapist's affective issues are believed to vary, depending on the type of therapeutic relationship. The dyads described below employ racial identity status, as presented in previous chapters.

The four types of relationships emerge when a client's and therapist's levels of racial identity are assessed and used to characterize the psychotherapeutic process (Helms, 1984). Each type of relationship, regardless of its racial composition, is associated with particular process dimensions and psychotherapeutic outcomes. The process dimensions believed to be salient in these psychotherapeutic relationship types are: (a) affective reactions and responses; (b) the therapists' and patients' perceptions and experiences of the therapy sessions, overall processes, and outcomes; and (c) the counselors' and clients' verbal and nonverbal strategies. Primarily, Black and White dyads will be used to describe the four relationship styles identified by Helms, because her model was designed specifically for understanding process issues in Black and White dyads.

PARALLEL RELATIONSHIP

A parallel relationship exists when a therapist and client share similar attitudes about Blacks and Whites; in a same-race dyad, a therapist and patient have the same level of racial identity, and in a cross-racial dyad, the participants share the same attitudes about Blacks and Whites. In a cross-racial dyad, a parallel relationship is formed when the Black participant has a predominantly Encounter status and the White participant exhibits a Disintegration status. For instance, in a Black dyad, a parallel relationship exists when both the client and counselor exhibit predominantly Pre-encounter statuses. However, it is important to keep in mind that even when the client and therapist hold similar racial identity statuses, the power differential between the two can impact on the therapeutic process and outcome.

The following case illustrates some of the process dimensions prevalent in parallel relationships. The therapist, Linda, is a brown-skinned

Black woman who was raised in an upper-middle-class White neighborhood. She was raised in a small family that consisted of her parents and her younger brother, and there was little contact with her extended family, which resided in other parts of the country. While growing up, she was always the only Black person among her peers, and she seldom thought of herself as Black. She excelled academically and attended a prestigious undergraduate college. At college, she had her first experiences with Blacks outside of her family. Many Blacks from various parts of the country attended Linda's college, and they often socialized and studied together. Initially, Linda interacted with her fellow Black students, but their behaviors made her uncomfortable. She felt more comfortable with Whites. Throughout college, she maintained her White social and personal network of friends, and her beliefs and behaviors remained consistent with theirs. More importantly, she found that Whites seldom, if ever, talked about race, and when they did, she agreed with their views.

After graduating from college, Linda pursued a doctoral degree in psychology. She received her training in a prestigious graduate program located in the Midwest. She was taught psychodynamic psychotherapy and did not take a course that focused on people of color or issues of culture. Additionally, during her training, she never worked with a person of color. During her internship, she is assigned a Black woman who is seeking counseling because of marital problems. Initially, Linda is apprehensive and angry at the staff for assigning her this patient.

The patient, Jackie, is a 27-year-old, middle-class Black woman who has lived in the Midwest all her life and has been married for five years to Gerald, a 29-year-old salesman. Jackie was adopted by a White family when she was young, and she has been raised to think of herself as a person and to de-emphasize the fact that she is Black. She has interacted with the other Blacks in her community, but these relationships have always been awkward and conflictual, primarily because her Black peers perceive her as feeling superior to them. In fact, Jackie does hold this belief, but not consciously. She does not understand other Blacks and resolves this conflict by not interacting with them.

The presenting problem centers around her husband's desire to have children. Whenever the issue is raised, Jackie becomes terrified and cannot discuss it. She does not understand her fear or its source. She is seeking therapy on the advice of her physician and because she thinks her marriage is in trouble. When she meets Linda, she feels a sense of doom and frustration and wonders whether she has been shortchanged because her therapist is Black. Nevertheless, Jackie decides to give Linda a chance.

During the course of therapy, the major theme discussed is Jackie's feelings about being adopted. This leads to an exploration of her feelings of inadequacy surrounding motherhood. These are key issues for Jackie, yet Linda and Jackie both avoid a critical factor—Jackie's husband is

White, so their children will be biracial. More importantly, their children might look like Jackie. Thus, having children with a White male raises central and critical questions for Jackie about race, race relations, and racial identity—topics that Linda does not believe are salient.

In this type of dyad, the client may feel resentment and anger for having a Black therapist, and the therapist may feel doubt and guilt for having negative feelings about working with a Black client. Consequently, both participants may use strategies that eschew or deny racial issues. In a parallel relationship, when both participants have low levels of racial identity, a client may leave treatment with minimal therapeutic gain, and a counselor may encourage a client to terminate or to seek treatment with another therapist. Moreover, in this example, even if Linda thought that the racial issues were important, her training did not equip her to broach these topics. In this particular therapeutic relationship, both participants collude to avoid racial issues, in part, because they do not believe race is important, which is consistent with their Pre-encounter level of racial identity.

An example of a parallel cross-racial dyad would involve a White counselor who has a predominantly Disintegration status (e.g., confusion and conflict) and a Black client who exhibits predominantly Encounter attitudes (e.g., confusion). In this type of dyad, both participants might try to raise the topic of race, but because the clinician and the client are both confused and conflicted, their efforts may come in false starts and be half-hearted. A White counselor with a predominance of Disintegration attitudes may be avoidant, paternal, or overidentified with the patient; depending on his or her resolution of racial identity, the client may respond with a mixture of apprehension and acceptance. When a client feels encouraged to talk about his or her struggle with race and racial identity, he or she may experience various reactions, including confusion and conflict, and gain little insight or symptom relief.

CROSSED RELATIONSHIP

A crossed relationship, involving participants of the same race or of different races, is characterized by a counselor and a client whose racial identity status about Blacks and Whites are in opposition. For example, in an all-Black crossed relationship, a client may have a predominantly Pre-encounter status, and a counselor may have a predominantly Immersion status; in an all-White crossed dyad, a client may have Contact level attitudes and a counselor may have Disintegration level attitudes. In an all-White crossed dyad, both participants, whether or not racial issues are discussed, might become angry, hostile, and anxious. Regardless of the participants' race, in crossed dyads, neither the client nor the counselor empathizes with the other's racial attitudes; however, both engage in educative strategies. These strategies may hinder the formation of a therapeutic relationship, which may lead the client and/or the counselor to become frustrated and terminate therapy.

PROGRESSIVE RELATIONSHIP

A progressive relationship exists when the counselor's racial identity status is at least one level above the client's. For example, in a Black dyad consisting of a client who has a predominance of Pre-encounter status attitudes and a counselor who has a predominance of Encounter status attitudes, the counselor may be apprehensive and excited, whereas the client may be angry and may attempt to avoid racial issues. In progressive dyads with people of color, the therapeutic process may prove productive if the counselor can focus the client on the treatment. For instance, a progressive White dyad in which a counselor has a predominance of Autonomy status attitudes and a client has a predominance of Disintegration status attitudes is characterized by a counselor who is accepting and empathic and a client who is genuine and willing to self-explore. In this type of relationship, the counselor can encourage the client to explore racial issues.

The following case study involves a White progressive dyad and illustrates several characteristics of this type of therapeutic relationship. John is a 30-year-old White male who is employed by a prestigious law firm. Recently, his firm hired several Black attorneys who have been assigned to John's work group. John is now the only White person in his work group. He is confused about his feelings; he believes people should be treated the same, but he cannot develop close relationships with his Black coworkers because his White peers have warned him about associating with the new "affirmative action hires." John enters therapy to help him cope with these and other work-related issues.

John's therapist is Pat, a 35-year-old White female who has struggled with these issues in her personal relationships with visible racial/ethnic group people, particularly Blacks, and with other Whites, including her family. She grew up in a middle-class home with several brothers and sisters. While growing up, she valued her interactions with her grandmother more than those with any other relative. Pat's grandmother retained her Polish ethnic identity by speaking Polish and by following the customs and the "old ways." Her parents, however, wanted to be American. Pat was conflicted for a period of time, but she decided to recapture her Polish ethnicity through different efforts, including traveling to Poland and visiting her extended family. She chose to go away to college and, while there, found herself interacting with people who were racially different from her. These relationships were difficult and painful at times, but she persisted, even though people discouraged her. Gradually, she began to understand that her race was more salient than her ethnicity in cross-racial relationships. She realized how her race affected her perceptions and experiences and how being non-White affected others. Nevertheless, Pat did not bend to social and peer pressures to conform to social racial standards and consequently evolved a more developed racial identity.

Pat's developed racial identity status enabled her to empathize with John's concerns, to help him explore his feelings, and to work toward developing ways to cope with his emotions. During the course of therapy, Pat wove together issues of racial identity, family, and peer relationships to help John discover his true feelings about his coworkers.

REGRESSIVE RELATIONSHIP

A regressive relationship exists when the client's racial identity status is at least one level more advanced than the counselor's. In this type of relationship, the process may resemble a power struggle; both participants may have strong affective reactions to each other, and conflict may characterize the relationship's dynamics. Highlights from a case involving a cross-race regressive dyad are presented below. The client has predominantly Pseudo-Independent status attitudes, and the counselor has predominantly Contact status attitudes.

Bob is a 28-year-old first-generation Asian American male who recently completed his training to be a clinical psychologist. Bob was raised in a working-class community on the East Coast. His parents are Chinese immigrants who came to the United States in their early twenties. They worked hard and long hours so that Bob could get a good American education. Bob was born in the United States, and being a good American is extremely important for him and his parents. His parents were eager to be seen and accepted as Americans. They both obtained U.S. citizenship and chose to live among Whites. Bob's desire and willingness to fit in were encouraged and supported throughout his education. As a staff psychologist at an area hospital, he is assigned to work with a Hispanic patient.

Bob's patient is Carmen, a dark-skinned, 30-year-old Puerto Rican woman who relocated to the West Coast to attend school. She was referred to the hospital clinic because she was having difficulty in her program. Carmen's presenting problem is depression. During the first few sessions, Carmen reveals feelings of isolation, marginality, and intense anger, and states that these feelings have surfaced since entering graduate school. She talks about experiencing racist acts by faculty and students and about being mistaken for a Black American. She is shocked at how racist people are toward her. She has felt some support from Black Americans, but she is not Black and feels they do not completely understand her. She finds White Americans simply confused, and often distant and superficial. To Carmen, these experiences are particularly disturbing because in Puerto Rico she was more aware of class differences than racial conflicts.

Bob believes that Carmen's concerns are rooted in her family history and her personality formation, and argues that race is not an issue. He thinks that Carmen needs to learn to be more social than she currently is and to accept things as they are in the United States. She, on the other hand, rejects Bob's perspective and spends a considerable amount of time trying to show Bob that Whites mistreat her. Bob interprets her observations as her projections and insecurities. Often, Carmen leaves the sessions feeling more isolated, marginal, and angry than when she entered. Bob sees Carmen as deeply resistant to therapy.

CONCLUSION

In summary, Helms's (1984) interaction theory, which builds on her racial identity theory, describes how race influences the treatment process and its outcome. This theoretical foundation can be the basis for systematic, empirical investigations of race and its effects on the therapeutic process.

Traditional clinical and empirical approaches to understanding race's influence on the therapeutic process assume that it is the sole stimulus for racial effects. This assumption centers on the presumed racial beliefs and attitudes that patients bring to therapy—typically, as transference and resistance. Some clinicians argue that therapists also bring racial issues, in the form of countertransference, to therapy. I argue, however, that if the goal is to fully understand race in therapy, then an examination of race alone is inappropriate and inadequate. To do otherwise promotes the use of racial stereotypes, focuses on visible racial/ethnic group members as racial people, and ignores the fact that Whites belong to a race. Nevertheless, the debate highlights the fact that race is a more complex phenomenon than has been previously considered. The inclusion of racial identity theory adds to the debate.

The debate in the counseling and culture-specific literature on the influence of race in the psychotherapeutic process suggests that racial identity affects a client's and counselor's style, and the manner in which they interact. To date, only Helms's (1984, 1990) interactional model explains how these factors influence the quality of the counseling process.

Implicit in this interaction model (Helms, 1984) is the idea that a counselor's actions are a result of his or her racial identity status attitudes, which influence a client's reactions, and that a client's racial identity status attitudes might influence a counselor's behaviors (i.e., intentions). Such a sequence would occur if the racial identity status of each member of the dyad influenced the other's overt behavior in a discernible way. It is reasonable to speculate that a counselor is influenced by something his or her client does and that a client is influenced by something his or her counselor does. Therefore, a more in-depth and empirically based discussion of the interactive effects of racial identity statuses on the therapeutic process is warranted. Each type of therapeutic relationship (e.g., parallel, regressive) and selected process variables associated with the client's and counselor's racial identity statuses have been presented and discussed in terms of how each dyad member's racial identity status may influence the counselor's intentions and the client's reactions.

Empirical investigations based on a theory are critical because a theoretical framework enables a researcher to formulate testable hypotheses, conduct investigations to test these hypotheses, and extend and/or modify a theory based on empirical findings. Scientifically based knowledge is acquired through the process.

This chapter has explored whether race influences the counseling process in the manner(s) proposed by Helms (1984). Her interaction theory suggests that all psychotherapeutic pairs can be described in terms of their racial identity combinations or as a particular type of relationship (e.g., progressive, crossed). Each of the four relationship types is characterized by distinct differences in a patient's and a therapist's cognitions, behaviors, strategies, and processes. Based on these differences, the participants in each type of relationship, regardless of the clinician's or client's race, should have distinct perceptions of the session and the therapeutic outcome. Also, the client's and counselor's assessment of each other's affective responses should differ across the four types of dyads.

For example, in a progressive relationship where the counselor's racial identity status is at least one level higher than the client's, the counselor may be empathic and accepting, while the client is self-exploring. In this type of relationship, one would expect low levels of anger and anxiety, and the sessions should be evaluated as positive and beneficial by both members of the dyad.

On the other hand, in a regressive relationship where the client's racial identity status is at least one level higher than the counselor's, the process and outcome will be very different. In this regressive relationship, one would expect the client to have more negative reactions to the counselor's statements and intentions than in the aforementioned progressive relationship. Additionally, in this regressive relationship, the counselor's intentions will differ from those used by a counselor in a progressive relationship.

Certain client reactions, including hostility, anxiety, and anger, are more likely to be present in some dyad types than in others. If different levels of counselor and client affect, counselor intentions, and client reactions do occur, then clients and counselors in dyads characterized by negative affect and process might experience the relationship more negatively than would counselors and clients in relationships characterized by more positive processes. Additionally, a counselor's and a client's racial identity attitudes alone may influence the counseling process. A counselor's racial identity attitudes may be related to his or her intentions, and a client's racial identity status may be related to his or her reactions.

Critical to the interactional framework is the notion that one's racial identity level is an integral aspect of a person's personality. Before the basic tenets of the process model can be tested, evidence must be set forth that racial identity levels are associated with specific psychological, emotional, cultural, and behavioral variables.

If the racial identity and interactive models are correct, then (a) the counselor's and client's racial identity statuses should influence the behavior of each in therapy; (b) the counselor's and client's racial identity statuses should, regardless of the race of the therapy participants, differentially influence the internal reactions of each to the other; and (c) the combinations of participants' racial identity statuses should contribute to qualitatively different types of interactions.

In Part Three of the book, the interaction model mentioned here will be explicitly tested, and four questions raised by the racial identity and relationship type theory will be investigated:

1. Are racial identity statuses differentially related to specific predicted variables?

2. Does race or racial identity influence the therapeutic process in same-race and cross-race dyads?

3. Does the quality of the therapeutic relationship vary by relationship type?

4. How does race influence overt therapeutic processes?

Part Three will also examine various other questions raised by the racial identity and relationship type theory.

How Do We Know?
Research Evidence

Much of the traditional literature on race in psychotherapy has been based on clinical observation, intuition, personal experience, racial myths, and stereotypes. Little systematic investigation has been used to examine and explain racial influences in psychotherapy. Moreover, empirical studies have not been grounded in theory. Typically, a client's race has been used to determine his or her intrapsychic life and human worth. This book attempts to integrate theory, research, and clinical insight to understand racial influences in psychotherapy. Part Three is a step beyond speculation and a step toward systematic inquiry. It tests specific aspects of the Racially Inclusive Model of Psychotherapy. In particular, it examines the proposition that racial identity ego statuses are aspects of personality. This proposition is tested in Chapter 9 by exploring whether different levels of racial identity are related to emotional, psychological, social, and cultural perspectives.

A second proposition is the notion of interactional process, described in Chapter 8, where race's influence in psychotherapy is interactive. Chapters 10 and 11 explore these propositions, and Chapter 12 presents case studies that highlight racial identity issues and process in psychotherapy on an overt (response category) level.

Although it may be unusual to present research in a clinical book, findings are offered as a way to transcend speculation and theory and to demonstrate the relevance of racial identity for clinical practice.

CHAPTER 9

Racial Identity and Psychosocial Correlates

Racial identity models can be used to examine psychological differences within racial groups (cf. Cross, 1991; Helms, 1990). Traditional psychological approaches for understanding race have used social, economic, cultural, and familial influences as constructs for explaining the mental health needs of various racial groups. Racial identity theory, the central feature of my Racially Inclusive Model of Psychotherapy, accounts for psychological complexity within individuals, groups, and therapeutic pairs regardless of one's racial group membership. As noted earlier, racial identity ego statuses include attitudes, thoughts, feelings, and behaviors toward oneself as a member of a racial group, and toward another racial group. It describes how an individual looks at himself or herself and at the dominant racial group. In the United States, for visible racial/ethnic group people, the dominant racial group is Whites, and for Whites, the out-group is people of color.

Furthermore, each level of racial identity is presumed to be associated with a distinct worldview that corresponds to emotional, psychological, social, and interpersonal preferences consistent with that worldview. Thus, one's racial identity resolution is believed to be integrated into personality.

RACIAL IDENTITY MEASURES

As is the case with many theories, empirical research and instruments have not kept pace with theory building. For example, Helms's current version of racial identity theory, which explains ego status, and other modifications of theory (Parham, 1989; see Chapter 5), are not directly assessed by existing measures.

To date, three racial identity measures have been used in empirical research. Before providing an overview of each instrument, it is important to note that the current measures assess attitudes and do not measure emotions or behaviors. They do not capture the many emotional and behavioral elements posited in each theoretical level of racial identity. However, Carter (in press) has found that these measures do capture theoretical dimensions appropriately, particularly when raw scores are transformed into percentiles. The first measure, the Black Racial Identity Attitude Scale (BRIAS), developed by Helms and Parham (in press), is based on a four-level racial identity model that does not include the Internalization–Commitment level and does not measure the phases within each level of the Black racial identity theory. The BRIAS is used to assess attitudes (as opposed to statuses) that reflect critical aspects of the four racial identity levels.

The White Racial Identity Attitude Scale (WRIAS), developed by Helms and Carter (1990), is based on a five-level racial identity model. The levels are Contact, Disintegration, Reintegration, Pseudo-Independence, and Autonomy. This instrument differs from the White racial identity model presented in Chapter 6 in that the Immersion–Emersion level is not included. Helms and Carter note: "Although the attitudinal scales are based on a model that proposes discrete [statuses] of racial identity, it is probably best to use all five of a respondent's scores to form a profile rather than single scores to assign her or him to single [levels]" (p. 69). It also does not measure all the statuses; rather, only five of the six statuses are measured. The Immersion–Emersion status is not yet a scale in the existing measure. Also, the White Racial Identity Attitude Scale is an attitude instrument just like the Black scale. It should be noted that Helms (in press) and Carter (in press) have offered new information regarding how these measures should be scored and used in research and practice.

The White and Black racial identity instruments have been more widely used in research than the visible racial/ethnic identity (e.g., Asian, Hispanic, Native American) measure (Helms & Carter, 1986). The instrument for visible racial/ethnic identity was used in the counseling process study summarized in Chapter 10.

With the racial identity models in mind and after an overview of the instruments used to examine these models, key empirical studies of racial identity are reviewed. These studies focus on psychological and clinical issues associated with the Black and White racial identity models; however, these findings can be extended to other visible racial/ethnic groups that have similar sociopolitical histories. Research findings will be presented according to racial identity levels. Therefore, findings from one study will appear in several places because the majority of investigators examined all racial identity levels in their studies.

BLACK RACIAL IDENTITY STUDIES

Pre-Encounter

Pre-encounter is characterized by a dependency on White society for self-definition and approval. Racial identity attitudes toward Blackness are negative, and White culture and society are seen as the ideal. Race is not a salient aspect of one's identity.

Psychological Findings

Looney (1988) examined the relationship between Black racial identity and Loevinger's model of ego development. According to Loevinger (1976, 1979), ego is central to personality and evolves, through seven stages, from a simple to a complex and highly integrated ego structure. Looney (1988) found that Pre-encounter attitudes were inversely related to ego development; when Pre-encounter attitudes dominated one's worldview, the ego structure was weak. This study also suggested, as Looney notes, "if an individual has a strong ego, he or she defines self; if the individual's ego is weak, others define self" (p. 49). This finding supports the contention in racial identity theory that lower levels are externally defined. Looney points out that this finding is consistent with the idea that ego is a universal aspect of a person's development that combines elements of character and interpersonal and cognitive style. Thus, one's ego unifies the personality.

Taub and McEwen (1992) examined how racial identity attitudes in Black and White women were related to various aspects of psychosocial development. In particular, they studied personal autonomy and interpersonal maturity. For Black women, they found that high Pre-encounter attitudes were associated with low levels of autonomy and difficulty with interpersonal relationships. Again, the theme of dependence on others, immaturity, and less complex relationships is associated with the Pre-encounter status.

Pre-encounter attitudes have also been found to be related to high levels of anxiety (Carter, 1991; Parham & Helms, 1985a), low self-regard, low self-esteem, and high self-actualization tendencies (Munford, 1994; Parham & Helms, 1985a; Pyant & Yanico, 1991). Thus, although a person with high levels of Pre-encounter attitudes may have a poor self-image, a weak ego, and low self-regard, he or she is able to move toward self-actualization, but not without psychological cost. Carter (1991) found that Pre-encounter attitudes were strongly related to psychological dysfunction. These attitudes were predictive of memory difficulties, hypersensitivity, suspicion of others, and alcoholic tendencies. Pyant and Yanico (1991) and Munford (1994) reported that high Pre-encounter attitudes were related to low scores on a measure of psychological well-being, self-esteem, and high scores on the Beck depression scale. Both Pyant and Yanico and Munford used samples of adults and college students in the South East of the United States. Another study found that a person characterized by these attitudes would prefer to seek professional help from a White counselor (Parham & Helms, 1981).

Social Findings

In a sample of Black working adults and churchgoers who were between the ages of 15 and 55, Parham and Williams (1993) investigated how various demographic variables such as gender, age, racial designation, income, birth city, and developmental experiences (i.e., race-specific messages from parents) were associated with the four racial identity attitudes. These investigators found that income was the only demographic variable related to Pre-encounter attitudes: high Pre-encounter attitudes were linked to high incomes. Additionally, they found that, of the four racial identity attitudes, Pre-encounter was the only one affected by where a person grew up. People who grew up in the South had higher Pre-encounter attitudes than those who grew up in the West. However, people born in the West had significantly higher Pre-encounter attitudes than people who were born in the East or South. Martin and Nagayama-Hall (1992) reported that Pre-encounter attitudes, as assessed in a sample of noncollege women ranging in age from 18 to 75 (mean age of 47), were related to endorsement of *Colored* and *Negro* as racial self-designations.

Watts (1992) studied middle-class Black adults at different levels of racial identity to determine which racism reduction strategies were preferred. Watts asked respondents to rate eleven strategies for confronting racism, and found that only four were rated positively. Two of these four strategies involved legal remedies for reducing discrimination, and two involved educating Whites about racism and working with Blacks. Strategies that were rated negatively included convincing Whites of the personal effects of racism, participating in activities to help Whites and Blacks "get to know each other," and advocating for proposals to withdraw and/or separate the races. Watts developed the Strategies for Reducing Racism Scale (SRRS) based on several of the favored strategies. When this scale was used in conjunction with the BRIAS, Pre-encounter attitudes were negatively related to the scale. Watts (1992) points out:

> [T]hose high in Pre-Encounter preferred strategies that emphasized personal and social contact, integration, and socializing with European Americans. . . . Since Pre-Encounter attitudes reflect an identification

with Whites and a rejection of Black culture, it makes sense that their perspectives would be comparable to that of Whites. (p. 12)

Watts and Carter (1991) explored the perceptions of racism in organizations at three levels (personal, work group, and policies and procedures) and found that Black adults with higher levels of Pre-encounter attitudes had relatively favorable perceptions of the racial climate (work group, policies and procedures) and did not perceive themselves to be subject to personal discrimination in the workplace. Mitchell and Dell (1992), in a study of West Coast Black undergraduates, found that students with high levels of Pre-encounter were less likely to participate in Black-oriented campus activities.

Summary

To the extent the research evidence involving Pre-encounter can be generalized, it suggests that this racial identity status is, on the one hand, a psychologically and socially White-oriented motivational force that seems to be associated with income gains and a sense of acceptance in one's work setting. However, some psychological distress is also related to this status. Perhaps these findings reflect the passive and active phases of Pre-encounter as proposed by Helms (1990) (see Chapter 5). It is also likely that a person characterized by this racial identity status might struggle with issues such as depression, low self-esteem, or interpersonal conflicts at work or with family members.

Encounter

The next level of Black racial identity, Encounter, begins when an individual has a personal and challenging racial experience. The Encounter status is marked by confusion about the meaning and significance of race and an increasing desire to become more aligned with one's Black identity.

Psychological Findings

Looney (1988) found that ego development and Encounter attitudes for Black males were positively associated. High Encounter attitudes were related to greater ego strength. Taub and McEwen (1992) found that high Encounter attitudes were consistent with emotional independence, high anxiety, low self-esteem, and an inability to accept cultural differences. Pyant and Yanico (1991) found that Encounter attitudes were predictive of low psychological well-being, low self-esteem, and high depression scale scores. Munford (1994) also found Encounter to be related to high depression and low self-esteem. In other studies, Encounter attitudes for Black college students were associated with low anxiety, high self-actualization, and high self-regard (Parham & Helms, 1981, 1985b).

Social Findings

The social findings with respect to Encounter relate to the personal and therapeutic relationship. Martin and Nagayama-Hall (1992), in their study of feminism, racial self-designation, and locus of control in Black adult women, found that Encounter was related to an external locus of control in which one had a strong belief in chance and luck. Such persons also tended not to accept legitimate authority. Mitchell and Dell (1992) found that Black students with a predominance of Encounter attitudes were more likely to be involved in Black-oriented campus activities. With regard to therapeutic relationships, Bradby and Helms (1990), in a study of mixed racial counseling pairs, found that Black clients with high Encounter attitudes had high scores on a measure of counselor satisfaction when seeing a White therapist. However, Encounter attitudes were also associated with fewer sessions with White counselors. Pomales, Claiborn, and LaFromboise (1987) found that subjects with Encounter attitudes rated their culturally sensitive counselors as expert and culturally competent, and had favorable perceptions when viewing a White female counselor's discussion of racial issues in a simulated session with a Black male client. In a similar study, Richardson and Helms (1994) found that Encounter attitudes were predictive of Black males' reactions to White counselor/Black client counseling simulations; high Encounter attitudes were negatively associated with a willingness to self-disclose to a White counselor and with general reactions to the sessions. These mixed findings suggest that Encounter attitudes are transient and difficult to measure and that the two phases of Encounter may contribute to these inconsistent results.

Interpersonal relations may be uncomfortable for an individual in Encounter, because he or she has not yet acquired a solid Black identity and may move between racial worlds. McCaine (1986) reports that Encounter attitudes are associated with a desire to affiliate with people of a clearly specified race. However, Denton (1986) suggests that individuals with Encounter attitudes feel positively about affiliation with Blacks. These inconsistent findings may be a result of the dual phases in this level.

Summary

It seems that Encounter has two distinct psychological trends, supporting Helms's contention that there are two phases to this status. One dimension of Encounter seems to be associated with depression, poor self-image, and anxiety. This aspect of Encounter may reflect the initial phase that is connected to emotional turmoil. The other dimension involves a strong ego, less anxiety, a high self-concept, and active implementation of one's plans. These characteristics seem consistent with the second phase of Encounter, when an individual has decided to search for the meaning of his or her Blackness. At either of these two phases, an individual seeking mental health assistance may prefer a Black counselor (Parham & Helms, 1981, 1985b).

Immersion–Emersion

The Immersion–Emersion status follows the Encounter experience and is characterized by positive feelings toward Blacks and idealizing of Black culture, while having intense negative feelings toward Whites and White culture.

Psychological Findings

Looney (1988) found that high Immersion attitudes were consistent with high ego development. Thus, people with a preponderance of these attitudes were more likely to have strong egos. Parham and Helms (1985a) found that Immersion attitudes were associated with low self-actualizing tendencies, low self-regard, and high anxiety and hostility. Munford (1994) reports these attitudes to be related to high depression scores. Taub and McEwen (1992) also found Immersion–Emersion for Black women to be related to high anxiety, low self-esteem, and emotional dependency, a finding consistent with that of Parham and Helms (1985b). Carter (1991) reports that Immersion–Emersion attitudes were predictive of a few memory problems and concerns about drug use. Austin, Carter, and Vaux (1990) suggest that people with high levels of these attitudes may believe that seeing a counselor is stigmatizing and reflects personal weakness. Thus, Blacks characterized by Immersion–Emersion attitudes may be unwilling to use mental health services.

Social Findings

Parham and Williams (1993) found that high Immersion attitudes were consistent with less educational attainment. Immersion–Emersion, the change from a race-is-not-salient to a Black-oriented view, also seems to reflect a shift in group affiliation, ideology, cultural frame of reference, values, and worldview. Carter and Helms (1987) found Immersion–Emersion attitudes to predict preferences for Afrocentric cultural values (e.g., Harmony with Nature, Collateral). Cross et al. (in press) found that these attitudes were associated with a strong, emotional anti-White orientation; an emphasis on separating the self from things perceived to be White, such as appearance, clothes, and speech; and a blaming-the-system perspective. Its intense emotional quality makes this an uncompromising level of identity development.

Watts (1992), in a study on racism reduction, found that individuals with high Immersion attitudes preferred to engage in active racism reduction strategies that mobilized Blacks. In their study of perceptions of racism in an organization, Watts and Carter (1991) found that Immersion attitudes were related to perceptions of personal discrimination and institutional racism. Mitchell and Dell (1992) reported that Black students characterized by these attitudes were likely to be involved in Black-oriented campus activities. Also, Black women with a predominance of Immersion attitudes did not endorse feminist beliefs. This finding was interpreted as evidence of a strong investment in a Black worldview where other social group issues were less important (Brookins, 1994; Martin & Nagayama-Hall, 1992).

Summary

The psychosocial research findings are quite consistent. Immersion–Emersion is clearly an emotionally volatile and distressing status. It also seems to be related to a single-mindedness and an emphasis on Black issues and concerns where an individual begins to invest in the Black experience, although the journey is fraught with intense self-examination, tension, and anxiety.

Internalization

During Internalization, one realizes that Blacks and Whites have strengths and weaknesses. In addition, one's Black identity is experienced as a positive, important, and valued aspect of the self. An individual in this status respects Whites and tolerates their differences. In Internalization–Commitment, the last level, an individual actively promotes the welfare of Black people.

Psychological Findings

Studies have revealed fewer correlates for Internalization attitudes and other psychological variables. Looney (1988) did find that high Internalization attitudes were related to lower ego development. Perhaps, an internalized Black identity leads to a more fragile ego state. This inference is supported by Carter (1991), who investigated the relationship between psychological symptoms and racial identity attitudes. His results indicated that the Internalization level of racial identity was characterized by a suspiciousness of Whites, which can be considered hypersensitive or culturally adaptive. Martin and Nagayama-Hall (1992) found these attitudes were positively related to internal locus of control. These authors concluded that this finding shows "the healthy positive personality characteristics that were found for internalization in other research" (p. 513). Munford (1994) found Internalization to be related to high self-esteem and low depression. According to Helms and Carter (1991), a person with a predominance of

Internalization attitudes would be skeptical about seeking counseling services and would prefer a Black counselor. Austin, Carter, and Vaux (1990) suggest that people with high levels of these attitudes may believe that counseling will be ineffective for them. Perhaps, a major issue for internalized Blacks is whether they can self-disclose in therapy without educating the therapist.

Social Findings

Parham and Williams (1993) found that high incomes were associated with low Internalization scores. Cross et al. (in press) suggest that Internalization is associated with a strong Black cultural orientation, a commitment to a pluralistic society and to protection of Black culture, and beliefs that promote the importance and value of Black identity. This contention is supported by Mitchell and Dell's (1992) finding that Black students with a predominance of Internalization attitudes were more likely to participate in general campus activities. These findings are supported further by the work of Carter and Helms (1987), who found that Internalization attitudes were predictive of Afrocentric cultural values (e.g., Harmony with Nature, Collateral (group) relations, and Doing activity). These findings are supported by Brookins (1994). In addition, Watts's (1992) study of social change strategies indicates that people at this level endorse a racism reduction strategy that mobilizes Blacks. Pomales, Claiborn, and LaFromboise (1987) report that Internalization subjects are considerably negative in their perceptions of both culturally sensitive and insensitive counselors.

Summary

Empirical studies regarding Internalization are mixed. According to some studies, a person at this level of racial identity seems to be clearly invested in a predominantly Black worldview. Yet, mistrust and a somewhat weak ego are also associated with this status. Again, it is possible that the findings show the complex inner layers of this racial identity ego status.

Empirical support for Black racial identity strongly suggests that the theoretical models have considerable merit. Research also reveals the complexity of one's psychological orientation to his or her Black reference group membership at each level of Black racial identity. It is reasonable to conclude that a person with a specific racial identity resolution will have varying types of psychological and emotional issues and symptoms. Next, empirical studies will be presented that examine how racial identity for Whites might influence their perceptions of themselves and other racial/ethnic group people, an area that has been given minimal attention in the psychological literature. Tables 9.1 and 9.2 present the findings in uniform groupings to facilitate comparison.

TABLE 9.1 Black Racial Identity and Research Findings

Status	General Theme	Emotional Themes	Psychological Themes	Social Issues
Pre-encounter (active)	idealization of Whites	anxiety, low self-esteem	• weak ego • dependent • high anxiety	• high income • work with Whites for social change • prefer White counselor • no personal discrimination at work
Pre-encounter (passive)	denigration of Blackness	defensiveness	• low self-esteem • depression • psychological distress • self-actualized	• prefer Black counselor
Encounter (events)	confusion	bitter, hurt, angry	• high anxiety • low psychological well-being • high depression	
Encounter (discovery)	conscious of race	euphoria	• low anxiety • high self-regard • self-actualized • emotional independence	
Immersion	idealization of Blackness	rage, depression	• low self-esteem • low self-actualization • emotional dependence • strong ego	• less education • focus on Blacks to reduce racism • anti-White/system blame • separatist • aware of racism • Afrocentric cultural values
Emersion	distance from Whites	acceptance		
Internalization	Black-oriented worldview	self-confident, secure	• weak ego • suspicious ("culture paranoia")	• focus on Blacks to reduce racism • Afrocentric cultural values
Internalization Commitment	group activism			

TABLE 9.2   White Racial Identity and Research Findings

Status	General Theme	Emotional Themes	Psychological Themes	Social Issues
Contact	unaware of race	discomfort with unfamiliar people and situations	• low anxiety • poor self-image • dependent • immature interpersonally	• cross-racial comfort • Euro-American cultural values • supports organization and management efforts to promote equity
Disintegration	conflict/confusion	anger, guilt	• immature interpersonally	• prefers White counselor • confused by Blacks • Euro-American values • supports organization and management efforts to promote equity • negative view of racial issues in work place
Reintegration	idealizes Whiteness devalues other races anti-Black	fear, anger	• high anxiety • immature interpersonally	• holds racist views • Euro-American values • supports organization and management efforts to promote equity • negative view of racial issues in work place
Pseudo-Independence	cognitive understanding of racial difference	defensive	• lacks affect • mature interpersonally	• prefers White company • interracial dating OK • comfortable cross-racially • shift in work and cultural values • mixed racial views in workplace, some negative
Autonomy	nonracist/accepts race as pos– sitive part of self and others	calm, secure, self-confident	• mature interpersonally • self-actualized • inner-directed	• supports racial integration • balanced view • shift in work and cultural values • positive racial view of work place

149

WHITE RACIAL IDENTITY STUDIES

Contact

The first or lowest level of White racial identity development is Contact; at this level, the person is unaware of him or herself or others in racial terms; in other words, a person at this level of development denies the importance of race and racial issues.

Psychological Findings

McCaine (1986) found this level of identity to be related to low anxiety. Tokar and Swanson (1991), in a study of self-actualization and White identity, concluded that "people who do not consider racial matters (i.e., Contact) have a weak sense of self and do not exhibit independent ideas and behavior" (p. 299). They also found that people at this level may lack the ability to develop close, meaningful relationships with other human beings, regardless of race. Carter and Parks (1994), in a study of White racial identity and psychological symptoms, found that Contact attitudes for White men were related to obsessive/compulsiveness and memory impairment. These findings were thought to reflect the psychic energy needed to deny the significance of race. Also, Pope-Davis and Ottavi (1994) found Contact to be more characteristic of women than men.

Social Findings

McCaine (1986) found that individuals with high Contact attitudes are not likely to seek social contact with others. Helms (1990) reports that high levels of Contact attitudes are related to endorsements of statements such as:

> [A] family of the same socioeconomic status can move in next door re-
> gardless of race, "it is easy to understand Blacks' complaints about racism
> on campus," and "Blacks and Whites should room together, even if
> Whites object." Higher contact attitudes were related to stronger dis-
> agreement with the attitudinal statement, "government and news media
> respect Blacks too much." (p. 73)

Carter (1990), in a study of the relationship between White racial identity and racism, found that White women with high Contact attitudes were unlikely to endorse racism but were likely to ignore race, which itself can be racist when race is salient to the other individual. But, it is possible that Whites at this level are unaware of race. Pope-Davis and Ottavi (1992), in a replication of Carter's (1990b) study, found that high Contact attitudes for White men were related to endorsement of racist beliefs. Claney and Parker (1988) found that White identity and comfort with Blacks were characterized by a curvilinear relationship. Individuals with high Contact attitudes felt more comfortable with Blacks than those with less of these attitudes. Block, Roberson, & Neuger (1995) studied Whites reactions to interracial situations in organizations, using a sample of working adults and part-time business students. They assessed Whites attitudes regarding issues such as equity, discrimination, reverse discrimination, tokenism, affirmative action, work comfort, social comfort, and personal, management and organizational interventions. They found that people with Contact attitudes are "likely to support both organization-wide and management interventions to promote equality in the workplace" (p. 81). In addition, they found support for the Claney and Parker results with Contact in that there were positive reactions to interracial contact with Blacks. In terms of worldview, Carter and Helms (1990) found that Contact attitudes were predictive of many traditional American cultural values (e.g., Evil or Mixed human nature, Mastery over Nature, and Achievement orientation). These attitudes reflect a curious and humanistic perspective. It is also the case that one is dependent on others for racial self-definition.

Summary

The Contact status psychologically is characterized by low self-actualization, dependency, psychological symptoms for men and a basic denial of race. These psychological issues seem to be apparent in social situations and interactions. In general, this level socially seems to be associated with subconscious endorsements of racism and a strong investment in American cultural patterns.

Disintegration

At Disintegration, a person becomes aware of social norms and pressures associated with cross-racial interactions as a result of confusing experiences with Blacks or negative reactions by Whites to interracial associations. In this status, a person realizes and acknowledges that he or she is White. According to Helms (1984, 1990), an individual at this level is "caught between internal standards of human decency and external cultural expectations" (p. 10).

Psychological Findings

Taub and McEwen (1992) found that Disintegration status attitudes were negatively related to immature interpersonal relationship styles. Helms and Carter's (1991) study of racial identity and counselor preference revealed that participants with high Disintegration status attitudes preferred a counselor with characteristics similar to their own.

Social Findings

According to Helms (1990), people who are characterized by high levels of Disintegration attitudes have a difficult time understanding Blacks' expression of anger and believe that Blacks need help in their academic endeavors. Pope-Davis and Ottavi (1994) found these attitudes to be associated with racism. Yet, in work preferences and values, Carter, Gushue, and Weitzman (1994) found that Disintegration attitudes were associated with work values consistent with traditional White American mainstream worldviews such as "getting ahead." Block et al. (1995) found that individuals characterized by high Disintegration attitudes are likely to "react negatively toward interracial situations at work such that they do not endorse principles of equality" (p. 79), do not think discrimination against Blacks is real, are not comfortable with Blacks in work-related social situations or as colleagues, but think reverse discrimination exists. They consider Blacks to be tokens, are against affirmative action and any effort, interpersonal or by management, to make the workplace more equitable. People with high Disintegration attitudes were also likely to support efforts at the organizational and management level to promote racial equality in the workplace. Block et al. (1995) thought these attitudes were indicative of racism at all levels. Also, Carter and Helms (1990) found that Disintegration attitudes were predictive of many traditional American cultural values (e.g., Evil or Mixed human nature, Mastery over Nature, Achievement orientation, and Future time focus).

Summary

People characterized by Disintegration attitudes seem to be interpersonally immature and confused by Blacks, and hold traditional work and cultural values. Additionally, the research indicates that clients in this level prefer to see therapists with similar characteristics.

Reintegration

During Reintegration, a person is fearful, angry, and hostile toward Blacks. This individual develops anti-Black and pro-White attitudes and sees Blacks stereotypically. However, "if the individual uses these feelings to become more aware of [his or her] Whiteness and attempts to understand the socio-political implications of being White in a racist society, then it is possible that feelings of anger and fear will dissipate" (Helms, 1984, p. 11).

Psychological Findings

Tokar and Swanson (1991) found Reintegration attitudes to be associated with an inability to develop intimate relationships, irrespective of race.

White males were also found to have higher levels of anxiety than men and women in other statuses. Taub and McEwen (1992) found that Reintegration attitudes were related to immature interpersonal relationships, too. Carter and Parks (1994) found that high Reintegration attitudes for White men were associated with psychological distress. "They have significantly higher levels of paranoia, concerns about drugs, and they wonder if some things they see and hear are real" (p. 18). In general, it appears that an individual in this status is characterized by psychological rigidity.

Social Findings

Carter (1990b) reports that Reintegration status attitudes are related to symbolic racism. Westbrook (as cited in Helms, 1990) found that the statement "affirmative action gives Blacks too many jobs" was evidenced by people at this level of racial identity. Carter (1990) found these attitudes to be predictive of racist attitudes among White males, a finding replicated by Pope-Davis and Ottavi (1992, 1994) for students and faculty at a Midwestern university. The faculty study also found women's Reintegration attitudes to be related to racism. In the student study, age was found to be related to the endorsement of racist beliefs. Similar to the Disintegration level of White racial identity, Carter, Gushue, and Weitzman (1994) found that Reintegration attitudes were associated with traditional American work values. Block et al. (1995) found that individuals characterized by high Reintegration attitudes were also strongly negative about interracial situations at work. They did not endorse principles of equality, did not think discrimination against Blacks was real, were not comfortable with Blacks in work-related social situations or as colleagues. Conversely they thought reverse discrimination existed for Whites, considered Blacks to be no more than token employees, were against affirmative action and any effort—interpersonal or by management—to make the workplace more equitable. These researchers reported that this level of racial identity resembled "old-fashioned racism . . . the tendency to endorse pre-Civil War negative racial stereotypes about Blacks and to be opposed to all aspects of integration" (p. 84). Carter and Helms (1990) reported that Reintegration attitudes were predictive of a number of traditional American cultural values (e.g., Evil or Mixed human nature, Mastery over Nature, and Achievement orientation).

Summary

In a way, the Reintegration worldview is similar to Disintegration in that both statuses reflect an externally defined racial identity. However, they are dissimilar in that a person with Reintegration attitudes feels less confused than a person with Disintegration attitudes. Reintegration also has a strong anti-Black element.

Pseudo-Independence

The next level of White racial identity, Pseudo-Independence, is characterized by an acceptance of differences and similarities between Black and White cultures. However, the Pseudo-Independent person only recognizes these distinctions intellectually, while remaining emotionally distant about racial issues.

Psychological Findings

Taub and McEwen (1992) found that Pseudo-Independence status attitudes were positively related to mature interpersonal relationships, that is, more mature interpersonal relationships were found than among lower-scoring individuals. Neither McCaine (1986) nor Carter (1988) found an association with any particular affect among participants in their studies. Helms and Carter (1991) found these attitudes to be predictive of a preference for White counselors—more specifically, White female counselors. Thus, under psychological distress, the Pseudo-Independent person's intellectual distancing regarding race can be seen in a preference for a White counselor. Carter and Parks (1994) report that these attitudes are associated with memory difficulties and obsessive psychological defenses. This was thought to mean that such people need to hold race at a cognitive level.

Social Findings

At this level of racial identity, a shift in social understanding is apparent. Helms (1990) reported that individuals with high Pseudo-Independence attitudes approved of interracial dating and marriage. Claney and Parker (1988) found these attitudes to be related to comfortableness with Blacks in various situations; Pope-Davis and Ottavi (1994) found them to be inversely related to racism. But when age was considered, racism was endorsed by Whites 20 years and younger. Ottavi, Pope-Davis, and Dings (1994) linked these attitudes with prediction of self-reported multicultural competence (skills, knowledge, awareness, relationships) in a sample of counseling graduate students. Carter et al. (1994) found less endorsement of traditional work and cultural values (i.e., getting ahead) (Carter & Helms, 1990). Regarding Pseudo-Independent attitudes Block et al. (1995) reported that high levels were associated with support of management and institutional efforts toward equity in the organization. They go on to note that their findings revealed "a negative side to Pseudo-Independence attitudes. It suggests that attitudes reflecting knowledge and understanding of Blacks, although not overtly negative, are associated with negative attitudes toward interventions to achieve work force integration and the perception that Whites are discriminated against in many organizations. This attitude may be similar to symbolic or modern racism" (p. 83).

Summary

Again, these findings indicate a distinct shift in worldview. The Pseudo-Independence level seems to show a shift from a less mature personal style to a self-reliant one. However, this shift lacks emotional content and may be primarily cognitive. The emotional learning may lag behind the intellectual understanding of racial identity.

Autonomy

Autonomy is the final status of White racial identity, and its attitudes are related to a transcendent level of racial development. When compared to the other four levels of White racial identity, Autonomy represents the most accepting and flexible of the racial identity attitudes.

Psychological Findings

Taub and McEwen (1992) found that Autonomy attitudes were positively related to mature interpersonal relationships. Tokar and Swanson (1991) found that "a secure appreciation and acceptance of oneself and others (autonomy) appears to be associated with a liberation from rigid adherence to social pressures and with a strong inner reliance (inner directedness)" (p. 299). When seeking mental health services, Helms and Carter (1991) found that individuals with high Autonomy attitudes indicated no preference for a White counselor, unlike prospective clients with Pseudo-Independence attitudes. It appears that an individual with a predominance of these attitudes has shifted from being externally to internally defined with respect to racial identity.

Social Findings

Westbrook (as cited in Helms, 1990) found that individuals with high Autonomy attitudes supported racial integration and believed that Blacks and Whites committed an equal number of crimes on campus. With respect to work and cultural values, Carter et al. (1994) found Autonomy attitudes to be inversely related to traditional American work values. In the Block et al. (1995) study high Autonomy attitudes were related to endorsing management and organization interventions to promote equity in the workplace. Also, they were more likely to see discrimination, less likely to see reverse discrimination, did not see Blacks as tokens, supported affirmative action, and were comfortable with Blacks in work and work-related social situations. Carter and Helms (1990) reported that Autonomy attitudes were predictive of the cultural belief that people were subjugated by nature. This finding may indicate that individuals at this level of racial identity have learned that they have little control over their environment.

Summary

These research findings suggest that individuals with Autonomy attitudes have both an intellectual and an emotional understanding of their racial identity. This understanding stems from a shift from an externally to an internally defined racial identity.

RESEARCH FINDINGS: AN OVERVIEW

Both the Black and the White racial identity theories have been examined empirically, using the BRIAS and the WRIAS. These quantitative studies have included varied participants; however, like most psychological research, several studies have used college samples. The results described have supported the theoretical models, suggesting that each level of White and Black racial identity is related to various psychological, behavioral, social, and cultural variables.

Therefore, it is reasonable to argue that a therapist or patient will bring an array of feelings, attitudes, and perceptions to the counseling situation. These elements will be consistent with his or her level of racial identity resolution and will influence and guide behavior and interpersonal interactions.

Racial identity theory goes beyond racial group-based inferences and offers a psychologically grounded perspective with which to understand race. This racially inclusive perspective also uses race as a socially meaningful group characteristic that allows for individual psychological variation. Moreover, it allows for a description of specific ways that a client's and counselor's racial identity attitudes influence both self and others' affect and behavior.

CHAPTER 10

Does Race or Racial Identity
Influence the Therapy Process?

I have reviewed traditional approaches to understanding race in psychotherapy and have presented an alternative Racially Inclusive Model of Psychotherapy, which uses a psychological race-based approach for describing how race influences psychotherapeutic interactions. The empirical evidence presented suggests that different levels of racial identity are associated with specific psychological, emotional, attitudinal, social, and cultural characteristics. These investigations offer support for the racial identity theories, but they do not indicate whether and in which way race or racial identity affects the therapeutic process. Therefore, it is important to determine whether the race or racial identity perspectives and the therapeutic process have merit. Currently, little empirical evidence exists to support either perspective.

The first and longest held notion, as outlined in Part One, assumes that racial group membership in and of itself influences the psychotherapeutic process. In particular, various authors have proposed that the patients' and therapists' socially derived racial attitudes have an effect on this process. Advocates of the race per se assumption who also use transference and countertransference assert that racial stereotypes affect the psychotherapeutic process only in cross-race dyads. They argue that race stimulates subconscious positive and negative transference and countertransference reactions and responses. According to this traditional view, White dyads should not be influenced by race (see Chapter 2), because race is considered only when either a patient or therapist is a visible racial/ethnic group member.

A majority of writers who argue that race, alone, is the primary influence on the therapeutic process have discussed transference and countertransference from a historical, political, and sociocultural perspective

---

Portions of this chapter are reprinted with permission from "Does Race or Racial Identity Attitudes Influence Counseling Process in Black and White Dyads?" by R. T. Carter, 1990. In J. E. Helms (Ed.), *Black and White Racial Identity*. Westport, CT: Greenwood Press. Copyright 1990 by Greenwood Press.

that emphasizes cross-racial relationships in North American society. Some authors have suggested that the racial stereotypes and cultural biases that exist in American society may also be present in cross-racial therapy relationships (see Chapter 2). According to this race per se perspective, psychotherapeutic interactions are affected by cultural biases and racial stereotypes only if the therapist and client are from different racial groups. In most of the literature on race's influence in therapy, Black and other visible racial/ethnic group clients and White counselors' interactions have been studied. However, little attention has been given to other types of dyads such as a Hispanic therapist/White client, a Black therapist/Black client, an Asian therapist/Hispanic client, or an Asian counselor/Asian client. I would argue that racial dynamics might emerge in racially similar, as well as racially mixed, therapeutic pairs. Psychological projections stimulated by race are said to mirror racial group members' social views and attitudes, but, to date, only a few studies support this view. Therefore, one would assume that if it were possible to categorize therapists' and clients' covert behaviors, they would be influenced by each participant's race.

Two studies by Jones (1978, 1982) have investigated the psychotherapeutic process and outcomes using racial group membership as a predictor variable, rather than racial identity attitudes. Jones (1978) used transcripts from the first ten sessions of ongoing therapy, therapist and client postsession reports, and rater evaluations of the therapeutic process to determine the influence of race.

In this study, data for the psychotherapeutic process were gathered from written transcripts of tape recorded sessions, therapists' notes, and a postsession measure. A Black and a White judge read the transcripts and interpreted the meaning of the interactions by using content analysis. Outcome was assessed by examining the client and therapist responses to an instrument that measured each participant's satisfaction with the therapy and perception of the other participant. Additionally, each therapist was asked to evaluate the client's progress and the therapeutic outcome.

The design of the study helped Jones to isolate and assess racial influences in the process and outcome of the treatment. The outcome was the same for each therapist/client pair (Black/Black; White/Black; Black/White; White/White). The psychotherapeutic process was examined along seven dimensions that emerged from the data:

1. Client openness/motivation.
2. Race salience (i.e., therapist's emphasis on race).
3. Rapport/liking.
4. Depth/efficacy (i.e., did therapist come to understand the client).

5. Therapist activity.
6. Erotic transference (i.e., patient's sexualized feelings for therapist).
7. Therapist tolerance/support.

A comparison revealed no differences in client motivation, therapist activity, or therapist support by racial pairs. However, results indicated that race salience was greater for Black clients than for White clients and was highest in Black/Black pairs. In the Black/Black dyads, the degree of salience exceeded that of Black therapist/White client and White client/White therapist pairs. The White/White dyads were rated as significantly greater in rapport/liking than Black/Black pairs, and Black/Black pairs showed greater depth/efficacy than White/White pairs.

Jones (1978) also investigated how therapy changed over the ten sessions. In particular, he examined whether race influenced the type or direction of change during the treatment process. He found that, regardless of race, the process was characterized by a strong working alliance. As a group, Black clients more frequently discussed race, tested the therapists' commitment to them, and then grew more trusting. The White clients showed an increase in rapport and liking, which Jones (1978) suggests is an indication of fewer process issues and a greater liking of the therapist.

Overall, Jones found that race influenced the psychotherapeutic process but not its outcome. All clients were expected to have successful outcomes because they were young, well educated, and good candidates for therapy. The results revealed that Black clients' process was facilitated in same-race pairs and suppressed in racially dissimilar pairs. Thus, Jones's (1978) study provides strong support for the racial group membership perspective.

The instruments Jones (1978) used can be considered global or macro-process measures and outcome measures in that they do not assess the covert, interaction experiences of the participants, but rather evaluate the overt statements or verbal exchanges. It is also unclear how race was discussed in therapy. It is therefore difficult to determine how therapists and patients may experience therapy at a covert level, that is, in what covert ways patients may experience therapeutic interventions. Moreover, Jones used racial group membership as the primary race variable, which means he did not consider within-group psychological variation of the therapy participants.

In a more recent study, Jones (1982) explored psychotherapists' impressions of treatment outcome for different racial pairs. In this investigation, Jones used archival data of case records and controlled for demographic variables. The selected racial pairings were: Black clients/White therapists, White clients/White therapists, White clients/Black therapists, and Black clients/Black therapists. Each therapist was asked to complete an adjective checklist and an outcome instrument two to six weeks after terminating with his or her client.

In this study, based on the data generated by the therapists, Jones found that Black and White clients benefited equally from therapy. Black therapists rated their clients as improving more than did White therapists. Jones also found that Black and White therapists differed in their assessments of psychological disorders; White therapists tended to report that their Black patients were more seriously impaired than did Black therapists. This finding was most pronounced when White therapists were assessing the quality of family relationships. Jones notes that these findings "possibly . . . represent[s] differences in culturally influenced notions about what constitutes psychopathology and what characterizes good family relationships" (Jones, 1982, p. 730). Jones's findings that racial differences exist in defining psychological disorder are supported by other researchers' results. It appears that Blacks and Whites hold varying conceptions of mental illness and that certain forms of behavior considered to be a sign of disturbance by a White clinician may in fact serve an adaptive function for a Black client (Grier & Cobbs, 1968).

Jones's studies indicate that race is an important variable in the psychotherapeutic process and outcome, but they do not suggest the nature of the influence. At best, one can conclude that racial differences actually reflect cultural differences. But the lack of a consistent theory makes this conclusion tentative. Moreover, Jones's research has considered global or macrolevel processes as opposed to psychological or microlevel processes, that is, in-session interactions.

Racial identity theory suggests that identity resolutions that affect personality, attitudes, and behavior directly affect psychotherapy. Similarly, the psychotherapy literature suggests that a therapist's and client's cognitive and verbal behavior may vary as a function of their racial attitudes, and that a considerable amount of affect may be associated with cross-racial dyads as well as dyads with a Black client and a therapist of any racial group. However, neither the psychotherapy literature nor the race-specific literature considers how a client's or therapist's racial attitudes interact with and influence each participant's thoughts, feelings, and behavior.

If the race per se perspective is conclusive, one would expect that race alone, without consideration of racial identity status attitudes, would influence the psychotherapeutic process at a microlevel. However, if the interactional model involving racial identity is correct, one would expect to find that counselors' and clients' racial identity attitudes would be related to the counseling process at a microlevel in both same- and cross-race therapy dyads. Two studies tested these notions. The first study is described and discussed in this chapter, and the second study is presented in Chapter 11.

METHODS AND PROCEDURES FOR EMPIRICAL EVIDENCE

Sample

The participants in the studies presented here and in the next chapter were drawn mostly from people who attended cross-cultural training conferences in New York, California, and Maryland. However, only those workshop attendees who participated in simulated counseling sessions were included in the analyses.

Participants ranged in age from 20 to 63 years. The groups included Blacks, Whites, Asians, and Hispanics. The education of the participants ranged from high school to doctoral level. With regard to occupation, the majority of participants reported that they were in a mental health occupation; graduate students comprised less than half of the participants. Participants reported an average of 7 years' work experience in the mental health profession with a range of 1 to 30 years.

Instruments

The measures used in these two studies were: (a) the Black Racial Identity Attitude Scale (BRIAS), (b) the White Racial Identity Attitude Scale (WRIAS), (c) the Visible Racial/Ethnic Identity Scale, (d) the Therapist's Intentions List, and (e) the Client Reactions List.

Intentions and Reactions Measures

According to Hill and O'Grady (1985), a counselor's intention is defined as a "therapist's rationale for selecting a specific behavior, response mode, technique or intervention to use with a client at any given moment within the process of the session" (p. 3). Thus, "counselor's intention" seems to refer to one of the 19 reasons for a therapist's choosing a particular intervention or response. The therapist's intentions are: get information, give information, support, focus, cognitions, feelings, insight, change, challenge, therapist needs, set limits, clarify, hope, cathart, behavior, self-control, reinforce change, resistance, and relationship.

Hill, Helms, Spiegel, and Tichenor (1988) reported on a system that consists of 19 positive, negative, and neutral client reactions. The measure consists of 14 positive reactions in which the client: felt supported, understood, hopeful, relieved, more clear; had feelings, negative thoughts or behaviors, better self-understanding; took responsibility; was challenged; got unstuck; gained a new perspective; felt educated; learned new ways to behave. The system included four negative reactions in which the client felt: miscommunication, worse about self, a lack of direction, ineffective therapist intervention. The one neutral reaction was: no particular reaction (see Appendix).

Relationship Measures

The *Session Evaluation Questionnaire (SEQ—Form 4)* (Stiles & Snow, 1984) is composed of two dimensions: Perceptions and Affect. The Perception dimension consists of Depth and Smoothness, which measure independent evaluative aspects of counselor and client perceptions of the session. The Affect dimension includes Positivity and Arousal, which measure aspects of client and counselor postsession affect. The Depth scale assesses the perceived power and value of the session. The Smoothness scale is an evaluation of how the session was experienced—that is, whether the session was pleasant, relaxed, and comfortable. The postsession measure of Positivity reflects the extent to which the counselor and client felt confident and happy, and whether there was an absence of fear or anger. The Arousal scale is reflective of feelings of excitement and activity.

Affective Measures

The *State-Trait Anxiety Inventory (STAI)* (Spielberger, Gorsuch, & Lushene, 1968) is a measure of anxiety that consists of two distinct self-report scales: Trait Anxiety and State Anxiety. The State Anxiety scale, a measure of momentary feelings, was used in the current study.

The *Hostility Dimension of the Symptom Checklist-90 Revised (SCL-90R)* (Derogatis, 1984) is intended to reflect behavior, thought, or affect associated with angry feelings.

Procedures

Group leaders, knowledgeable about Helms's (1984) racial identity model and familiar with the Hill and O'Grady (1985) therapist intentions list and the Hill et al. (1988) client reactions system, led small groups in the audio-videotaped simulated counseling sessions. The participants who chose to be clients were given a list of potential racial topics and were asked to select, for discussion during the simulation, a topic with which they had personal experience.

The therapists were instructed to counsel the clients drawing on their therapeutic skills. At the completion of a brief session, each client and counselor completed the session evaluation scale (SEQ) and the affective measures (STAI and SCL-90R's Hostility subscale) and reviewed the videotaped session. During this process, each client recorded his or her reactions to each of the counselor's statements, using the Hill et al. (1988) client reactions system, and each counselor indicated his or her intentions underlying each statement, using Hill and O'Grady's (1985) therapist intention system.

RACE ALONE OR RACIAL IDENTITY: WHICH HAS THE GREATEST IMPACT ON THE THERAPEUTIC PROCESS?

The following types of therapeutic pairs were formed by considering the counselor's and client's race:

   8 White counselor/Black client pairs (W/B)
   4 Black counselor/White client pairs (B/W)
  19 White counselor/White client pairs (W/W)
   5 visible racial/ethnic group pairs (VR/VR).

The VR/VR pairs consisted of 3 Black, 1 Asian, and 1 Hispanic counselor, and 3 Asian, 1 Black, and 1 Hispanic client. The term racial identity attitude will be used in the research section in order to be consistent with the measures used in the studies.

Race Alone

Analyses of variance were conducted to examine the effects of race on therapist intentions, client reactions, session evaluations, and affective states. These analyses revealed that two counselor intentions were significantly different for Black and White therapists. White counselors' intended to clarify and elicit feelings more often than Black therapists, suggesting that White counselors more frequently intended to explore feelings and seek elaboration and specification from clients than Black clinicians.

Black and White client reactions did not differ significantly. The analyses of variance for session evaluations (Depth, Smoothness, Positivity, and Arousal) and affect (Anxiety and Hostility) for Black and White clients and counselors indicated that Blacks had significantly higher mean scores for Positivity and Hostility than did Whites. Thus, racial differences were most evident in Blacks' expressed mood and Whites' reactions to feelings. However, fewer differences were found than would have been expected by chance.

These results confirm the assertion that race alone (i.e., without considering racial identity development) may not have a particularly strong effect on the psychotherapeutic process, when assessed at a microlevel or speaking turn within sessions.

Racial Identity within Racial Dyads

This study also examined whether therapist and client racial identity attitudes are correlated with therapist intentions and client reactions. These analyses compared four dyads with varying levels of racial identity to determine whether these attitudes were related to the therapy process and, if so, how they were associated.

Implicit in this interactional model is the notion that a counselor's actions, which result from his or her racial identity attitudes, influence a client's reactions and that a client's racial identity attitudes influence a counselor's behaviors (measured as therapist intentions). Such an interaction would occur if a counselor's or client's racial identity attitudes influenced his or her behavior in a manner that was discernible to either participant. Although counselor and client behavior was not investigated directly in the present study, it seems reasonable to speculate that the counselors' intentions were influenced by the clients' actions and that the clients' reactions were influenced by the counselors' actions. If these speculations are warranted, then it is reasonable to discuss the finding in the present study interactively.

The four groups of pairs (i.e., W/B, B/W, W/W, and VR/VR) described above were used. For each group of therapeutic pairs, the counseling process variables (i.e., intentions and reactions) associated with each counselor's and each client's racial identity attitudes were presented and discussed in terms of how their racial identity attitudes may have influenced the counselors' intentions and the clients' reactions. For example, in the W/B group, the counselor intention and client reaction associated with the counselors' Contact attitudes were discussed, and so on.

White Counselor/Black Client Counseling Dyads

The assumption being examined in this study was the extent to which racial identity attitudes, as they interact with race, are better predictors of the counseling process than race by itself. Figure 10.1 shows that in White counselor/Black client dyads, racial identity attitudes were significantly related to counselor intentions and client reactions. For example, White counselor Contact attitudes were not associated with counselor intentions but were related to Black client reactions.

This interaction can be understood by considering Contact attitudes: the person does not see race as salient, so differences due to race are ignored. If a therapist with a predominance of Contact attitudes either ignores racial issues or believes they are unimportant, he or she may not see possibilities for changing or clarifying these feelings when presented by a client.

White Counselor/Black Client
(N = 8)

White Counselor Intentions	White Counselor Racial Identity Attitudes	Black Client Reactions
	Contact ↔	(+) Supported (−) More clear (−) Negative thoughts and behavior
Set limits (+) ↔	Disintegration ↔	(+) Lack direction
	Reintegration	
Set limits (+) Support (−) Resistance (−) ↔	Pseudo-Independence ↔	(−) Learn new behavior (−) Ineffective
	Autonomy	

White Counselor Intentions	Black Client Racial Identity Attitudes	Black Client Reactions
Set limits (+) Hopeful (+) Behaviors (+) ↔	Pre-encounter	
Cathart (+) ↔	Encounter ↔	(−) Relief
	Immersion–Emersion ↔	(+) Understood (−) Relief (−) Got unstuck
	Internalization ↔	(−) Hopeful

Figure 10.1   Correlations among counselor intentions, client reactions, and counselor and client racial identity attitudes for White counselor/Black client dyad types.

Note: Arrows show intentions and reactions correlated with racial identity attitudes; (+) indicates positive relationship, (−) indicates negative relationship.

A therapist with a high level of Contact attitudes would be less likely to attend to race-related material that is an important aspect of a client's personality or presenting problem. This therapist, believing that race is not salient, would fail to see its importance in the identity formation of others. Thus, counselor Contact attitudes are related to the Black client feeling supported but at the expense of being clear or learning about maladaptive thoughts and behaviors.

A counselor characterized by Disintegration attitudes feels uncomfortable in situations with racial significance and uncomfortable reacting to negative experiences with Blacks and Whites. A person at this level of racial awareness has just discovered the implications of being White and has begun to confront the conflicts and emotions (e.g., guilt, depression) associated with this discovery. Because the counselor with Disintegration attitudes intends to set limits, he or she is not understood by the client or the client experiences a lack of direction regarding problems with racial issues.

White counselors with a predominance of Pseudo-Independent attitudes indicated the counselor intention of set limits, and were less likely to provide support or deal with client resistance. The client felt that he or she did not learn a new perspective while working with a counselor characterized by Pseudo-Independent attitudes, and viewed the counselor as ineffective. Pseudo-Independent attitudes were hypothesized to reflect an intellectual understanding of racial similarities and differences. It is possible that when a White counselor high in Pseudo-Independence attitudes works with a Black client, he or she can provide structure, but has difficulty being supportive or working with emotional issues.

The findings with respect to Disintegration and Pseudo-Independent attitudes seem to be consistent with racial identity theory: Disintegration attitudes reflect a transitional and uncertain racial identity structure, and Pseudo-Independent attitudes are associated with a distant, White "liberal" attitude orientation. Consequently, a counselor with a high level of Disintegration attitudes may be able to structure the process because of his or her own uncertainty with respect to identity. Pseudo-Independence attitudes may contribute to a counselor's ability to perceive accurately the goals that need attention, but has trouble with emotional work.

When examining a Black client's racial identity attitudes and their influence on the counseling process with a White counselor, it appears that Pre-encounter and Encounter attitudes affect counselor intentions, whereas Encounter, Immersion–Emersion, and Internalization attitudes influence client reactions. Black clients with high Pre-encounter attitudes may influence White counselors to provide structure, convey expectations that change is possible, and provide feedback about the client's inappropriate behavior when racial issues are discussed. Thus, when a White counselor intends to provide structure, this intervention may be appropriate with a Black client who has high Pre-encounter attitudes. Because Pre-encounter attitudes are related to anti-Black/pro-White attitudes, such clients, when attempting to discuss racial issues, may desire structure and direction, as well as specific information about how to change. This information may be best received from a White counselor.

Black clients with a predominance of Encounter attitudes were associated with White counselors' intention to help the clients relieve tension and unhappy feelings. This finding might reflect the clients' need to cope with the emotional upheaval that accompanies this level of racial awareness. At the same time, Encounter attitudes were negatively related to clients' feelings of relief. Therefore, although Encounter attitudes are related to the counselor's desire to be cathartic, a client may not derive many benefits from releasing tension and unhappy feelings with a White counselor.

Black clients with high Immersion–Emersion and Internalization attitudes were not related to counselors' intentions, but were related to clients' reactions in White counselor/Black client dyads. Black clients with high Immersion–Emersion attitudes felt understood by the White counselors, but did not experience relief from anxiety or tension, and felt that they could not remove obstacles to change (get unstuck). Black clients who were immersed in Black culture and had anti-White/pro-Black attitudes felt understood by White counselors. Internalized Black clients were less likely to focus on their cognitive processes but hoped that change was possible.

In summary, the counseling process for White counselor/Black client dyads is influenced by each participant's racial identity attitudes. In general, lower levels of the White counselor's racial identity attitudes were related to the counselor's desire to provide structure. Black clients' reactions to these interventions were primarily negative (e.g., ineffective, lacked direction). When a White counselor had higher levels of racial identity attitudes, the Black clients felt supported but did not necessarily learn skills for behavioral change (e.g., learn new behaviors) or feel emotionally supported. Black clients high in Pre-encounter attitudes were also associated with White counselors who provided structure and hope and identified inappropriate behavior. Black clients with Pre-encounter attitudes seemed to benefit most from interventions from White counselors. However, Black clients with high racial identity attitudes, when working with White counselors, felt understood but did not learn appropriate behaviors or feel that the setting was a place for exploration. Thus, such clients in these dyads would not necessarily experience any growth or symptom relief.

The psychotherapy literature has focused primarily on White counselor/Black client dyads. Although the assumption is that Whites are unable to counsel Blacks, these results suggest that counseling effectiveness depends on the client's and counselor's racial identity attitudes more than race. Interestingly, in the former case, Disintegration and Pseudo-Independent attitudes seem most problematic. In the latter case, Pre-encounter and Encounter attitudes seem to contribute to the most cognitive "work" on the White therapist's part.

Black Counselor/White Client Dyads

The characteristics and effectiveness of Black counselor/White client dyads have received minimal attention in the therapy literature. In general, the literature has focused on White clients' negative reactions toward Black counselors therapeutically.

In the present study, the best evidence of what Black counselors *think* they should do in Black/White dyads is reflected in the relationships (correlations) of Black counselors' racial identity attitudes and their counseling intentions (see Figure 10.2). These relationships for Black/White dyads were strong; the correlations had to be greater than .90 to be significant (N = 4).

When a Black counselor was high in Pre-encounter attitudes, he or she did not intend to indicate an opinion that the White client did not need to change his or her manner of handling racial issues or that the counselor felt ill-equipped for handling racial matters. Another possibility for the

Black Counselor/White Client
(N = 4)

Black Counselor Intentions		Black Counselor Racial Identity Attitudes		White Client Reactions
Hopeful (−)	↔	Pre-encounter		
Feelings (+)	↔	Encounter	↔	(+) Better self-understanding
		Immersion-Emersion		
		Internalization	↔	(+) No reaction
Black Counselor Intentions		**White Client Racial Identity Attitudes**		**White Client Reactions**
		Contact		
		Disintegration	↔	(+) Lack direction (+) Ineffective
		Reintegration	↔	(+) Lack direction (+) Ineffective
Hopeful (+)	↔	Pseudo-Independence		
		Autonomy		

Figure 10.2   Correlations among counselor intentions, client reactions, and counselor and client racial identity attitudes for Black counselor/White client dyad types.

Note: Arrows show intentions and reactions correlated with racial identity attitudes; (+) indicates positive relationship, (−) indicates negative relationship.

relationship is that the counselor perceived the client's behavior to be appropriate. The client may have understood what to do and how to act in the therapeutic interaction.

Black counselors with high levels of Encounter attitudes intend to deepen the White client's emotional awareness (feelings) of the racial issues being discussed. The counselor's desire to focus on emotions may reflect his or her willingness to confront difficult feelings that both the client and counselor may be struggling to understand.

The relationships between White client reactions and Black counselor racial identity attitudes pertain to clients' perceptions of Black counselors who (presumably) exhibit different levels of the various Black racial identity attitudes. When a Black counselor had high levels of Encounter attitudes, the White clients felt a deeper self-understanding and acceptance. When a Black counselor had high levels of Internalization, a White client had a neutral reaction.

Emotional turmoil associated with their own Encounter attitudes facilitates counselors' abilities to encourage White clients to be more accepting of themselves when racial issues are the topic of counseling. The relationship between Internalization and no reaction on the part of the White client may reflect the client's misunderstanding of the Black counselor's internalized interventions or possibly the Black counselor's tendency to intellectualize racial issues when his or her Internalization attitudes are high.

One significant relationship was found between the White clients' racial identity attitudes and the Black counselors' intentions in these dyads. Pseudo-Independence attitudes were related to Black counselors' intentions to convey expectations that change was possible. Black counselors may be responding to the White clients at this level of racial identity by offering reassurance that the clients can work through the emotional issues associated with race.

Information concerning White clients' reactions to Black counselors is provided by the relationships between White clients' reactions and their racial identity attitudes. Disintegration and Reintegration attitudes were negatively related to the clients' reactions of lack of direction and ineffectiveness in the counselor. Clients with high levels of Disintegration and Reintegration, in most instances, had strong negative reactions toward the Black counselor.

The Disintegration client enters counseling in a state of confusion with respect to racial matters. Therefore, any intervention by a Black counselor that increases such confusion may be perceived as lacking direction or being ineffective. Reintegration attitudes are described as involving negative feelings toward Blacks. Thus, Reintegration attitudes may be a protective function, contributing to a White client's resistance toward exploring uncomfortable racial issues. A White client, using these defenses, may perceive a Black counselor as ineffective and incapable of directing the counseling process.

In summary, Black counselor/White client dyads were strongly influenced by each participant's racial identity attitude development. A Black counselor who has high Pre-encounter attitudes when working with a White client believes that racial discussions are a worthwhile endeavor. Furthermore, if the counselor's Encounter attitudes are high, attempts to focus on a client's emotional experiences may lead the client to increased self-knowledge. If the counselor has internalized his or her Black identity, the White client may respond neutrally. On the other hand, a Black counselor, when working with a White client who has high Pseudo-Independence attitudes, may enhance expectations that change is possible. However, if the White client's Disintegration and Reintegration attitudes are high, the Black counselor is seen negatively, and the client receives little benefit from working on racial issues with the counselor. Perhaps this level of racial identity development, with its strong defenses, limits a positive therapeutic exchange.

White Counselor/White Client Dyads

Little has been written about race in White counselor/White client dyads. Results from this dyad indicate that each level of racial identity is related to a counselor intention (see Figure 10.3).

Counselors with high levels of Contact attitudes allowed the client to establish the agenda (i.e., set limits), but they neither encouraged the client to be clear and complete in the problem presentation (i.e., clarify) nor provided the client with a sense that change was likely or possible (i.e., hope). When the counselors expressed Contact attitudes, the White clients felt that they were able to become aware of themselves but were not able to experience relief from anxiety or tension.

When race was the topic of counseling, counselors with high Contact attitudes avoided dealing with the issues. The counselors provided little encouragement for the clients, but the clients still gained self-knowledge.

A White counselor with Disintegration attitudes communicated that change was possible and gave feedback about the clients' inappropriate behavior. Counselors' Disintegration attitudes were related to White clients' reactions such that they felt able to release tension and anxiety (relief) and overcame barriers (got unstuck). In contrast to their positive reactions, clients perceived that counselors with high Disintegration attitudes were ineffective. These findings may reflect the ambivalence regarding racial issues associated with Disintegration attitudes.

A White counselor with high Reintegration attitudes provided structure, conveyed an expectation for change, and identified problematic behaviors, but did not encourage the clients to explore deep feelings. These

White Counselor/White Client
(N = 19)

White Counselor Intentions	White Counselor Racial Identity Attitudes		White Client Reactions
Set limits (−)	↔ Contact	↔	(+) Better self-understanding
Clarify (−) Hopeful (−)			(−) Relief (−) No reaction
Hopeful (+) Behaviors (+)	↔ Disintegration	↔	(+) Relief (+) Got unstuck (−) Ineffective
Set limits (+) Hopeful (+) Behaviors (+) Feelings (−)	↔ Reintegration	↔	(+) Lack direction
Get information (+) Self-control (+)	↔ Pseudo-Independent		
Hopeful (−) Behaviors (−)	↔ Autonomy		
White Counselor Intentions	White Client Racial Identity Attitudes		White Client Reactions
Support (+) Feelings (−) Reinforce change (+)	↔ Contact	↔	(+) Supported (+) Understood
Set limits (−)	↔ Disintegration	↔	(+) Ineffective
Cathart (−)	↔ Reintegration		
Get information (−) Cognition (−)	↔ Pseudo-Independent	↔	(+) New perspective
Get information (−) Change (−) Relationship (−) Therapist needs (−)	↔ Autonomy	↔	(−) Relationship (−) Lack direction

Figure 10.3 Correlations among counselor intentions, client reactions, and counselor and client racial identity attitudes for White counselor/White client dyad types.

Note: Arrows show intentions and reactions correlated with racial identity attitudes; (+) indicates positive relationship, (−) indicates negative relationship.

racial attitudes seem to inspire the White counselor to control the situation when race is an issue for a White client. From the client's reaction to the counselor's Reintegration attitudes, it seems that the client felt the White counselor lacked direction. A counselor with these attitudes superficially confronts racial issues but is unable to manage a client's deeper feelings and reactions about these issues. These behaviors may reflect the counselor's ambivalence about racial matters. Perhaps counselors with high levels of Reintegration attitudes are in conflict about their own racial attitudes and their humanistic counselor training. Although the counselor tries to focus the session, a White client experiences these interventions as ineffective.

Counselors with Pseudo-Independent attitudes were associated with intentions to acquire specific information about a client's history and psychological functioning, and to encourage the client to understand and control his or her feelings, thoughts, and behaviors. It appears that Pseudo-Independent attitudes influence the White counselor to emphasize cognitive aspects of the White client's situation.

Finally, counselors high in Autonomy attitudes were less likely to convey an expectation for change or to identify inappropriate behaviors. Counselors' Autonomy attitudes seemed to lessen the counselors' need to influence the counseling process; at the same time, clients did not seem to feel any particular influence from the counselors' Autonomy attitudes.

Just as the counselors' racial characteristics in White/White dyads have been overlooked, so too have the clients' racial attitudes. When clients had high Contact attitudes, counselors perceived that the clients needed feedback regarding their efforts to change, and a warm, supportive environment. White clients with high levels of Contact attitudes understood counselors' beliefs that clients' emotional experiences should not be more intense (feelings). White clients' Contact attitudes were related to feelings that White counselors liked, understood, and supported them. These clients may have experienced their White counselors as supportive and understanding because they had no other experiences by which to evaluate them or because they were receptive to members of their own race.

When working with clients high in Disintegration attitudes, White counselors provided structure and established goals. Disintegration attitudes were related to clients' feeling that the counseling interventions were ineffective. Therefore, any intervention by a White counselor that increased the White clients' confusion regarding racial issues may have been perceived as not being in tune with the client.

However, the clients' verbal expressions of Reintegration attitudes seemed to have led counselors to feel that they should not protect clients (or themselves) from a full expression of feelings.

Clients gained a new perspective when their Pseudo-Independent attitudes were high. Counselors responded to these attitudes by restricting cognitive discussions and not gathering information. Perhaps this finding reflects a new perspective from their White counselors: the Pseudo-Independent clients' openness to a new cognitive perspective, and their desire to gain information about racial matters.

Clients' Autonomy attitudes influenced the White counselors to avoid: seeking information about the White clients' history and functioning, building new coping mechanisms to analyze relationships, and focusing on the counselors' anxiety. The clients' Autonomy attitudes seemed to contribute to their feeling less responsible for the racial problem as well as feeling that the process did not lack direction. Thus, the clients' Autonomy attitudes appear to have influenced counselors and clients to accept the situation as it was. Clients with high levels of Autonomy attitudes did not feel responsible for causing the situation, and the counselors did not appear motivated to change the racial issues presented by the clients.

In summary, White counselor/White client dyads, when addressing racial issues, are influenced differentially by the counselors' and clients' level of racial identity development.

Visible Racial/Ethnic Counselor/ Visible Racial/Ethnic Client Dyads

In the five visible racial/ethnic counseling pairs, there were three Black counselors, one Asian, and one Hispanic. The Black and visible racial/ethnic identity attitudes can be used to describe process relationships (see Figure 10.4). In these pairs, when the counselor's Pre-encounter or Conformity attitudes were high, he or she focused on a client's emotions and was less likely to give information, discuss relationship issues, tend to his or her own needs, or explore feelings. From the clients' perspective, Conformity or Pre-encounter attitudes were related to their having little affect, and feeling that the counseling session lacked direction. On the other hand, a counselor with Encounter or Dissonance attitudes conveyed the expectation that change was possible, but did not attend to the client's feelings. When a counselor's Resistance or Immersion attitudes were high, the counselor intended to help the client gain insight. But when the counselor's Awareness or Internalization attitudes were high, he or she simply gathered information.

In this study, five pairs included three Asian clients, one Black, and one Hispanic. When a client had high Conformity or Pre-encounter attitudes, the counselor was influenced to confront the client and help him or her develop self-mastery. No correlational findings existed between

Visible Racial/Ethnic Counselors/Visible Racial/Ethnic Clients
(N = 5)

Visible Racial/Ethnic Counselor Intentions		Visible Racial/Ethnic Counselor Racial Identity Attitudes		Visible Racial/Ethnic Client Reactions
Cathart (+) Give information (−) Feelings (−) Relationships (−) Own needs (−)	↔	Conformity or Pre-encounter	↔	(−) Feelings (+) Lack direction
Hopeful (+) Feelings (−)	↔	Dissonance or Encounter		
Insight (+)	↔	Immersion–Emersion Resistance		
Get information (+)	↔	Awareness Internalization		
Visible Racial/Ethnic Counselor Intentions		Visible Racial/Ethnic Client Racial Identity Attitudes		Visible Racial/Ethnic Client Reactions
Challenge (+) Self-control (+)	↔	Conformity or Pre-encounter		
Information (+) Feelings (−)	↔	Dissonance or Encounter	↔	(+) Hopeful
Hopeful (−)	↔	Resistance or Immersion–Emersion	↔	(+) Hopeful
Hopeful (+) Set limits (−) Self-control (−) Direct guidance (−)	↔	Awareness or Internalization	↔	(−) Learn new ways to behave

Figure 10.4 Correlations among counselor intentions, client reactions, and client racial identity attitudes for visible racial/ethnic group dyads.

Note: Arrows show intentions and reactions correlated with racial identity attitudes; (+) indicates positive relationship, (−) indicates negative relationship.

the counselor's Encounter or Dissonance attitudes and any of the client's reactions, but the counselor was influenced to give information and to avoid dealing with intense feelings. The client felt a sense that change was possible (hopeful). Clients with high Immersion or Resistance attitudes did believe change was possible, although the counselors were influenced to convey the possibility that change was not possible. Clients with high Awareness or Internalization attitudes led counselors to convey the expectation that change was possible, but the counselors offered less structure, did not focus on client self-mastery, or guide the client. Additionally, when a client had high Awareness or Internalization attitudes, he or she was unlikely to learn new ways of thinking.

SUMMARY OF STUDY

The counseling process in visible racial/ethnic pairs shows patterns similar to those in the other dyads. When the therapists' racial identity attitudes were low, they engaged in avoidance behavior, and clients did not feel that the therapeutic work was of great benefit. Midlevel racial identity development (Resistance and Immersion) resulted in counselors' focusing on intrapsychic issues (insight). Clients did not feel they would grow much, yet influenced the counselors to hold out hope. Internalization and Awareness attitudes seemed to function in the way that Autonomy attitudes did in White counselor/White client dyads. The counselors seemed less involved in directing the session, and, as a consequence, the clients were able to learn and grow.

In general, across all four types of therapeutic pairs, more counselor intentions than client reactions were related to counselor and client racial identity attitudes, a finding similar to Carter's (1988); that is, in White/White dyads, a counselor's intentions are more salient than a client's reactions. Nonetheless, it seems that White racial identity attitudes are related to counseling process variables, as suggested by Helms's interactive counseling model.

On the one hand, based on these findings, it can be said that considering the race of counselors and clients in the absence of within-group racial psychological variability (e.g., racial identity attitudes) was not particularly useful for describing the counseling process. On the other hand, racial identity attitudes were more useful for understanding the counseling process than race alone. In general, this study revealed that racial identity attitudes were related to counselor intentions in White counselor/White client and visible racial/ethnic group dyads, to client reactions in Black counselor/White client dyads, and to client reactions in White counselor/Black client dyads. However, racial identity attitudes were less likely to be related to counselor intentions in cross-race dyads than in same-race dyads. More specifically, Black clients with Immersion–Emersion attitudes were most often related to positive reactions; for White clients, the same was true of Contact attitudes.

The results of this study provide support for the racial identity perspective and little, if any, support for the race perspective. The study also demonstrates how racial identity attitudes go beyond traditional explanations of race. I think that using racial identity and its various levels, as described in the Racially Inclusive Model of Psychotherapy, goes beyond established perspectives that use traditional social ideas to describe broad phenomena due to race. Also, because racial identity is psychological in nature, with corresponding correlates to other domains of self and others, it allows for a more varied and complex analysis of race's influence on psychotherapy. Moreover, racial identity's theoretical foundation helps guide explanations and observations and is, as demonstrated above, subject to empirical investigation in addition to clinical judgment. However, the study described in this chapter pertains only to racial identity's direct relationship to therapeutic process in same- and cross-race pairs. These findings do not pertain to the relationship types model.

CHAPTER 11

Relationship Types: An Examination of Qualitative Aspects of Therapeutic Process and Outcome

Thus far, three major findings have emerged, each of which supports propositions of the Racially Inclusive Model of Psychotherapy:

1. Race alone (i.e., race per se) is not as important a variable in the psychotherapeutic process as some researchers (e.g., Jones, 1978) have proposed;
2. Racial identity statuses vary and influence a therapist's and a client's thoughts and behaviors;
3. Racial identity status attitudes affect a dyad's interactions.

These findings provide evidence that racial identity statuses in all types of dyads (i.e., same-race and cross-race) influence the therapeutic process. Additionally, the argument has been made (see Chapter 8) that the psychotherapeutic process can be defined and understood in terms of the interaction between the therapist's and client's racial identity statuses. That is, distinct types of therapeutic relationships can be formed, each with its own interactional dynamics, outcome, and affective issues. In this chapter, I present a research study that was designed to explore whether evidence supports this contention. The study examines therapeutic process and outcome in three of the four relationship types described in Chapter 8.

Few empirical studies have examined the influence of racial identity statuses on the counseling process and its outcomes, even though speculation about their role abounds. For the most part, the existing psychological literature has focused on broad questions, such as whether White counselors can be effective with Black clients, or has used narrow nonpsychological definitions of race (e.g., participants' racial category or racial group membership) to understand and investigate the influence of racial issues in psychotherapy.

Recently, Helms (see Chapter 8) proposed an interactional model that attempts to overcome some of the shortcomings in previous attempts to understand race's influence in psychotherapeutic interactions for all racial groups. This interaction model differs from other race-specific approaches; it uses racial identity, a within-group psychological variable, to define the quality of therapeutic interactions, and it categorizes psychotherapeutic dyads according to similarities and dissimilarities in their racial identity statuses, rather than race per se. Other race-specific approaches simply characterize all cross-racial dynamics in terms of presumed racial group characteristics and do not address same-race dynamics (see Chapter 2). Helms's model suggests a focus on the way racial identities interact in therapeutic relationships, and she posits four relationship types (i.e., parallel, crossed, progressive, and regressive) to facilitate our understanding of how dyads' racial identity statuses might interact.

Helms uses the interaction of racial identity attitudes as the basis for the proposed types of relationships: parallel, crossed, progressive, and regressive. These relationship types were described in detail in Chapter 8, and will be only briefly outlined here. A parallel relationship exists when a counselor and a client are at similar levels of racial identity development. A crossed relationship occurs when a therapist and a patient have opposite attitudes about racial groups. In an all-Black crossed dyad, for example, the therapist has anti-Black/pro-White attitudes and the patient has pro-Black/anti-White attitudes. A progressive relationship involves a counselor whose racial identity development is at least one level more advanced than the client's. An example might be an Asian therapist who has developed to the third level, Resistance, and a Native American patient who has developed to the second level, Dissonance. A regressive relationship exists when a client's level of racial identity is at least one level more advanced than the counselor's. Thus, in Helms's (1984, 1990) interactional model, the counselor's and client's races do not characterize relationship types; rather, the interaction of their racial identity statuses does.

Helms (1984) suggests that cognitive reactions, affective states, behaviors, and perceptions of the counseling relationship can be used to characterize counselors and clients according to the different relationship types. For example, she suggests that progressive relationships can be characterized by a client who engages in self-exploration and a counselor who recognizes racial issues and displays genuine race-based empathy and acceptance. In this type of relationship, one would expect the sessions to be perceived as positive and beneficial by both the client and the counselor, and one would find moderate levels of anger and anxiety. Unlike a progressive relationship, a regressive relationship is described as conflictual. The client and the counselor may have negative impressions of the sessions and may experience high levels of anxiety and hostility, partly because each participant is struggling for control of the sessions when racial issues are discussed.

RESEARCH QUESTIONS

This study was designed to explore two research questions about Helms's interactional model:

1. Do the counselor and the client in each relationship type have identifiable patterns of covert cognitive behaviors and emotional responses?
2. If each relationship type is qualitatively different in terms of (a) the strategies used by the client and the counselor and (b) their emotional responses, then do the participants' in-sessions perceptions of the therapeutic process vary?

In this study, process is measured by counselor intentions, the therapeutic purpose of counselor statements (Hill & O'Grady, 1985), and client reactions to the counselor, assessed at a speaking turn or microlevel (Hill, Helms, Spiegel, & Tichenor, 1988). Counselor and client postsession emotional reactions (e.g., hostility, arousal) and perceptions of the relationships (e.g., session impact) in the simulated counseling sessions were also examined.

Therefore, what aspects of the therapeutic process, defined as participants' intentions and reactions to one another, describe the four different racial identity relationship types?

CLASSIFICATION OF RELATIONSHIP TYPES

To classify dyads according to the four relationship types, a client's and a counselor's raw scores on the racial identity attitude scales (i.e., WRIAS, BRIAS) were transformed into percentile scores using preliminary White (Helms & Carter, 1990) and Black (Helms & Parham, in press) norms. Once these transformations were made, the therapeutic dyad was placed in one of the four relationship types by comparing each participant's level of racial identity. Using this procedure, dyads were classified in the following manner:

Parallel—the counselor's and client's highest percentile scores reflected conceptually equivalent attitudes;

Crossed—the counselor's and client's highest percentile scores were conceptual opposites;

Progressive—the counselor's highest percentile score was on a more developmentally advanced attitudinal scale than the client's highest score on an attitudinal scale;

Regressive—the counselor's highest percentile score was on a less advanced attitudinal scale than the client's highest score on an attitudinal scale.

In forming these relationship types, dyads were collapsed across racial combinations (i.e., Black/Black, White/White, White/Black, and Black/White), meaning that the pattern of racial identity attitudes, rather than race, was used to classify relationship types. This is consistent with Helms's theory, which states that the pattern of racial identity attitudes is more salient than the individual attitudes. Thirty-three dyads from the sample described in Chapter 10 participated in this study, and, using the aforementioned classification procedure, they were categorized as follows: 17 were parallel; 7 were progressive, and 9 were regressive. None of the dyads was classified as crossed.

Procedures as outlined in Chapter 10 were also used in this study. To examine the qualitative and interactive patterns of specific counseling process variables (e.g., therapist's intentions, client's reactions, each participant's perception of the session), correlations between different measures were used. For example, the therapist's intentions were correlated with his or her perception of and emotional responses to the session. From these correlations, the types of motives or strategies used by a therapist were determined and related to the therapeutic process for each relationship type. Remember, the two areas of interest are how a therapist's intentions relate to his or her emotional experience and impression of the session, and how a therapist's and client's behaviors influence or interact with each other (i.e., how a therapist's intentions are affected by the client's experience and emotions).

To explore these complex interactional process questions within each relationship type, counselor and client variables (i.e., perception of session and affective measures) were correlated with the counselor intentions and the client reactions. Thus, by using the criss-cross analyses as described in the previous paragraph, it is possible to capture each participant's behavior as well as how the participants affected one another.

The counselor's process measures (i.e., intentions) and how the intentions were related to the counselor's emotional and session experiences were correlated. How the counselor's intentions matched or differed from the client's experience in the session was also investigated. The client's reactions and their relationship to his or her session experiences, and the relationship between the client's reactions and the counselor's session experiences were examined.

The results of these analyses are described in this chapter. Each relationship type has its own section, and within each section there are four subsections: counselor intentions, counselor intentions and client behavior, client reactions, and client reactions and counselor behavior. These analyses are discussed in terms of racial identity attitudes because the instruments assess attitudes. The attitudes, however, reflect important aspects of the statuses.

PARALLEL RELATIONSHIPS

Counselor Intentions

Seventeen of the 33 dyads were classified as parallel relationships. A parallel relationship is defined as a dyad in which the counselor and the client share the same or similar racial identity attitudes. In these 17 dyads, a total of 23 significant correlations were found among the counselor intentions, session evaluations, and emotional responses. Approximately half of these correlations were between the counselor intentions and two emotional responses: positivity and anxiety.

The pattern regarding the counselor intentions and positivity and anxiety reveals that a counselor felt positive about the session when he or she tried to educate or provide factual information, to convey the belief that change was possible, to give reinforcement or feedback about the client's efforts to change, and to resolve relationship issues (see Figure 11.1). When a counselor was pleased, his or her joy was mixed with anxiety. Specifically, a counselor felt anxious when confronting relationship issues, conveying the belief that the client could change, and encouraging the client to own or control his or her feelings, thoughts, and behaviors.

Overall, counselors evaluated the sessions more favorably than clients. Counselors perceived the sessions as positive when they facilitated good therapeutic work and when they focused on the client. To the extent that they focused on themselves, counselors reported feeling anxious and uncomfortable.

Helms (1984) characterizes the interaction between a counselor and a client in a parallel relationship as angry, and perhaps hostile. However, the findings (see Figure 11.1) from this analysis suggest that a counselor in this type of dyad might find himself or herself in conflict and anxious when racial issues are discussed. This conflict might involve a counselor's attempts to help the client without revealing his or her own racial attitudes. It can be argued that the counselor should focus on the client and not on himself or herself; however, the counselor can become

Parallel Dyads (N = 7)

Counselor Variables Correlated with Counselor Intentions	Counselor and/or Client Session Evaluations and Affect		Client Variables Correlated with Counselor Intentions
Cathart (−) Cognitions (−)	↔	Depth ↔	(+) Set limits (−) Clarify (−) Cognitions (−) Resistance (−) Therapist needs
Support (+) Feelings (+) Reinforce change (−)	↔	Smoothness ↔	(−) Resistance
Cathart (−) Give information (−) Hopeful (+) Reinforce change (+) Relationship (+)	↔	Positivity ↔	(+) Set limits
Get information (+) Focus (−)	↔	Arousal ↔	(−) Clarify (−) Cognitions (−) Resistance (−) Therapist needs
Support (−) Focus (−) Hopeful (+) Self-control (+) Relationship (+)	↔	Anxiety ↔	(−) Clarify (−) Cognitions (−) Resistance (−) Therapist needs
Get information (+)	↔	Hostility ↔	(+) Cognitions (+) Behaviors (+) Self-control (+) Relationship (−) Support

Figure 11.1   Significant correlations among counselor intentions and counselor and client session evaluations and affect for parallel dyads.

Note: Arrows show counselor intentions correlated with various session evaluations and affective measures; (+) indicates positive relationship, (−) indicates negative relationship.

anxious regardless of whom he or she is focused on. Therefore, the counselor's anxiety seems related to racial issues raised in the therapeutic setting. This is consistent with the notion that anxiety is associated with relationship issues such as helping the client believe that change is possible and assisting the client to control his or her psychological life, especially regarding racial issues.

Counselor Intentions and Client Behavior

It is instructive to examine the impact of the counselor intentions on the client session evaluations and postsession affect measures. The analysis to examine the relationships among counselor intentions and client session evaluations and affect reveals that client depth, hostility, and arousal were most often related. A client perceived the sessions as deep and positive when a counselor intended to structure the treatment and establish goals and objectives, whereas sessions were considered worthless and shallow when a counselor tried to protect himself or herself or to appear superior to a client. In these parallel relationships, a client experienced sessions as fairly positive when a counselor was cognizant of and focused on creating order and direction and being self-involved (see Figure 11.1).

Sessions were assessed by a client as rough (opposite of smooth) when a counselor tried to overcome barriers to change or progress. A client perceived the sessions as slow, calm (opposite of arousal), and anxiety-provoking when a counselor attempted to encourage elaborations, identify irrational thinking, overcome obstacles to change, or protect himself or herself. A client felt angry when a counselor intended to resolve relationship issues, encourage the mastery of feelings and thoughts, and identify the client's maladaptive behaviors. In a parallel relationship, the client appears (as does the counselor) uncomfortable with the counselor's efforts to change the client's perceptions or behaviors. A counseling process that, in general, is structured, supportive, and perhaps avoids focusing on specific client change characterizes the client's and counselor's reactions to the counselor intentions in a parallel dyad (see Figure 11.1).

Client Reactions

Turning to the client reactions in a parallel relationship, most of the significant correlations among a client reactions, session evaluations, and affect were associated with the client's level of hostility followed by his or her perceptions of the session's depth. Client reactions were directly connected to the therapist's overt statements, and client session perceptions were related to how the client found the entire interaction.

The client perceived sessions as valuable when he or she felt that the counselor's interventions allowed him or her to explore deep feelings. Sessions were smooth and produced hostile feelings when the client reported feeling reassured about his or her ability to change. These two sets of relationships suggest that although a client may value the exploration of feelings, he or she may become hostile because such exploration can lead to change.

Sessions were considered positive, but also generated anger, when the client felt that he or she had developed a new understanding of someone or some situation. Receiving specific ideas for coping with particular problems, gaining new knowledge or information, and feeling confused, puzzled, distracted, or misunderstood by the counselor all contributed to the client's feeling angry. These client reactions seem to indicate resistance to change. Moreover, in a parallel relationship, anger and hostility seem to dominate the client's reactions. It should also be noted that these feelings are mixed with experiencing sessions as positive and deep. In parallel relationships, the correlations among client reactions support the view that a client may be resistant to confronting racial issues. These findings are illustrated in Figure 11.2.

Client Reactions and Counselor Behavior

Client reactions to a counselor's session evaluations and postsession affect may offer information about the observation that a client in a parallel relationship may be resistant to confronting racial issues. The measurement categories most often correlated with client reactions were counselor postsession affect and depth of session. Counselors seemed to view sessions as worthless (not deep) when the client was able to explore feelings, be involved in the counseling process, or had no reaction. Sessions were perceived as smooth when the client felt understood by the counselor. According to the counselor, sessions were positive when the client reported feeling liked, accepted, and reassured that change was possible. The counselor was aroused by sessions in which the client felt an increasing awareness of his or her maladaptive thoughts and behaviors, whereas the counselor experienced high levels of anxiety and hostility during sessions when the client felt responsible for himself or herself and learned new coping strategies. The counselor was less angry when the client reported no reactions or liked himself or herself better (see Figure 11.2).

Parallel relationships seem to be related to a counseling process that involves strategies designed to avoid racial issues, even though these strategies are often associated with considerable affect, including anger, hostility, arousal, and positivity. The intentions and reactions that related to a counselor's and client's assessment of the session as deep seemed to involve maintaining a pleasant, nonthreatening environment. When a counselor attempted to deal with issues, he or she seemed angry and anxious about the interactions, and the client seemed to react similarly. Other studies (Atkinson, 1987; Garfield & Bergin, 1978) have suggested that when a client and a counselor have similar attitudes, the counseling process and its outcome are generally favorable. However, the results from this study indicate that parallel relationships may be counterproductive

Parallel Dyads (N = 17)

Client Variables Correlated with Client Reactions	Counselor and/or Client Session Evaluations and Affective Measures		Counselor Variables Correlated with Client Reactions
Feelings (+) New perspective (+) Challenge (−) Ineffective (−)	↔	Depth ↔	(+) Feelings (+) Got unstuck (+) Felt worse (+) Ineffective (+) No reaction
Hopeful (+) Relief (+)	↔	Smoothness ↔	(+) Understood (−) Better self-understanding
Support (+) Hopeful (+) New perspective (+)	↔	Positivity ↔	(+) Support (+) Hopeful (+) New perspective
Challenge (−)	↔	Arousal ↔	(+) Negative thoughts and behavior (+) Miscommunication
Challenge (−)	↔	Anxiety ↔	(−) Better self-understanding (+) Responsibility (+) Learn new behavior (+) Lack direction
Hopeful (+) Understood (+) Responsibility (+) Challenged (+) Learn new behavior (+) Miscommunication (+) Felt worse(+)	↔	Hostility ↔	(−) Better self-understanding (−) New perspective (−) No reaction (+) Learn new behavior

Figure 11.2   Correlations among client reactions and counselor and client session evaluations and affective measures for parallel dyads.

Note: Arrows show client reactions correlated with various session evaluations and affective measures; (+) indicates positive relationship, (−) indicates negative relationship.

when racial content is involved; even though a counselor and a client may have similar racial identity attitudes, the dyad may be unable to deal effectively with racial issues.

PROGRESSIVE RELATIONSHIPS

Counselor Intentions

A counselor in a progressive relationship has a racial identity that is at least one level more developmentally advanced than that of the client. Therapists in these relationships (seven in all) perceived the sessions as deep, anxiety-producing, and hostile when they tried to resolve problems in the relationship or to overcome obstacles to progress. All sessions were evaluated as smooth and resulted in low anxiety levels and less arousal when a counselor tried to assist a client to stay on track and did not focus on structuring the session. When a counselor did not try to structure sessions, he or she reported feeling aroused and anxious. Sessions were perceived as positive by the counselor when he or she tried to explore the client's feelings.

The counselor intentions of therapist needs, and cathart were related to the counselor's anxiety level. When a counselor did not encourage a client to reduce his or her tension or unhappy feelings, the counselor reported feeling anxious. When a clinician intended to provide a client with support, the counselor reported feeling anxious and hostile.

Based on these findings (see Figure 11.3), it appears that a counselor who has a more highly developed racial awareness than the client experiences more anxiety and anger when he or she attempts to focus on therapeutic issues involving race. In this type of relationship, a client may respond slowly to the counselor's interventions, thus causing the counselor to be upset with the client.

Counselor Intentions and Client Behavior

A client perceived the sessions as deep, smooth, and arousing when the counselor intended to bring structure to the session. When a counselor intended to identify maladaptive behaviors, the client evaluated the sessions as deep, smooth, positive, and arousing, and reported low levels of anxiety. When a counselor intended to instill in his or her client the expectation that change was possible, the client assessed the sessions as deep, smooth, positive, arousing, and less anxiety-provoking than other sessions. Also, when a counselor tried to encourage the client to develop adaptive skills, the client perceived the sessions as smooth, positive, exciting (arousal), active, and less anxiety-producing. A client

Progressive Dyads (N = 7)

Counselor Variables Correlated with Counselor Intentions	Counselor and/or Client Session Evaluations and Affect		Client Variables Correlated with Counselor Intentions
Resistance (+) Relationship (+) Therapist needs (+)	↔	Depth ↔	(−) Resistance (+) Set limits (+) Support (+) Behaviors (+) Change
Focus (+) Set limits (−) Support (−) Hopeful (−) Insight (−) Therapist needs (−)	↔	Smoothness ↔	(+) Set limits (+) Hopeful (+) Behaviors (+) Change
Feelings (+)	↔	Positivity ↔	(−) Give information (−) Clarify (+) Hopeful (+) Behaviors (+) Change
Focus (−) Set limits (+) Support (+) Hopeful (+) Behaviors (+) Insight (+) Challenge (+) Therapist needs (+)	↔	Arousal ↔	(−) Focus (+) Hopeful (+) Behaviors (+) Change
Focus (−) Cathart (−) Set limits (+) Hopeful (+) Behaviors (+) Insight (+) Relationship (+) Therapist needs (+)	↔	Anxiety ↔	(−) Hopeful (−) Behaviors (−) Change (+) Get information (+) Give information (+) Clarify (+) Cognitions (+) Self-control
Support (+) Relationship (+) Therapist needs (+)	↔	Hostility ↔	(+) Get information (+) Clarity (+) Relationship (+) Therapist needs

Figure 11.3 Correlations among counselor intentions and counselor and client session evaluations and affective measures for progressive dyads.

Note: Arrows show counselor intentions correlated with various session evaluations and affective measures; (+) indicates positive relationship, (−) indicates negative relationship.

reported feeling anxious and angry when the counselor intended to get information, give facts, and solicit elaborations from the client (see Figure 11.3).

Thus, these results suggest that, in progressive relationships, the counselor and the client respond differently to the counseling process. In progressive dyads, the counselor perceived the counseling process as favorable when he or she focused on therapeutic issues such as exploring the client's feelings. The client, on the other hand, perceived sessions as favorable when the counselor intended to provide support and hope, or to identify problematic behaviors. However, the client reported anger and/or hostility when the counselor tried to focus his or her attention on details.

Client Reactions

When client contributions to the therapeutic process were examined, his or her reactions seemed to be related most often to anxiety and positivity (see Figure 11.4). In general, when a client reported feeling understood by the counselor, he or she perceived the sessions as deep, smooth, and arousing, and reported low levels of anxiety. Also, when a client reported feeling encouraged and confident about changing and reported learning new ways of coping, the client perceived the sessions as deep, smooth, positive, and arousing, and anxiety was low. However, during sessions that were perceived as shallow, arousing, and anxiety-provoking, a client reported relief, which in this study refers to feeling less depressed, angry, or anxious than before. Sessions were considered less positive, anxiety-producing, and hostile when the client's reactions were more clear, feelings, and better self-understanding. It appears that a client evaluated the sessions as favorable experiences when he or she believed that the counselor's interactions were supportive and instructive about other people or situations, and encouraging about change. However, the client reported feeling anxious, hostile, and perhaps uncertain and afraid when he or she perceived the counselor's interactions as promoting growth via self-exploration.

Client Reactions and Counselor Behavior

The counselor perceived the session as deep (i.e., not worthless) when the client reported feeling relief (i.e., less depressed or anxious than before the session) and believing that some of the counselor's interventions were ineffective. The client's reaction of ineffectiveness was also associated with the counselor's anxiety, anger, and perceptions that the sessions were rough, not smooth. When a client reported the reaction of

Progressive Relationships (N = 7)

Client Variables Correlated with Client Reactions	Counselor and/or Client Session Evaluations and Affect		Counselor Variables Correlated with Client Reactions
Understood (+) Hopeful (+) Learned new behavior (+) Relief (−) Got unstuck (−)	↔ Depth ↔		(+) Relief (+) Got unstuck (+) Ineffective
Understood (+) Hopeful (+) Learned new behavior (+) Got unstuck (−)	↔ Smoothness ↔		(−) Challenge (−) Ineffective
Hopeful (+) Learned new behavior (+) Miscommunication (+) More clear (−) Feelings (−) Better self-understanding (−) Educated (−)	↔ Positivity ↔		(+) Negative thoughts and behaviors (+) Better self-understanding
Understood (+) Hopeful (+) Relief (+) Learned new behaviors (+)	↔ Arousal ↔		(+) Understood (+) Learned new behaviors (+) Felt worse
More clear (+) Feelings (+) Negative thoughts and behaviors (+) Better self-understanding (+) Educated (+) Understood (−) Hopeful (−) Learned new behaviors (−)	↔ Anxiety ↔		(+) Understood (+) Lack direction (+) Ineffective (−) Miscommunication
Relief (+) More clear (+) Negative thoughts and behaviors (+) Responsibility (+) Ineffective (+)	↔ Hostility ↔		(−) Miscommunication (+) Responsibility (+) Ineffective

Figure 11.4   Significant correlations among client reactions and counselor and client session evaluations and affective measures for progressive dyads.

Note: Arrows show client reactions correlated with various session evaluations and affective measures; (+) indicates positive relationship, (−) indicates negative relationship.

miscommunication, the counselor seemed to feel less anxious and hostile. However, the counselor felt anxious when the client thought that he or she did not receive enough guidance from the counselor, felt shaken up, or was forced to confront issues (see Figure 11.4).

It is possible that, in progressive dyads, counselors' goals are different from those of their clients, and the counselors believe that facilitating their clients' learning about and understanding of racial issues might involve unpleasant emotional experiences for their clients and themselves. Progressive relationships may produce more tense environments than other relationship types; however, this heightened uneasiness seems to be beneficial to the counseling process.

REGRESSIVE RELATIONSHIPS

Counselor Intentions

Regressive relationships are defined as those in which a client's level of racial awareness is at least one status more developmentally advanced than a counselor's. In the study's nine regressive relationships, the correlations pertaining to the postsession evaluations indicated that counselors perceived the sessions as deep, smooth, and less anxiety-provoking when they attempted to encourage an understanding of the underlying reasons for or the unconscious motives of the clients' feelings, thoughts, or behaviors (see Figure 11.5). Sessions were also evaluated as deep when the counselor tried to develop the client's coping skills or improve the client's assumptive system. Sessions were seen as exciting, arousing, and producing anger when the counselor intended to provide a warm, empathic, and supportive environment. Depending on the counselor's intentions, his or her level of anxiety varied: anxiety was low when the clinician intended to identify irrational thinking, and anxiety was high when the counselor attended to his or her own needs. Counselor hostility was related to the counselor's keeping the client on topic, structuring the session, getting information from the client, providing support, encouraging the client to gain mastery, and facilitating relief.

In a regressive dyad, a counselor seems more comfortable when he or she tries to explore on a deep level the client's intrapsychic dynamics or unconscious motivations, and less comfortable and more hostile when he or she intends to provide structure, deal with relationship issues, or acquire specific information from the client. Possibly, in this relationship type, a counselor feels threatened by the client's better grasp or awareness of racial issues when compared to his or her own.

Regressive Dyads (N = 9)

Counselor Variables Correlated with Counselor Intentions	Counselor and/or Client Session Evaluations and Affect		Client Variables Correlated with Counselor Intentions
Insight (+) Change (+)	↔	Depth ↔	(+) Negative thoughts and behaviors (+) Challenge (+) Educated (+) Felt worse
Insight (+)	↔	Smoothness ↔	(+) New perspective
		Positivity ↔	(+) Change (+) New perspective (+) Educated (−) Miscommunicated (−) Lack direction (−) Ineffective
Support (+) Cognitions (−) Challenge (−)	↔	Arousal ↔	(+) More clear (+) Negative thoughts and behaviors (+) Educated (+) No reaction (−) Hopeful (−) Responsibility
Resistance (+) Therapist needs (+) Cognitions (−) Change (−)	↔	Anxiety ↔	(+) Miscommunication (+) Ineffective (−) New perspective
Set limits (+) Get information (+) Support (+) Clarify (+) Cathart (+) Self-control (+)	↔	Hostility	

Figure 11.5 Significant correlations among counselor intentions and counselor and client session evaluations and affective measures for regressive dyads.

Note: Arrows show counselor intentions correlated with various session evaluations and affective measures; (+) indicates positive relationship, (−) indicates negative relationship.

Counselor Intentions and Client Behavior

In general, a client believed that the session was deep and positive when the counselor tried to identify irrational thinking (see Figure 11.5). When a counselor intended to intensify or facilitate a client's acceptance of his or her own feelings, the client described the session as deep, exciting, or arousing. A client assessed the sessions as smooth, positive, and arousing when a counselor tried to encourage the client to understand his or her underlying dynamics or unconscious motivations. The client appeared to feel anxious and angry when the counselor used specific intentions (i.e., set limits, get information, support, resistance, and therapist needs).

Based on the session evaluations and postsession affect measures, it seems that a client perceived the session as more favorable when the counselor intended to focus on feelings, irrational thoughts, and insight, which are characteristics of intense therapeutic work. Perhaps, in a regressive dyad, the client's higher level of racial identity motivates him or her to deal more directly with racial issues. When the counselor intended to structure the sessions, give support, and gather information, the client seemed to feel anxious and hostile, possibly because these interventions, from the client's perspective, did not address the client's concern (see Figure 11.5).

Client Reactions

An examination of the client reactions, session evaluations, and postsession affect (see Figure 11.6) might clarify the client's experience. In general, when a client reported becoming aware of negative thoughts and behaviors, he or she evaluated the session as deep and exciting. When a client indicated that he or she gained knowledge and information, the session was seen as deep and positive. The client also described the session as deep when he or she felt challenged or worse about himself or herself. A session was considered smooth, positive, and less anxiety-producing when a client reported that he or she gained a better understanding of another person or situation. A client's hopefulness was associated with feeling less arousal, and feeling less arousal was related to a client's feeling more responsible for himself or herself. A client perceived the session as arousing or exciting when he or she felt understood by the counselor and had gained a better self-understanding. However, a client felt that the session was anxiety-producing and either unpleasant or negative when he or she believed that the counselor's interventions were ineffective and miscommunications had occurred during the session.

Regressive Dyads (N = 9)

Client Variables Correlated Client Reactions	Counselor and/or Client Session Evaluations and Affect		Counselor Variables Correlated with Client Reactions
Negative thoughts and behaviors (+) Challenge (+) Educated (+) Felt worse (+)	↔	Depth ↔	(+) Relief (+) New perspective (+) Educated (+) Learn new behaviors (+) Felt worse (−) Feelings
New perspective (+)	↔	Smoothness ↔	(+) Feelings (+) Negative thoughts and behaviors (+) Challenge (+) Educated (+) Felt worse (−) Hopeful (−) Lack direction (−) Ineffective
Challenge (+) New perspective (+) Educated (+) Miscommunication (−) Lack direction (−) Ineffective (−)	↔	Positivity ↔	(+) Challenge (+) Educated (−) Ineffective
Understood (+) More clear (+) Negative thoughts and behaviors (+) Educated (+) No reaction (+) Hopeful (−) Responsibility (−)	↔	Arousal ↔	(−) More clear (−) Better self-understood
Miscommunication (+) Ineffective (+) New perspective (−)	↔	Anxiety ↔	(+) Challenge (+) Negative thoughts and behaviors (−) Lack direction
		Hostility ↔	(+) Learn new behaviors (+) Miscommunication

Figure 11.6 Correlations among client reactions and counselor and client session evaluations and affective measures for regressive dyads.

Note: Arrows show client reactions correlated with various session evaluations and affective measures; (+) indicates positive relationship, (−) indicates negative relationship.

Client Reactions and Counselor Behavior

Counselors' session evaluations and clients' reactions indicated different and sometimes opposing patterns. In a regressive dyad, a client seemed to value a session in which he or she could discuss racial issues in ways that enhanced his or her understanding and ability to cope. A client seemed to feel less favorable and more anxious about the session overall when he or she had negative reactions, such as ineffectiveness. A counselor tended to evaluate sessions as shallow and smooth when a client reported increased awareness of his or her feelings. However, a counselor considered a session as deep when a client reported reactions such as relief, new perspective, educated, learned new ways to behave, and felt worse. Additionally, the client reaction of felt worse was associated with the counselor's perception of a session as smooth. A session was assessed as rough and anxiety-provoking when a client reported that the counselor lacked direction and was ineffective (see Figure 11.6).

In a regressive relationship, the client's reactions seemed to indicate that the client is struggling to deepen his or her knowledge and understanding of racial issues, while the counselor is struggling to maintain his or her power and authority in the therapeutic relationship. The counselor appears comfortable with racial issues only when they are discussed in terms of the client's dynamics and not the counselor's.

CONCLUSION

In summary, these three relationship types—parallel, progressive, and regressive—are associated with different qualitative experiences in terms of the client's and counselor's perceptions of and affective reactions to a session. It seems that these relationship types, which are based on the combination of the counselor's and client's highest racial identity attitudes, have different counseling processes and outcomes.

The studies described and reviewed in this chapter and in Chapter 9 offer evidence to support the propositions of the Racially Inclusive Model of Psychotherapy outlined in Part Two. The studies presented show the effects of racial identity on the therapist's and the patient's behaviors, perceptions, and feelings. The studies also demonstrate that the effects of racial identity on the therapeutic process vary, depending on the level of identity or the manner in which racial identity combines in the therapy dyad.

The interactions between the therapists' and clients' racial identity status attitudes, however, lead to predictable therapeutic environments. Unlike traditional concepts, which are atheoretical, this Racially Inclusive Model of Psychotherapy accounts for race's specific effects on personality, interpersonal interactions, and therapeutic relationships. This model suggests that all people in same-race and cross-race pairs are subject to racial influences that do not stem from racial group membership solely, but rather from one's psychological resolution to his or her racial group. One's racial identity resolution has numerous and often subtle effects on one's own behavior and perceptions as well as on the other participants in the interaction. Thus far, the evidence has been drawn from therapy simulations where race was a topic. Another question now arises: What happens in ongoing psychotherapy when race is not the central issue? This question is explored in the next chapter.

CHAPTER 12

Case Studies: Evidence of Race in Psychotherapy

A racial issue can be described theoretically, and studies can be designed to demonstrate its existence; however, a complex phenomenon ingrained in a person's behavior, lifestyle, or thinking is difficult to observe and discern. Even with a theory to guide the research, a phenomenon can be difficult to sort out when it is not specifically addressed. It is certainly easier to discover a person's racial identity resolution when the individual specifically asks or talks about race. When race is presented directly as an issue, a therapist has available specific information with which to determine the client's or other person's racial identity status.

In a general social context that sanctions or accepts racial discourse and debate, racial identity resolutions are more obvious. However, for most of American history, negative and derogatory beliefs about Africans, Native Indian Americans, Hispanics, and Asians were prevalent. These beliefs resulted in overt and covert discriminatory and oppressive behaviors. Whites and people of color socialized in this psychosocial and sociocultural climate were reared to believe in White superiority and in visible racial/ethnic group inferiority.

A byproduct or consequence of the 1950s to 1970s social activism is the shift from overt, explicit expressions of racial beliefs to subtle, symbolic forms of expression. For instance, racial euphemisms such as "inner city," "safe neighborhood," and "at risk," or statements such as "The issue is not race but economics" and "Differential racial treatment occurs for reasons other than race" tend to disguise, evade, or ignore race as a personality and sociopolitical reality in the United States. Furthermore, the implicit and subtle expressions of race are complicated by the recent emphasis on political correctness (see Chapter 2). Consequently, cognitive and behavioral expressions of race and racial identity are suppressed, disguised, projected, and distorted.

The purpose of this chapter is to describe expressions of racial identity in therapy that the client sought for personal reasons that were not related directly to race. Four cases are presented, and ways in which race and racial identity enter the therapeutic interaction are highlighted. In all four case studies, the therapeutic relationships were classified as progressive, and the clients, two Whites and two Blacks, were seen by a Black therapist.

RESPONSE MODES: OVERT PROCESS MEASURES

To categorize and describe the psychotherapeutic process in these ongoing cases, measures of the counselor's and client's response modes were used. Because obtaining the intentions and reactions in these cases was not possible, different types of process measures were used. Typically, response modes are gathered from verbatim transcripts of the therapy sessions. Using these transcripts, a grammatical unit is treated as a single response and assigned to a mutually exclusive nominal category by three people trained in this method. The response mode system used in this chapter was developed by Hill and her colleagues (Hill, Greenwald, Reed, Charles, O'Farrell, & Carter, 1981) and is designed to capture communication patterns in the therapy interaction. This procedure is similar to the one used by Jones (1982), described in Chapter 9.

Before defining the response categories that will be used to describe the therapeutic process in these four cases, a brief overview of the response mode literature is presented. Hill (1986) argues that response modes are important:

> They reflect communication styles or patterns . . . the specific choice of what type of response to make indicates the relationship between the two persons. For example, one person may communicate by asking questions, whereas another person might tell his or her own story (description) and not ask questions or express interest in the other person. These different response styles have different impact on the receiver. (p. 13)

For counselors, specific response modes seem to be related to their theoretical orientation and training (Hill, Thames, & Rardin, 1979). In other words, if a counselor's orientation and training emphasize being passive and supportive and forcing the client to take the initiative, then he or she might rely primarily on silence, minimal encouragement, and restatements. On the other hand, if a counselor is directive and action-oriented, then he or she might use direct guidance, giving information, and confrontation.

According to Hill (1986):

> Response modes describe the client's style of involvement in the interaction and predict the ability to participate in a verbal therapy interaction. A client who engages mostly in silence or description of the problem will

probably have a more difficult time in insight-oriented therapy than would a client who more readily engages in experiencing and insight. (p. 131)

Because the therapist and client have distinct roles in therapy—one facilitates awareness and change, and the other discusses and works toward awareness and change—two response mode systems are used to describe the process in each of the four cases presented here. Each case study will be described in terms of its response mode, and the most frequent response categories will be described. Also, I will identify the counselor's and clients' responses that are related to one another and how these response modes interact. Before presenting the case studies, a description of the clients as well as the counselor's and clients' verbal response system is in order.

Description of Case Study Participants

Case study participants are composites of various clients seen by several Black therapists. The core issues and exchanges were drawn from sessions involving two Whites (a female and a male) and two Blacks (a female and a male) in their twenties and thirties. Most clients sought treatment for reasons not directly related to race or racial issues. They consented to have the sessions tape-recorded and to participate in this study.

Procedures and Analyses

Aspects of sessions have been modified to illustrate how specific racial identity statuses may influence a person's presentational style and behavior in therapy. In many instances, the actual dialogue was altered in one of three ways: (a) some dialogue was taken from cases not analyzed; (b) the interactions presented were derived from the actual exchanges; and (c) the actual exchanges served as material to develop the dialogues presented here. However, some of the exchanges are taken verbatim from the sessions. Data analyses of response modes were based on transcripts.

Measurements

Counselor Verbal Response System (Hill et al., 1981) consists of 14 categories that are used to classify counselors' responses:

1. *Minimal Encourager*—a phrase or response that shows acknowledgment;
2. *Silence*—a pause that is longer than 5 seconds;
3. *Approval/Reassurance*—a response that offers emotional support or reinforcement;

4. *Information*—when a counselor provides specific information about counseling or some other matter;
5. *Direct Guidance*—a response wherein advice or a directive is given; this type of response may involve both parties or pertain to something outside of the therapy;
6. *Closed-Ended Question*—a response that asks for data that can be provided with a short phrase or one word;
7. *Open-Ended Question*—usually a probe for clarification or for exploration without clear limits;
8. *Restatement*—when a counselor repeats or restates the client's previous statement in specific and concrete terms;
9. *Reflection*—same as Restatement except it includes implied feelings and can be drawn from nonverbal cues or from the overall situation;
10. *Interpretation*—a statement that goes beyond the client's current understanding or statement and attempts to connect isolated events or experiences and identify feelings, defenses, resistance, or transference;
11. *Confrontation*—usually a response in which the counselor points out a discrepancy in the client's behavior or emotions;
12. *Nonverbal Referent*—a reference to nonverbal behavior;
13. *Self-Disclosure*—when a counselor shares his or her own personal experiences;
14. *Other*—an unclassified response.

Client Verbal Response System (Hill et al., 1981) consists of nine categories:

1. *Simple Responses*—a one- or two-word phrase that indicates agreement, acknowledgment, or disagreement; additionally, specific information unrelated to feelings, descriptions, or explorations is placed in this category;
2. *Request*—an effort to get direction from the counselor or to shift responsibility for solutions from the client to the counselor;
3. *Description*—when a client is reporting history (e.g., telling stories, reporting on events related to problems); emphasis is on what happened, not on understanding, emotional reactions, or experiences;
4. *Experiencing*—a statement that reveals an emotional understanding of behavior, events, and reactions; it lacks connection to causality and usually indicates an awakening experience;

5. *Exploration of the Client–Counselor Relationship*—a discussion of feelings, behaviors, and experiences that pertain to the therapeutic relationship;

6. *Insight*—a statement that shows the client comprehends themes and patterns in experiences, behaviors, and relationships;

7. *Discussion of Plans*—when a client reports future decisions and actions or possible outcomes;

8. *Silence*—a pause that is longer than 5 seconds;

9. *Other*—an unclassified response.

WHITE CASE STUDIES

These two cases, involving White clients who exhibit attitudes associated with the less mature racial identity ego statuses (i.e., Contact, Disintegration), illustrate the subtle and indirect influences race can have on the therapeutic process. In general, Whites are socialized to be unaware of their being White and how it impacts their personalities, and therefore are likely to have low levels of racial identity. Racial identity statuses that are externally defined are not well differentiated. As mentioned before, people with less well developed racial identity statuses typically act as if race creates no dilemmas for them, or they ignore race as a factor for themselves or others.

Case One—Tom

The first case, I argue, illustrates how defenses that are stimulated by race partially impede the counseling process. Tom is a White male whose racial identity status is predominantly Contact. Tom was raised in a fairly segregated environment and was taught that people were people, regardless of race.

Tom, who is in his mid-twenties, was a college freshman when he entered counseling. He sought counseling to explore vocational options before choosing a major. Tom was seen for approximately 12 sessions.

Tom grew up in a small rural town where his parents were businesspeople. While growing up, he often helped his parents run their business. Tom believed that he would be a good businessman because he had spent a considerable amount of time around businesses. Nevertheless, he wanted to explore all possibilities. In addition to finding an appropriate career path, Tom also wanted to develop a clearer sense of himself. Tom stated, "I don't know myself yet. I don't have any confidence in myself." Tom's case illustrates the ways in which race—specifically, the racial difference between the client and therapist—was not directly discussed or mentioned during the course of this short-term counseling.

Throughout Tom's treatment, the focus shifted from an emphasis on his career options to his lack of self-confidence. In the initial phase of therapy, Tom's objectives and goals were assessed and his expectations of the counseling process were discussed. Tom was eager to talk about and share his work and school experiences, but he had difficulty exploring and sharing his feelings when breakthroughs regarding his self-esteem were imminent.

Tom's expectations of the therapeutic process and his perceptions of the therapist (T) are reflected in the following exchange:

T: What do you hope to get out of counseling?

TOM: Just a better knowledge of what I do best, and I would like to learn how I can feel more confident, too.

T: What kinds of things do you see us talking about in counseling? What kind of expectations do you have?

TOM: I don't really know.

T: How do you see us pursuing the issues you raise?

TOM: Well, uh, I guess finding out about me for one, who I am, what I think, how I act, and how I deal with things. *(Pause)*

T: It must be hard to think about doing all of that.

TOM: Yes, it is. *(Pause)* Yeah.

T: What's going on?

TOM: I'm always uncertain. *(Silence)* It doesn't matter what I'm doing really. I don't have any confidence in myself.

T: So, maybe this process will help you to get a sense of who you are.

TOM: Well, if you want to know the truth, I always wanted to go to a psychologist. I just want people, other people's opinions. Because it kind of helps me to see whether I'm totally subjective or not. I don't have anybody to talk to. Like real friends, they're friends, but they're not someone you can say how you are or, you know, what bothers me.

T: So, you find it hard to share some of your thoughts and feelings with your friends. But you feel that you can talk to me. What makes you feel that way?

TOM: You need all kinds of people in your life. You seem more down-to-earth.

T: Mmm.

TOM: Well, you are superior.

T: How is that?

Tom: All kinds of ways. *(Laugh)* Let's start with education for one. You are superior with intelligence for another. You are superior. Well, you've been around longer than I have, so that definitely makes you superior. I'm a firm believer that older people can teach you a lot of things if you just listen to them.

On the surface, Tom clearly thought that the Black therapist, by virtue of age, education, and academic achievement (i.e., a doctorate) was superior. Tom did not mention race directly. And by not applying some of the commonly held Black stereotypes (e.g., uneducated, unintelligent) to his Black therapist, Tom was making the clinician an exception. However, his reference to the clinician as being "down-to-earth" can be interpreted as an indirect suggestion that the therapist, like other Black people, was more comfortable expressing emotions than Tom and other Whites.

During the middle phase of counseling, the pattern of opening up and then shutting down continued. It became apparent that Tom was more comfortable relating stories and describing incidents of assault to his self-worth than engaging in deeper self-exploration. One can understand Tom's behavior and need to idealize his therapist when his background is taken into account. Tom's rural background left him with distinct ideas about people of color, particularly Blacks. Although he tried to exempt the therapist from his stereotypes of Blacks, Tom seemed unable to share himself and his inner struggles in a consistent and productive way in the presence of his Black therapist. Tom's resistance to the therapeutic process may have been subconscious. Nevertheless, his racial identity status seemed to limit (restrict) his interactions with the therapist to retelling stories during the course of counseling, rather than self-disclosing and exploring issues.

In the beginning of the middle phase, Tom discussed his background and revealed that he grew up in a small community and led a fairly sheltered life until he entered college. Now, at college, he felt freer and more involved with different types of people than at any other time in his life. He described the small rural community in which he was raised as being racially homogeneous. Tom said that he went to schools where everyone knew everyone else and everybody was the same. Additionally, he stated that his parents taught him to treat everyone identically. From Tom's discussions, it seemed likely that race was seldom discussed in his family or among his peers.

Prior to the final session, Tom began to understand the relationship among his experiences, his self-concept, and his career options, but he continued to have difficulty exploring these issues in depth. Tom was emotionally closed and defended. During some sessions, he focused only on career issues and could not entertain the interpersonal problems he was experiencing. As both parties had agreed, counseling ended after the 12th session.

Race and the Therapeutic Relationship

As Tom's case illustrates, in many psychotherapeutic relationships where racial differences exist, therapists and clients may avoid addressing the significance and meaning of these differences. Also, given this particular client's presenting issue and his racial identity ego status, the client's and therapist's racial difference was not explicitly discussed; the client either ignored race or was more concerned with the therapist's personal qualities. Yet, the way the client experienced the therapist's personal qualities was racially based. For Tom, his therapist was seen as an exception. Pinderhughes (1989) points out that Whites may perceive professional Blacks as supercompetent as a way to cope with their own unstated expectations and feelings; the presence of "successful" Blacks must mean that they are different from other Blacks. A White person who is characterized by a Contact ego identity status, such as Tom, is likely to exhibit such beliefs when he or she is confronted with a Black therapist. The therapist, in this case, decided that exploring racial issues directly with Tom, who was unaware of race, was not warranted. Race does not have to be discussed directly; however, it can and should be part of the assessment process and considered when trying to understand a client's background, presenting problem, and interactional style.

Psychotherapeutic Process Measures

Client. Using the Client Verbal Response System (Hill et al., 1981), Tom's original responses were classified. Descriptions, Simple Responses, and Experiencing were the most frequent responses he used. Descriptions are defined as "discussions of history, events or incidents related to a problem. The person seems more interested in describing *what* happened than communicating affective responses, understanding or resolving the problem" (Hill, 1986, p. 137). A Simple Response, according to Hill (1986), is "a one- or two-word phrase that allows agreement or understanding, disagreement or disapproval or a brief response to a question of specific information" (p. 136). Experiencing refers to a response in which one is engaged in affective exploration, but the experiencing does not convey understanding or causality; it is an indication of growing awareness. Based on Tom's most frequent responses, response mode patterns were examined and related to his behavior. Tom was willing to tell his story and to reveal his emotions as they related to the story. He was less willing to seek or see solutions or to give the therapist some responsibility for finding answers.

Clinician.   The therapist's most common responses were Information, Closed- and Open-Ended Questions, Paraphrase, and Interpretations. Information is a response that involves giving information and is inversely related to Closed-Ended Questions. Typically, responses to Closed-Ended Questions are specific one- or two-word answers, whereas Open Questions are designed to probe and clarify feelings or to explore situations without limiting the patient's responses. Interpretation refers to a response that adds to "what the client has overtly recognized" (Hill, 1986, p. 135) and usually makes connections that may not be apparent to the client. These connections may involve themes, isolated events, defenses, and transference. The clinician's communication pattern was inconsistent during the course of therapy. In the early phase of Tom's therapy, the clinician used a lot of interpretations, and, in the latter part of the therapy, offered the client more information and guidance.

Interaction.   Further analyses of the interaction between the client's and clinician's response modes in this therapeutic encounter revealed that the counselor's use of the Approval response was related to the client's use of Simple Responses. The therapist's Information responses led the client to make Request responses. Closed-Ended Questions were correlated with the client's Experiencing responses. The clinician's use of Open-Ended Questions resulted in the client's using fewer Exploration responses that pertained to the therapeutic relationship. Finally, the therapist's interpretations tended to evoke a Silence response from the Client, while Confrontation responses led to Simple Responses and Experiencing responses by Tom.

The aforementioned response modes demonstrate how the client's behavior affected the therapeutic process and how the counselor's and the client's behaviors were influenced by each other. Additionally, the counselor's communication pattern in the therapeutic interaction was described. For the most part, the therapist engaged in efforts to get the client to open up, and his efforts were met with storytelling and minimal emotional reactions, typically stimulated by the stories. When the therapist attempted to be more active by confronting and interpreting, the client responded with Silence, Simple Responses, or more storytelling.

Based on the response mode technique, it seems that Tom was somewhat reluctant to open up during the course of his therapy, and his lack of exploration was related to the counselor's race. Also, it is possible that Tom was more strongly defended at the end than at the beginning of counseling. Because of Tom's level of racial identity, he found it difficult to share himself fully with a Black therapist, although he wanted very much to open up and explore issues that were touched on during counseling.

Case Two—Tina

Tina is a 32-year-old married White woman who grew up in the Midwest. She entered treatment because she wanted to explore ways to increase her sense of competence. She is a soft-spoken, thoughtful, and insightful person who wanted to feel more comfortable with herself and others. The treatment involved approximately 30 sessions over the course of a year. During the early phase of the therapy, race was not discussed directly, nor was it addressed. Instead, Tina struggled with how to relate to the therapist. The issue of race was raised by the client during the latter phase of the treatment.

Based on Tina's attitudes, she could be characterized as having a Disintegration racial identity status. She was aware of her Whiteness, but felt uncertain about how to discuss it or how to deal with her Black therapist. Additionally, Tina's actions indicated that she felt superior to her Black therapist, which is consistent with the Disintegration level of racial identity. For example, during the initial sessions, Tina made an effort to assert her authority. Her behavior led the therapist to interpret and to confront Tina's actions early in the relationship.

Tina's struggle to relate to her Black therapist was evident by her initial confusion and conflict about how she perceived herself and how she thought the therapist saw her. During the first few sessions, these perceptions were clarified. Tina seemed to feel that her attributions and her understanding of some childhood experiences were being minimized by the therapist's reframing of her descriptions and interpretations. She viewed the clinician's actions as ways to deny her self-development. Tina came to the third session angry and disturbed, and she shared these feelings. After pointing out that alternative explanations existed, the therapist observed that holding on to her anger and her perception of interactions might be related to her feelings of confusion and conflict in interpersonal relationships. This initial struggle led to the development of a strong working alliance. After this incident, Tina became more open and willing to examine her perceptions, and discovered that her interpretations of the therapist's actions were not entirely accurate.

The need for clarification is also related to the racial difference and each participant's racial identity status; often, a White client who works with a Black therapist needs to engage in a similar type of power struggle. A White person who has a developmentally low racial identity status (e.g., Disintegration) uses his or her own racial/cultural worldview to evaluate others who have a different perspective and cultural style. Applying a racially based cultural worldview to others can lead to the misperception of verbal and nonverbal communications. In the therapeutic setting, a White client may assume that a Black or visible racial/ethnic therapist should act, think, and feel as he or she does. The White client also believes that the non-White clinician will comply with the client's wishes and conform to the client's stereotypes. This results in a power struggle, because the therapist assumes that he or she is responsible for the direction of the psychotherapeutic process.

Once the therapeutic relationship was established, Tina and the clinician proceeded with the objectives she set forth. Not until the latter phase of the treatment did Tina begin to feel the need to address the racial boundaries that existed between her and the therapist. It is significant that race was not mentioned directly until late in the treatment. Perhaps the client felt that she had sufficiently bonded with the therapist and a deeper connection was needed. Tina may have felt that the therapist's race was an unstated but important part of the working relationship. However, the client's racial identity status was characterized by confusion, and, consequently, Tina became confused and distressed when race was raised.

The following excerpt, which occurred during the latter third of treatment, illustrates Tina's effort to connect with the therapist by demonstrating various ways in which she shared racial knowledge or experiences. In this exchange, Tina tells her therapist that a friend, who is light-skinned, told her she is lucky to have a Black clinician. The therapist encourages Tina to talk about race and tries to get her to stay with the topic.

TINA: I knew what he meant, a lot of people don't see that he's Black and so he hears an awful lot. He's had to struggle all his life, struggles with himself.

T: Had you had any thoughts about it [my being Black] before he said anything?

TINA: I know when I asked what you were like, it was just one of the things that was mentioned; yeah, I don't know what it would have been like if I'd come in and not known before.

T: So, that didn't conjure up any associations?

TINA: Well, I just *(Laughs; Pause),* I used to wish I was Black so that I would, I thought when I was a little girl, if I were Black, then I would have a purpose or I would have a cause or I would have a reason for feeling confused or whatever. I dated a Black man, I had a long-term relationship with a Black man, I don't know, I don't know, it was all right.

T: You were assuming what?

TINA: Mm-mm *(Pause)* I'm not sure it had a whole lot of bearing on anything. I think I just had to come in and feel what you were about. I don't think it registered any kind of, it didn't make any reservation in my mind or anything.

T: So, my being Black didn't generate any kind of association one way or another?

TINA: I'd suppose positive. I actually suppose it was kind of positive and I don't know *(Pause)* okay, interesting, yeah *(Laughs)*.

T: I thought you said earlier it had no bearing on anything?

TINA: Well, I don't know. This is getting reminiscent of the discussions I've had with G. where I try to say that I have some understanding of the Black experience and he says I have none.

T: So, it sort of feels like Black–White dichotomies exist.

TINA: Yeah.

T: I wanted to know whether my being Black added something to the experience that you were aware of? *(Silence)* Or took something away from your experience? *(Silence)*

TINA: I don't know. *(Silence)* About my being White? I mean, is that, I mean, are you really aware of your Blackness when you're in here? This probably doesn't have bearing on our relationship. I mean, mm.

T: What's your question?

TINA: Are you very much aware in here that I am White and you are Black? Because I'm not. *(Pause)*

T: Sometimes. *(Silence)* I mean, it's hard not to be aware that you're, White.

TINA: Yeah.

T: When I hear you talk about your experiences, then I think some of your experiences can only be understood by seeing you as White. The expectations and perspectives that you hold come about as a result of your racial experiences. So, I'm aware of that. I do have to understand you in the context of your race and gender.

TINA: I don't know what that means exactly.

T: Well, it means there're differences between people from various races, I might interact with you differently, talk to you differently; if you were Asian, for instance, our pattern of communication would be different. Thus, race affects our work. Do you see what I mean?

TINA: Yeah, I do.

The above exchange illustrates one way a White client's confusion about race might manifest itself.

The following exchange shows how difficult racial confusion can be and why a client might avoid a cross-racial therapeutic relationship.

Racial confusion is more difficult for a White client at a low level of racial identity because race arouses strong, intense emotions. Moreover, it is hard for a client to own up to the reality of his or her race and its effect on the therapeutic interactions. In this case, Tina needed the therapist to self-disclose before she could think about what she was feeling. But even after her self-disclosure, she remained unclear about race's influences on her, the therapist, and their interactions.

The next excerpt reveals Tina's approach-avoidance strategy for dealing with conflicts; in this instance, the conflict centers around her unexamined racial socialization and belief system.

TINA: After our last session, I was resenting the racial issue that happened to come up and I know that I brought it up. But, um, I just actually resented it being an issue because it hadn't been. I mean anytime I talk to you. I didn't feel a barrier between us due to racism until you talked about *(Pause)* my feelings about that. I end up sounding like all these other White people who say, some of my best friends are, I mean, you know, it sounds like, I didn't like that. I'm not saying you did that to me. I'm saying that I'm awkward in that position and it felt, um *(Pause)*, kind of like, I don't like that, because it's not me.

T: You felt anxious?

TINA: I don't like the awkwardness and I don't like the conclusion that I assume people jump to, that you would have jumped to about me. And then I resent it, even entering into my therapy.

T: Do you get confused?

TINA: No. Just, uh, mm, it doesn't seem right. It's just an entirely different issue to what goes on in here. I don't know. I would hope not. I would hope, I guess maybe it does harm in just the fact that I wonder how you perceive me. You know, with what I, if I fit into a certain category with White people.

T: And do you think if I have you in some kind of category that that would be harmful?

TINA: *(Sigh; Pause)* Yeah.

T: Tell me about it.

TINA: Well you wouldn't. I mean, it might interfere with you empathizing with me.

T: Because I put you in a category?

TINA: Yeah.

T: Do you feel like the category fits?

TINA: *(Pause)* I don't like to be categorized. Huh?

T: So, if I'm hearing you correctly, you feel if that does go on it would diminish how I would perceive you?

TINA: Yeah. *(Silence)*

T: How does it work in reverse?

TINA: *(Silence* = 8 seconds) You mean, do I categorize you?

T: Mm-mm.

TINA: I don't. I don't have any category right now for you because in this relationship, I'm the information giver really and I don't have much information about you.

T: Well, in terms of the things we were talking about, uh, in terms of race, are you saying that you don't see me as a Black person?

TINA: Yeah, I do, but you're a Black person, that is a category, but not who you are entirely.

T: That's part of who I am. Do you see that as harmful, seeing that characteristic as part of me?

TINA: Do I see that as harmful to you?

T: In your knowing me or interacting with me?

TINA: No.

T: So, those are categories.

TINA: I don't know.

T: What would be the categories that wouldn't be okay?

TINA: *(Long Pause)* I don't know how to go into it any deeper without, I mean I had discussions with A., a racial friend of mine who, you know, who just, it seems like the more I say it's out of my ignorance and coming from my, my, uh, background, but I just, you know, uh *(Pause)* I don't know. I don't know.

T: What I'm hearing you say is, "I'm afraid to share the things that I think of you because I may appear ignorant and bigoted and I don't want you to see me that way." You don't want to appear that way.

TINA: Well, no, and I don't want to dwell on it. That's not why I'm here.

T: Mm-mm. *(Pause)* Mm-mm. So, if I'm hearing you, what you're saying is that this stuff is real hard for you to talk about *(Pause)*.

TINA: I just don't know. *(Pause)* I find it hard to talk about without sounding like other people who say, people who really don't, um, *(Pause)* I acknowledge my prejudices. I acknowledge barriers between, you know, the cultures, but I don't want to be, I don't know how to talk about, that without sounding like so many other people who I hear who are really entrenched in prejudice.

T: It's hard, um?

TINA: Sure.

This discussion of race made Tina aware of her way of thinking about race and made her realize that she had to separate the therapist from other Black people or to ignore race to work effectively in treatment. The therapist facilitated Tina's awareness by not letting her avoid the issue and by helping her understand what racial barriers affected the psychotherapeutic process.

Psychotherapeutic Process Measures

Client.   Overall, this relationship was characterized by the use of Description, Experiencing, and Exploration responses. The therapist typically used Information, Open- and Closed-Ended Questions, and Interpretation responses. Over the course of the treatment, Tina used fewer Description responses and more Experiencing responses. During the latter phase of therapy, the client explored the therapeutic relationship more than during any other stage of treatment, and the therapist self-disclosed more. Experiencing was positively related to Self-Disclosure, which was linked to good therapeutic work on the client's part. The increased use of Experiencing responses indicates a growing awareness, because these responses reflect the client's affective exploration of issues but do not convey an understanding. A significant difference between Tom and Tina, the two White clients, is that Tina was more willing to explore issues in the cross-racial relationship. Her openness to explore issues in this setting may have resulted from her awareness of race as part of her identity.

Clinician.   The pattern is somewhat similar to the first case except for the counselor's use of Self-Disclosure statements. These are responses in which the counselor shares his or her personal experiences and feelings with the client.

Interaction.   In examining the response mode pattern of interactions within this dyad, it was found that Tina's Simple Responses were usually related to her Requests and Exploration of the Client–Counselor Relationship responses. And, her Experiencing responses led to Exploration utterances and Silence. Additionally, Experiencing utterances were correlated with Insight responses and corresponded with Tina's progress in therapy. Tina moved from minimal engagement to being responsible for the therapeutic work, which included examining her own feelings, gaining insight, and learning and understanding themes, patterns, and causal relationships.

BLACK CASE STUDIES

The two Black case studies illustrate two types of interactions with clients that have distinctly different racial identity resolutions. As with the White case studies, race was not part of the presenting problems; nevertheless, as the transcripts will reveal, race influenced the work even for the client who thought that race was irrelevant. It is also true that, for people of color, race is a more conscious aspect of their lives than for Whites, even when visible racial/ethnic people believe race is not important (Jones, 1982).

Case Three—Linda

Linda is a 29-year-old Black female. She entered therapy because she was having problems communicating with coworkers and, more recently, with her husband and parents. Her treatment took place over the course of a year and a half and consisted of approximately 25 sessions. The number of meetings was limited because of the client's business travel schedule.

Linda reported having considerable difficulty communicating with her parents, specifically her father. She felt that he treated her like a child, not an adult, by pushing his opinions and beliefs onto her without considering her point of view. Linda felt angry and frustrated, but she was unable to communicate these emotions. Linda was also unable to share her feelings with her husband.

As Linda progressed through the therapy, she began to talk about her childhood memories that might have shaped her maladaptive coping patterns in relationships. Midway through her exploration of developmental experiences and relationships, she began to realize that her self-concept and interpersonal style were greatly affected by her being one of a very few Black children in her schools and community. Linda found herself seeking approval and acceptance from her peers and family, while at the same time feeling the need to control and ignore race. Because Linda's parents and teachers emphasized that she should fit in and get along with others, Linda denied any awareness of racial differences.

Less mature externally defined levels of racial identity (i.e., Pre-encounter and Encounter) reflect a worldview in which race is not salient, and, based on certain experiences, an individual may question his or her worldview and become confused about the meaning and significance of race. Recall from the discussion of racial identity in Chapter 5 that different racial identity levels are present in an individual; however, one level is thought to predominate. In the work with Linda, what I call a "racial identity blend" was evident; she expressed some Pre-encounter (e.g., "I just want to be seen as a person") and Encounter attitudes, and showed some confusion about whether she denied her race. Midway through the therapy, she wondered aloud about how she thought about race. Having a Black therapist who considered racial identity as an integral part of her development and inquired about the racial context of her life and relationships facilitated her thinking about race and its influence on her.

After exploring some issues, including her relationship with her parents, Linda discovered that her emotional life was not as available to her as she previously had thought. Linda was discussing her feelings about her parents and how she was raised, and, in the midst, made connections among her upbringing, her emotional style, and her behavior at work.

LINDA: Yeah, although that was a feeling that I had about my mother, letting you know I was upset with her, I'm also reacting to the sometimes lack of feeling, when you ask me, "How do you feel about that?" There's almost a blank there. I don't feel anything and that kind of bothers me.

T: Say more about that.

LINDA: I don't know, I can't give you specific examples. But it's like, I couldn't link an emotion to it. I couldn't link a feeling to that particular incident and that feeling bothers me. I mean, if I do that, I'm wondering if I do that in conversations with people without being aware of it. To say something, and not really say anything. I'm wondering if suppressing my feelings with my parents has a carryover effect of expressing feelings about anything. It boils down to being perceived as—let me draw this analogy that I remember from a long time ago when I was a little kid— throughout the late '60s and '70s where the media portrayed people like H. Rapp Brown as militant, but people like Jerry Rubin as radicals. The Whites were radicals and the Blacks were militants and, you know, which word has the obvious derogatory meaning, you know, and so, I'm finding that I'm laying loose on my feelings because there's this perception that you can't be radical and be Black.

T: You're trying not to be perceived as a militant Black? If your emotions get involved in your expressions, you will be perceived negatively.

LINDA: Yeah, exactly, exactly. I wonder if I'm good at this. I'm looking at some of the things that have happened to me in my business life. I might play that game there, too.

T: How does that connect with you being Black?

LINDA: Emotions, I'm connecting it in a sense, and I'm trying to think it through, that since I've been good at suppressing my emotions, not saying what I feel, or having a hard time doing that in the professional environment, it may be perceived that I'm a team player when maybe I have feelings the other way on that issue and I am not able to articulate them.

T: The picture that I get when you say that is that you want to fit in. What does it mean to you to be a team player in a White environment?

LINDA: To be a team player for me is to *(Pause)* basically, do the best job I can. I mean that's the basic behavior. Being a team player is seeing how you can make things better. Why couldn't a statement act on its own instead of people coloring it with race?

T: It seems like you are equating being Black with being militant.

LINDA: Well, I don't want to equate it that way. I'm thinking that that's the way.

T: Those two things seem to be linked in your life.

LINDA: Yeah, they are.

T: Okay. Somehow, although you're not saying it, you seem to be suggesting that you can't be Black in these organizations because people will think you're militant and that will harm you, so you operate to be neutral. So you want them to deal with you as a person, not as a Black person?

LINDA: No. A person who is Black, but not as a Black person.

T: A person who is Black.

LINDA: Okay. That means to me, it means dealing with me, being me, and not dealing with me as being a representative of, I don't know if it's ever happened to you, but in certain situations, since you're the only Black person there, you are, in essence, a representative of all Black people, and I don't like being put in that category. It's like people saying, okay, you're a role model for Black people. I look at that statement as being well, that's well and good, but I can't be a role model for every Black person.

T: What I'm hearing you say is, your Blackness is secondary, that you want to be dealt with as a person.

LINDA: Yeah, that's probably, well, I wouldn't quite put it that way, but I would say it this way, that in, in any kind of context or any kind of social interaction, I would rather be seen as Linda, the person, instead of Linda, the Black woman.

T: It seems like you are asking people, and yourself, to move past that, and deal with you as a human being, somehow independent of your Blackness.

LINDA: All right. I'm wondering if my mobility in my profession is because I'm perceived as being *(Pause)* being closely associated with what is usually acceptable.

T: Okay. I am wondering how is that connected with suppressing your emotions or even keeping them suppressed? How are you feeling now?

LINDA: I don't feel uncomfortable. I think that there's some conflicting issues that I'm trying to sort out in my head. And, I think that talking with you, and you being a Black person, and me sharing this experience with you, I feel that, I have a feeling that maybe, well, I get the feeling that maybe I'm suppressing my Blackness and that's something that I am revealing. And the degree of comfort with your own self and my own self are clashing. They are clashing with each other.

T: And somehow, your being Black is central. You don't want people to deal with that part of you, so you hold it away?

LINDA: Let's start this question again. Okay. What does my relationship with other people, the way I control their behavior by not divulging information about myself, my vulnerability, that aspect there, have to do with my race?

T: You mean that it is possible to have a personal identity and that's different from you as a Black person. It seems that they have been different. That you have tried to keep your identity as a Black person away from your personal identity.

LINDA: No, no, no.

T: So, it seems from what you're saying that being Black has something to do with these issues of control, communication, power, etc. You said a few minutes ago that all of those things were intertwined and connected.

LINDA: Right, they are. They are. Quite frankly, that might be it. I see myself not being, being forthcoming with my feelings as a way to protect myself from being vulnerable. And I never really thought about that power of relationship with other people until just a few minutes ago, and it makes sense. My identity is centered around all of that. It is. It has to be. I know it is. How my identity as a Black person is centered around that, it's got to be in there as well.

Psychotherapeutic Process Measures

Client.   An analysis of response modes used during Linda's treatment revealed a process dominated by the client's describing events (i.e., Description) and some Experiencing responses (e.g., showing an emotional understanding of behavior, events, and reactions), and by the therapist's using mostly Interpretation responses, and, to a lesser degree, Direct Guidance and Information responses. For the client, the most frequent responses were Description, Experiencing, Requests, and Insight.

Clinician. For the therapist, the most common responses were Open-Ended Questions, Interpretation, and Paraphrase.

Interaction. Linda's Simple Responses were related to her Discussion of Plans and Request responses, and these were linked to her exploratory statements about the therapeutic relationship. In regard to the client–therapist interaction, an inverse relationship was found between the therapist's Information responses and the client's Experiencing responses; the more Information responses the therapist used, the fewer Experiencing responses Linda offered.

The process findings in Linda's case indicated that the pair's interactions were strongly influenced by the client's and the therapist's racial identity statuses. The process evidence revealed a pattern in which the therapist encouraged Linda to explore previously unexplored aspects of her personality, specifically their racial component. Linda's case also illustrates that when a person's racial identity status is blended, elements of different statuses are present and expressed in a person's personality. Moreover, this case demonstrates that racial understanding can facilitate the client's exploration of psychological and emotional dynamics. The therapist's ability to integrate race into the course of treatment resulted from having a mature and complex racial identity status. Because of this mature racial identity level, the therapist was able to effectively move with the client without a specific racial focus and without ignoring race either.

Case Four—Raymond

Raymond is a 33-year-old single Black male who was born in the West and later moved to the South. He is the first person in his family to graduate from college. He entered therapy because he wanted to understand why he had poor interpersonal relationships, specifically with women.

Raymond's therapy spanned some two years. From the initial contact, it was apparent that Raymond had a strong sense of himself as a Black person, which suggested an advanced level of racial identity, possibly Immersion–Emersion or Encounter, or a blend of the two. Raymond did not seem confused about race, but he was fighting to be seen in nonstereotypic ways, indicating that, in some ways, he had not fully established an internally defined racial identity.

Therapy began by assessing Raymond's initial complaint: poor interpersonal relationships with women. He seemed quite angry, yet he was only dimly aware of his anger's intensity. During the initial phase of treatment, he attempted to control the therapeutic agenda. This behavior was particularly hard to detect because he did it under the guise of being a "good client." Raymond controlled the first ten sessions by reviewing the previous meeting and launching into long, detailed stories of what happened. This behavior made it difficult to form an effective working alliance, because the therapist could not get a word in edgewise, and when he did, it was not for long. Midway through the first year of treatment, the clinician began to focus on Raymond's anger and his difficulties with relationships, in an attempt to develop a working alliance.

T: What makes you angry at women?

RAYMOND: *(Pause)* Uh, when I was a kid *(Pause),* lighter-skin boys were treated better. The girls liked them, uh, I remember listening to girls laughing. "Girl, uh, I don't like him. He's too Black." *(Pause)* "I don't like no dark skin men, uh-uh." The high yellow boys were the ones that were attractive to them. Uh, they were treated better by the girls and by people at large. My mother, until recently, would not go to a Black doctor, simply because he was Black and she would tell you that.

T: You say that when you grew up, girls in your neighborhood preferred lighter skinned boys?

RAYMOND: Yes, I felt ugly as a result of that.

T: You felt ugly as a result of them preferring lighter skinned guys?

RAYMOND: Yeah, I felt ugly. Uh, I remember when I was in college, and, uh *(Pause),* there, uh, a very pretty Black woman told me she thought I was good-looking. I thought she was lying. I sincerely thought she was lying. I thought she was making fun of me.

T: Mm-hmm.

RAYMOND: I didn't believe her. And it wasn't until, uh *(Pause),* I began dating women outside of my race—White girls or Spanish— and accomplishing some things at a young age, that I acquired some self-worth.

Raymond's discussion of how girls responded to his skin color triggered memories of his mother's racial views. It seems that Raymond's mother's racial identity status was actively Pre-encounter. Her distrust of Blacks was internalized by Raymond as a statement about how she felt about him. His mother's racial views, coupled with his social rejection by Black girls, made him feel devalued while he was growing up. The therapist shared this observation with Raymond and he affirmed it. Since his rejection came from women and it was hard as a young Black male to admit to feeling hurt, his pain turned to anger and Raymond felt angry toward Black women. Since he was raised primarily by his mother, who he thought did not value him, Raymond felt disconnected from his family, which made it hard for him to feel connected to and valued by people in general. His concern about Black women's perceptions of him also became a concern about what Black people thought about him.

Knowing that Raymond felt it was essential that he stay in touch with his roots while he pursued his education, the therapist tried to link issues around the family, relationships, and his own identity. The next excerpt reveals the difficulty he had with being an educated Black male.

T: Are you feeling defensive because you're educated?

RAYMOND: Um *(Pause)* yeah. I find myself *(Pause)* making sure I can still talk Black. I find myself making sure that I can switch my dialogue. And, I think it's because of the defensiveness *(Pause)*. Yeah, I find myself defensive.

T: Regarding?

RAYMOND: Regarding my identity, I guess. *(Pause)*

T: How so? Your identity?

RAYMOND: It goes back to me trying to relieve my conscience. What I'm saying is, I go out of my way to involve myself with bettering Black people.

T: What is it you're trying to relieve yourself of?

RAYMOND: Guilt, I guess.

T: Guilt?

RAYMOND: That I didn't turn out as bad as other Black males I grew up with, in spite of the fact that we had similar experiences.

T: And in some way, because of that, it's conceivable that you might feel left out of that world that they belong to, which is the part that may be related to wanting to leave your roots, and yet there also seems to be uncomfortableness with you living in this other world, which in some way you don't necessarily feel a part of.

RAYMOND: Correct. *(Pause)* Too Black for the Whites and too White for the Blacks.

T: *(Pause)* So that's the way you see yourself. I'm wondering what kinds of things contribute to your feeling that way.

RAYMOND: Because, uh, I feel I've been unjustly accused more than once of being a chocolate-covered White person.

Eventually, the explorations concerning Raymond's family and other people's racial attitudes led to a discussion of his own racial identity. In later sessions, which explored his family relationships and his identity, Raymond began to see how his family relationships affected his identity.

T: A lot of what I hear you talk about really has to do with how other people see you. Like you said, not Black enough for Blacks, not White enough for White people. In a way, those are the views of those people.

RAYMOND: Right.

T: I don't really get a good sense of where you are.

RAYMOND: I don't know, 'cause it hasn't been until the past few years that I have tried to focus upon what I want and what I need. I've always been preoccupied with pleasing other people most of my life. *(Pause)* So, I'm not sure where I fit in all of this.

T: You don't have to be sure. *(Pause)* Why don't you speculate?

RAYMOND: *(Pause)* Um, there's something, uh, about my perceptions or something about my upbringing that has caused me to conclude for some reason that, um *(Pause)* being well-off, um, not being hungry, not starving, not being a crack addict, not being a, um, gang member, means. *(Pause)* Because I'm not going through all of that, then I've lost touch, then I'm not Black. Um, *(Pause)* at times, when I have tried to tell friends or family, and when I say family I mean immediate family, about, um, different struggles and different frustrations I've had, it's always been a springboard for, "Like my problems are worse than yours," "Please give me your problems." So, it's like they won't even listen.

T: You may have moved away from their world and yet in some sense they are part of you. It seems that this is frightening, that you turn that fear and that anxiety into wishing they were different. If they were different, then you would be okay with what you're doing. And, that means you're not Black and somehow the struggle around your Blackness is clearly related to how you feel and see your family, how you see yourself fitting in. If you fit into it, then you're just like them, and then you're not, what you've done doesn't mean anything.

RAYMOND: Yeah.

T: If you don't fit in, that means you have to improve yourself, to better yourself, means the price you have to pay as a Black man in America is you had to give up your family, and all your ties, and all your roots for something or for people who don't accept you anyway.

RAYMOND: I think your analysis is quite accurate. Um, I catch myself, um, rationalizing that because I don't get caught up in my family. Somehow I think that they think that I don't care. Yet, I do get caught up in it.

T: What does it mean to be Black?

RAYMOND: What does it mean to be Black?

T: Yes, what does it mean to you to be Black?

RAYMOND: You're asking me what does it mean to be Black? And I'm trying to tell you that certain feelings are conjured by certain symbols that happen to me. Uh, it means that when I hear of certain conversations about affirmative action, correcting the wrongs of the past, then I get outraged because it's not correcting the wrongs of the past, it's correcting the wrongs of the present. That's what it means for me to be Black.

T: And when you start to list things intellectually about something that's emotional, and it also suggests that you're feeling the need to kind of defend yourself. In that way, it does not let the person know what you really feel.

RAYMOND: I feel a need to defend Black people, and for me that's what it means to be Black.

T: Defending against?

RAYMOND: Against, uh, emotions, against misunderstandings, against people who do not, who probably know about one Black person in their life and that's Eddie Murphy in a movie.

T: So, you're talking about Whites?

RAYMOND: Correct. *(Pause)* I'm like a mediator.

T: How does that translate into how you see yourself as a Black man? I hear you talk about how you feel about issues, I hear you talk about feeling caught between two worlds, being a defender, portraying yourself in a way that will not generate the stereotypical attitudes, etc., etc. What I get a picture of is you are not being yourself. I get a picture of you acting a part.

RAYMOND: I was brought up believing that you have to become White to get a degree, and I think that's what I was rebelling against.

T: Well, be that as it may, it seems like the effort to speak in slang was so that you could be identified as a Black person.

RAYMOND: Correct. And I do not have to be a chocolate-covered White.

T: It seems like you're unsure about that. You don't seem to be sure whether or not you are, in fact, a Black person.

RAYMOND: *(Long Pause)* I used to try to, uh *(Pause)* rationalize it intellectually, uh *(Pause)*. I used to check out guys like Paul Robeson. He became like a mixture of everything he ever experienced, and say that's what I am, and maybe there's a part of me that does in fact question.

In many ways, this dialogue shows some of the complexities surrounding the integration of racial factors with other personality variables to form an unconflicted identity. As therapy progressed, Raymond began to see how his personality and racial identity were merged and to learn that he could be himself and be Black without rejecting his family or his past. Additionally, he started to identify many of the triggers for his anger and the dynamics that governed his relationships.

Psychotherapeutic Process Measures

This dyad's top five responses were identical to those used in the previous three cases; however, in this therapeutic relationship, the responses were related differently and produced different results.

Client.   During Raymond's treatment, he consistently used Description responses, but as the therapy progressed, he began using Experiencing and Exploration of the Client–Counselor Relationship Responses.

Clinician.   The therapist had no particular response pattern across sessions. Interestingly, whether the counselor offered emotional support or reinforcement (i.e., Approval/Reassurance responses), asked for information (i.e., Information), or inquired using Open- and Closed-Ended Questions, Raymond did not show much insight. Instead, he gave one- or two-word phrases that indicated agreement (i.e., Simple Responses).

Interaction.   By examining the process via the response mode correlations (i.e., Descriptions, Simple Responses, Experiencing, Exploration of the Client–Counselor Relationship, and Silence), it was found that Raymond's pattern of responses consisted primarily of inverse relationships. For example, when he used more Simple Responses, he offered fewer Insight responses. Description utterances were related to Silence and linked to less experiencing, whereas Experiencing was associated with the likelihood that plans would not be discussed (i.e., Discussion of Plans responses).

The counselor's responses of Approval/Reassurance were related to Information, Direct Guidance, and Open- and Closed-Ended Questions. In addition, Open-Ended Questions were associated with Paraphrase and Confrontation responses. The interaction between the counselor's and client's responses suggests that when the counselor used an Approval/Reassurance response, the client uttered Simple Responses and decreased his use of Insight responses. The same was true for Information. Also, the clinician's Guidance and Open- and Closed-Ended Questions were correlated with the client's Simple Responses. Finally, the clinician's Confrontation responses were related to the client's Exploration of the Client–Counselor Relationship, and the therapist's Interpretations were linked to Raymond's uncategorized responses. These patterns of response modes suggest a far-ranging and complex therapeutic process.

CONCLUSION

These four cases illustrate the various ways a client's racial identity status can be expressed in therapy. The cases also show how a therapist's advanced level of racial identity can facilitate a client's awareness of the integration of race in his or her personality.

The four cases illustrate three critical issues in racial effects in psychotherapy, each of which has implications for clinical practice. First is the effect of race on treatment process when it is not discussed directly. This effect is reflected in the case of Tom. Second, racial effects due to racial identity statuses are shown. Each client's ability to deal with race was related to his or her level of racial identity development. Lastly, the influences of relationship types on the process of therapy and on the client's ability to learn about racial influences were shown. How these factors should be integrated in clinical practice, assessment, and training are discussed in Part Four.

What Do We Do with Race?
Clinical Applications

This section of the book provides a bridge for practitioners and educators who want to apply the Racially Inclusive Model of Psychotherapy. To this end, in Chapter 13, a number of different ways to integrate race into treatment are discussed, and in Chapter 14, a clinical assessment is described that examines emotional, psychosocial, and sociocultural influences associated with the different levels of racial identity development. In addition to the clinical assessment, this chapter extends the understanding of racial identity and its complexities by providing practitioners and educators with an more integrated framework of racial identity. Chapter 15 discusses five approaches for understanding racial-cultural differences and the advantages and disadvantages of each approach. I argue that the race-based approach is the most comprehensive and I outline a training model based on the race-based or racially inclusive model. The final chapter summarizes suggestions for future theoretical and clinical research areas.

CHAPTER 13

Race and Psychotherapy: Clinical Applications in a Sociocultural Context

As noted in Chapter 1, many mental health professionals are ill-equipped personally and/or professionally to help their clients learn about, cope with, and grow in understanding of race in their personal and interpersonal lives. The mental health professional's limited ability to help clients with their racial perspective results from the racial boundaries that exist in this society, and, specifically, from the education mental health professionals receive(d) and the delivery system in which they work which tends to deal with difference as if it were universal, ubiquitous, or traditional but seldom race-based. Consequently, many Americans are poorly served by mental health providers in their efforts to help clients cope with life in the United States.

Even though race has been a topic in psychological thinking and writing for years, considerable controversy still exists regarding the validity of race as a biological reality and, for some, a sociopolitical category. Some scholars have suggested that race, with its unclear definition, should be substituted for ethnicity or culture (Phinney & Rotheram, 1987). Nevertheless, race has come to have a powerful sociopolitical meaning that is derived from its earlier usage, which was based on biological factors (Gotunda, 1991). In North America, race is a powerful social and political factor that presumes certain psychological group characteristics and social status assignments that are determined by skin color, physical features, and, in some cases, language (Pinderhughes, 1989).

In this book, I define race as a visible sociopolitical variable that one individual or group uses to assign worth to another individual or group based on racial group membership. Additionally, a person can use this sociopolitical variable to determine his or her own self-worth. Implicit in this concept of race, as a social construct, is the notion that it is a psychosocial category that has associated with it unchangeable and permanent qualities (Smedley, 1993). Race has been and continues to be a critical aspect of psychological, economic, social, and political life in the United States. But, despite the central and enduring significance of race in North American society, the fields of psychology, psychiatry and mental health have failed to include race in their human development and personality theories. This omission is one reason for racial barriers in psychotherapy (Pinderhughes, 1973; Thompson & Jenal, 1994).

In this chapter, following an introduction of the issues associated with race in clinical practice, I discuss the clinical applications for using the Racially Inclusive Model of Psychotherapy.

FROM THEORY TO PRACTICE

Transitions from theory to practice often present a myriad of problems. Typically, theoretical models seem abstract and distant when a clinician considers possible ways to apply them and intervene with an individual client or group of clients. As with any theory, the Racially Inclusive Model of Psychotherapy becomes ambiguous and unclear when a clinician applies it to a specific client. When a clinician is thinking about using such models, he or she usually asks numerous questions, including:

1. Should the therapist wait for the client to introduce questions of race?
2. How should the issue of race be discussed when it arises?
3. What should the therapist do if the client denies the meaning of race?
4. How does one distinguish between racial influences and poor psychological functioning?
5. What are some of the ways race might influence therapy interactions?

In this chapter, I discuss each of these questions.

Should the Therapist Wait for the Client to Introduce Questions of Race?

Underlying this question are a couple of assumptions that are often implicit when clinical issues involving race are discussed. The first is that the therapy dyad is racially mixed or comprised of visible racial/ethnic group members. Another assumption is that race has an explicit or direct relevance in therapy only when it is part of the patient's presenting problem. These assumptions are being challenged directly here. This book's thesis is that race is an invisible backdrop against which North Americans live and interact; therefore, race is always salient in interpersonal relationships and in intrapsychic development, regardless of the specific racial groups involved. Race is not always apparent, but it is always present because it is part of each person's personality and it is part of our institutional and social structure.

To comprehend how race affects a person's life and psychological development, I believe that it is essential to have a model that includes race as part of one's personality. The Racially Inclusive Model of Psychotherapy has been presented as a way to represent the various race-based influences that affect people's psychological development.

Thus far, I have presented several elements that together, comprise the Racially Inclusive Model of Psychotherapy. I have also supported the suppositions of the model with empirical evidence and case studies.

Overview: Racial Socialization

The model posits that race or racial group membership creates the context for personality and human development because members of North American society are implicitly or explicitly socialized within the context of their racial group. Consequently, a person is taught to believe that he or she has certain qualities, characteristics, attributes, opportunities, or barriers because of his or her race. Therefore, in a psychotherapeutic relationship, race is always present in terms of each participant's racial identity status and the sociopolitical context, as well as the type of therapeutic relationship (e.g., progressive, parallel and so on, as determined by the participants' racial identity level) and its distinct process and outcome.

To fully grasp how race influences an individual's development and functioning, it is essential that one understands race's role in this complex, interdependent, interacting system known as North American society. In American society, therapists and patients have a shared racial history that stems from the historical-cultural role of race in the larger system, and, more specifically, from the dominant cultural patterns of White European-Americans (see Chapters 2 and 3). Every system or society operates to maintain its equilibrium or status quo, and, in so doing, it remains active and purposeful, as well as self-regulating. Where race is concerned, the equilibrium involves White superiority and visible racial/ethnic group subordination, with little or no consideration for individual psychological variations related to race. As a consequence of racial segregation, each racial group has evolved its own racial-cultural subsystem that functions within the superordinate, dominant cultural system.

Every person develops a racial component to his or her personality. The family is also shaped and influenced by the sociopolitical influences of the surrounding community and societal institutions (e.g., media, schools, churches, businesses, employers, recreational clubs). Thus, an individual's personality and psychological life are shaped by how he or she interprets and responds to the messages about his or her racial group. The general society, by way of its racial, social order, affects an individual's participation in American life, in his or her family, and in the community (see Chapters 2 and 4). The racial context gives meaning and significance to one's physical features, such as skin color, eye color, facial features, body shape, and hair texture. These physical attributes, in turn, affect one's self-concept and, at the same time, influence how others respond to the individual. A person's response to the racial context also may influence the structure, size, and resources of one's family and community, because social rewards and punishments are distributed on the basis of a racial hierarchy and one's adherence to its rules and norms (Andersen & Collins, 1995; Frankenberg, 1993; Rothenberg, 1995).

The context of race influences access to and opportunities in the nation's institutions (e.g., education, jobs, housing, and health care) and affects the selection of the country's cultural symbols and media images. The racial context of our socialization shapes our understanding of the meaning, value, and significance of our own and others' racial group memberships. Americans and immigrants, regardless of racial-ethnic origins, are socialized to believe that the values, communication patterns, lifestyles, and family structures of Whites, who comprise the dominant group in the society, are preferred and normative.

Mental health trainees enter their training with strongly reinforced beliefs about race; these have been described in earlier chapters. For instance, in elementary, secondary, and postsecondary schools, the experiences, contributions, and perspectives of European-Americans are emphasized, while those of people of color are seldom mentioned and, when they are mentioned, it is in a tangential or nonintegrated manner (e.g., Black history). This educational experience is mirrored in mental health professionals' training, which is typically based on traditional theories and models of personality and human development that omit race as a variable. As a result of the omission of race from these theories and models, a clinician believes that race and issues stemming from race belong to a special, isolated area of psychology. Textbook chapters and courses that pertain to people of color only reinforce this notion by using terms such as *special populations, minority,* or *diversity* in their titles. The evidence, presented in Part Three of this book, indicates that race through racial identity affects each person's perceptions, emotions, beliefs, attitudes, and behaviors during therapy. The data from therapeutic dyads and from the relationship type study (e.g., progressive, parallel, regressive) suggests that a therapist's actions (i.e., intentions) and affects, perhaps because of his or her position of power, have a greater impact on the psychotherapy process than a client's reactions. These findings strongly indicate the importance of training a therapist to explore the meaning and significance of his or her own race and to understand how race influences perceptions of the self and the client. This notion is analogous to psychoanalytic training that requires the analyst to submit his or her own analysis. Similarly, a mental health professional must start with self-development if he or she is to effectively understand race in psychotherapy.

How Should the Issue of Race Be Discussed When It Arises?

In part, this question relates to how therapists are trained. Little or no information about race in psychotherapy is provided in the education or training of mental health professionals. This silence about racial influences teaches mental health professionals to ignore or deny racial influences in treatment, supervision, and psychological development.

Franklin, Carter, and Grace (1993) point out that most mental health professionals are taught traditional theories of personality and human development, which ignore psychological issues associated with a sociocultural context, and that mental health training is devoid of such considerations. These authors state: "In our training, there is virtually no emphasis on evolving a theoretical orientation from first an insight about the patient's human condition, social ecology or 'psycho-ethnic history'; this in spite of the fact that our theory building comes from our knowledge of, and interaction with, a patient population having distinct personal legacies" (p. 466).

I have argued strongly that traditional models that assume difference due to culture arising from country, social groups affiliation, or individual differences are limited where race is concerned; however, I am not advocating that the baby should be thrown out with the bath water. I do not totally reject beliefs that are widely held about treatment, human development, and psychological functioning. Rather, I propose integrating the basic tenets of many traditional therapeutic approaches (e.g., psychodynamic, humanistic, behavioral) with the Racially Inclusive Model of Psychotherapy. I believe that each individual is deeply and profoundly affected by early life experiences, which can be the basis for the defense and coping mechanisms that come to characterize a person's psychic structure. The people around us when we are growing, I believe, influence the particular styles of interpersonal relating and living that we eventually adopt. A person's interpretations of his or her experiences are critical to his or her emotional life and personality formation, and reinforced actions, thoughts, and feelings shape a person's responses, attitudes, and behavior. I think that a person's sense of worth is affected by many factors, both internal and external, that directly and indirectly influence the process of development over the lifespan. I also accept that there are intrapsychic dynamics, operating outside of conscious awareness, that direct people's feelings and guide behavior. Nevertheless, I contend that these personality and developmental processes occur within a racial context.

The answer to the question of how race should be dealt with if it is raised directly is best answered, "It depends." In Chapters 2 and 3, the review of the literature indicated that race and its meaning for patients or therapists can take many forms. It can be used to test the therapist's level of competence with issues of race. The client might be guarded about discussing race. He or she might be deeply involved in racial conflicts or simply be in denial about its significance. Or, the client may be confused. How race is discussed and in what depth depends on the type of relationship (e.g., regressive, progressive, and so forth) the dyad has formed. The relationship type will reflect how both participants understand race's personal meaning and significance. We also know from Chapters 10 and 11 that the emotional responses and interactional dynamics (process) in psychotherapy when race is the topic will depend on the relationship type (see also Thompson & Jenal, 1994).

Even when a client understands that race is a part of, or related to, his or her presenting concerns, the client's level of racial identity development will dictate how these issues are experienced and understood. If a client is confused about the role of race, or is making a transition from denying race to recognizing it, or is beginning therapy with a clinician who is unable to integrate race into treatment consistent with the client's issues, then the client is likely to deny race, vacillate, and contradict himself or herself about race's significance. Thompson and Jenal (1994) found very different client-counselor interactions when counselors were race-avoidant. It is also possible that racial elements and related symptoms will merge and be hard to discern. Under these circumstances, a therapist should not conclude that race has no influence on his or her interactions with clients. Instead, I suggest that the clinician integrate the unstated or denied racial elements that contribute to the clients' functioning, just as he or she would look for pivotal events that contribute to clients' symptoms and defenses.

At other times, the relationship among race, racial identity, and clients' symptoms will be pronounced because of the clients' struggle to reconcile their beliefs and thoughts about race with their personality. American culture, for instance, values independence, an esteemed mode of self-expression. So, a person is often distressed and feels dependent when he or she needs other people or worries about what others think. These symptoms can and often do have racial components, because, despite the dominant societal norms or messages (e.g., independence is the mark of maturity), racial group norms operate according to racial criteria. However, independence is not a desirable cultural quality for some racial groups; yet, it is necessary if group members want to be accepted by and succeed in mainstream society. A client may feel depressed, socially isolated, or treated differently at work because he or she cannot form a clear and positive connection to his or her racial group. The case of Raymond (Chapter 12) involved a struggle for a comfortable and secure identity and interpersonal relationships in a context of societal racial practices such that Raymond felt a need to reject and guard against. His resistance to stereotypes of Black men contributed to his feeling angry, worthless, and invisible.

As an individual becomes more conscious of race, he or she begins to create an internally derived identity status. As he or she attains the advanced levels of racial identity, race is a somewhat less obvious factor in psychological and emotional distress than during earlier levels, but the person is still just beginning to accept what race means to him or her. More complex symptoms or expressions are likely to emerge with a client who is at high levels of racial identity development (e.g., interaction of self-esteem with external reality of racism). In some way, each racial identity level will shape the type or form of a client's psychological symptoms because these symptoms are filtered and influenced by the client's racial environment outside of therapy.

Clinicians who think race is an indirect aspect of personality or human development (i.e., Level One Racial Identity Status) or who are confused about race (i.e., Level Two Racial Identity Status) will ignore race more often than not in a therapeutic setting and in the diagnostic process. For the most part, DSM-IV authors, and the clinicians who use it without modifications, completely overlook or ignore race. A clinician who denies race in his or her own racial identity resolution (e.g., Contact, Pre-encounter) and ignores the role of race in society will consider race only in ways accepted by mainstream society (i.e., reinforcing racial images and stereotypes). This perspective on race and its influence is typical of a person with a lower level of racial identity. Such clinicians in cross-racial dyads will want to discuss race directly and then dismiss it. The question of race is often no longer pursued once asked and answered.

A clinician with a more advanced racial identity status (i.e., Internalization, Awareness, Autonomy) can understand race and its influence on human functioning, incorporate system effects, diagnose with race in mind, and see a patient in an integrated and complex fashion. A therapist who uses racial identity theory when working with a client can go beyond transference and countertransference in his or her efforts to comprehend the dynamics and personality structure of the client. In this way, the therapist can discern how societal messages about group-specific behaviors are absorbed by the client. In addition to the clinician's psychological sophistication, the racial climate of the therapeutic dyad and of the work site institution will affect whether and how race will be considered in treatment.

What Should the Therapist Do If the Client Denies the Meaning of Race?

Race is always meaningful and significant, but it can be subtle and indirect. To fully grasp the effects of race in clinical practice, it is necessary to include Whites as well as people of color. Additionally, race must be acknowledged as a psychological, social, and structural aspect of life in the United States. Given the subtle nature and hidden pervasiveness of race in American life, a clinician is not likely to encounter racial issues directly in psychotherapy. Usually, the impact of race and its intrapsychic and interpersonal manifestations will be interwoven with a client's symptoms and denied more than acknowledged.

Therefore, as the therapist considers various clinical syndromes and their etiologies, it is imperative that he or she also take into account the racial context in which a particular syndrome might emerge. In a therapeutic setting, when a clinician examines the client's history, background, and development milestones, he or she should not view the client's race as a descriptive characteristic but as a psychological and sociopolitical factor. A therapist must learn about and understand the sociopolitical ramifications of a client's racial group membership and must reflect on how the client has integrated race in his or her intrapsychic dynamics. Under these guidelines, the clinician need not discuss race directly with the client or raise the issue specifically during the course of treatment; rather, it is proposed that race, in all its complexities, be incorporated into the clinical assessment and treatment planning processes. For every patient, regardless of his or her specific racial group membership, some type of symptom can be seen to vary according to his or her racial identity status. This is evident from the research findings reported in Chapter 9.

For instance, Level One attitudes were represented by the racial identity of Contact, Conformity, and Pre-encounter. For Blacks, Pre-encounter attitudes have been linked to high levels of anxiety, psychological dysfunction, depression (Carter, 1991; Parham & Helms, 1985a), and low self-regard and self-esteem (Parham & Helms, 1985a; Pyant & Yanico, 1991). Blacks with Pre-encounter attitude are also likely to ignore racism in their environments. Similarly, for Whites, Contact attitudes have been linked to low levels of anxiety, denial of the significance of race, and a preference for traditional American cultural values (Carter, 1990a). A patient at this level of racial identity development will probably see his or her clinical concerns in terms of individual behavior, not group normative behavior.

Taken together, these factors indicate that race is always present in psychotherapeutic interactions. For both the client and the therapist, the presence of race can be seen in their personality structures and in their interpersonal orientations to race. Additionally, for the client, the presence of race is evident in his or her symptomatology.

How Does One Distinguish between Racial Influences and Poor Psychological Functioning?

A client's presenting problem involves self-assessment, developmental transitions, personal trauma, interpersonal difficulties, or a variety of other symptoms and complaints, some more specific than others. In most cases, a client, regardless of race, will be primarily concerned with his or her particular problem, as will the therapist. Therefore, in psychotherapy, race is woven into the client's presenting problem and subsequent therapeutic issues. The effects of race are determined by the way the person understands himself or herself racially. Race can be invisible and silent, but it can also be a powerful environmental and psychological reality in an individual's development. Race becomes deeply embedded into one's subconscious, and it forms a filter through which thoughts, feelings, experiences, and behaviors operate. Race, as an aspect of ego functioning, organizes an individual's perceptions and interpretations as well as his or her internal emotional and psychological life. Consequently, it is possible that a person's mental status may have deteriorated to the point that he or she is functioning poorly. Under these circumstances, I would advocate, as the first priority, focusing on the person's mental status and restoring functioning to the best level possible. But I would not say that race is not salient; rather, I would suggest that it is deeply embedded in the person's abnormal behavior. Discovering its role is central to restoring functioning ultimately. I do not think poor psychological functioning is completely separate from race or from the racial context in which we all live.

For instance, consider the case of John, a White 37-year-old male, who enters therapy because of a series of failed relationships. John grew up in a suburban area of the Northeast, and he graduated from college with a business degree. He reports that, since high school, he has had problems maintaining relationships with women. He wants to marry and have a family. His family and friends interpret his inability to maintain a stable romantic relationship as a sign of a personal defect; John's self-worth appears to hinge on whether he marries and has children. He states that his family's expectations of him were that he would be successful occupationally, marry, and have children. These expectations were unspoken but clearly communicated. John's parents had a stable but stormy relationship.

John's relationship issues can be seen as solely personal or family-related; however, through the lens of the racially inclusive model, this client can be viewed as a product of a racial climate that taught him his efforts and abilities would bring him the usual rewards for White males: a wife, children, and occupational success. Because John does not consciously consider his racial group's norms and expectations, as communicated by his parents and family members, his sense of responsibility and failure intensifies. This perspective does not need to be introduced directly into his treatment, but, with this viewpoint, a therapist can see John's individual dynamics as well as his racial group's powerful expectations.

When the clinical issue or treatment is indirectly related to race, it may be more important to focus on a client's symptoms while remembering that they have a racial component. A patient, for instance, who presents with depressive symptoms may have experienced traumas or losses that gave rise to the depression. It is important that the therapist unearth the particulars regarding the traumas or losses while remaining aware that racial socialization and sociopolitical experiences can contribute to the depressive symptoms.

What Are Some of the Ways Race Might Influence Therapy Interaction?

The Racially Inclusive Model of Psychotherapy should be used as a heuristic to guide a clinician's recognition and understanding of race as a psychological phenomenon, not just a social characteristic. The primary advantage of a psychologically grounded model of race is its capacity for racial influences to be understood in terms of a complex matrix of interacting and dynamic influences within and between individuals. Using the racially inclusive approach, in terms of the client's understanding of race in his or her life, a therapist is introduced to the client's racial world. From this information, the clinician can determine the client's racial identity level and begin to understand how deeply race-related issues matter to the client. Moreover, the therapist can start to comprehend race's role in the client's intrapsychic and interpersonal relations. However, being client-focused is insufficient to fully understand the process of psychotherapy; the therapist's own racial world must also be addressed.

Interactional Racial Dynamics

The interactional model hypothesizes that race influences the psychotherapeutic process differently, depending on the type of relationship created by the therapist's and the client's racial identity attitudes. Four types of relationships (i.e., parallel, crossed, progressive, and regressive) can form, and they can be used to characterize the client's behavior and the counselor's strategies during the psychotherapeutic process (see Chapter 8). Additionally, each type of relationship, whether same- or mixed-race, is associated with certain dissimilar process dimensions and psychotherapeutic outcomes. The process dimensions believed to be salient in all four types of psychotherapeutic relationships are: (a) affective reactions and responses; (b) the therapist's and patient's perceptions and experiences of the therapy session, the overall process, and the outcome; and (c) the counselor's and client's verbal and nonverbal strategies. The data pertaining to the relationship types and their process dimensions are based on research involving only Blacks and Whites.

The four relationship types, described in depth in Chapter 8, are briefly restated here. A *parallel* relationship exists when a therapist and a client of the same race have the same level of racial identity, or when the dyad's participants, although of different races, share similar attitudes about Blacks and Whites. A *crossed* relationship is one in which a counselor and a client have opposite attitudes about Blacks and Whites and belong to opposite levels of racial identity. A *progressive* relationship occurs when the counselor's racial identity is at least one level more advanced than the client's, and a *regressive* relationship, the opposite of a progressive relationship, occurs when a client's racial identity development is at least one level more advanced than the counselor's. In a regressive relationship, one expects the process to resemble a power struggle; both the client and the clinician have strong affective reactions to each other, which can lead to conflicts.

Regarding these relationship types, empirical evidence has suggested that each type of relationship, except crossed, has a qualitatively different process, meaning that the therapists and clients experience sessions differently, use distinct strategies, and report varying emotional reactions. Additionally, depending on the type of relationship, the therapeutic outcomes vary, and the data offer little symptom relief for clients in regressive and parallel relationships. The therapist's stance or perspective is usually guided by the theoretical orientation he or she has adopted.

Relationship formation is critical to the psychotherapeutic process. In American society, open and honest discussions of race, either in public or in private, are rare, because most Americans are taught that race is not and should not be a critical or central concern to them, regardless of their experiences. This view leads a clinician to believe that he or she should ask about race only when racial differences exist, and this should be done early in the relationship-building process. Generally, a counselor is instructed to ask a client, "How do you feel about having a therapist of my race?" as a way of introducing race, or to inquire whether the client thinks race has something to do with the problems or concerns being discussed. These types of questions tend to marginalize race, and I advocate that a therapist alter his or her assumptions and work to build a relationship, assuming race is present and operating in the client's and the therapist's psychic and interpersonal lives and interactions. With this approach during the initial phase of treatment, a therapist is able to inquire about and explore the client's racial climate, environment, and racial identity status, without asking specifically about race. The therapist's assessment of the client's racial identity status helps to guide his or her efforts to bond with the client, especially if the assessment is carefully done and incorporates the racial components of the client's symptoms.

A client's behavior in therapy is influenced by the type of therapeutic relationship he or she is in. As noted earlier, the therapeutic process is affected by the interplay between the client's and the therapist's racial identity attitudes. A client's level of comfort with his or her therapist seems to be affected more by the therapist's level of racial identity than by his or her race (see Chapters 10 through 12). When both participants in a therapeutic dyad assume that race is not salient, regardless of their racial group memberships, they are working in a parallel relationship. In this type of relationship, both participants are interacting in a way that is mutually reinforcing, and the client is likely to experience minimal symptom relief, regardless of the length of treatment. In a parallel dyad, the client and therapist operate as if they are color-blind; nevertheless, they tend to base their actions on unspoken and subconscious assumptions about each other. Regressive (i.e., client has a higher level of racial identity than counselor) and crossed (i.e., client and counselor have opposite racial attitudes) therapeutic relationships are characterized by confusion and conflict. In these relationships, the client is likely to experience strong, persistent feelings of disconnection, anxiety, or hostility, and may struggle to be heard by the therapist. The therapist, on the other hand, is likely to be preoccupied with his or her authority as the expert. Typically, a therapist who has a lower level of racial identity (i.e., Contact, Disintegration, Encounter) engages in this type of struggle.

Tyler, Brome, and Williams (1991) describe this type of dyad between two White women. The client, Mary, is a 46-year-old married White woman whose working-class family consists of her heavy-drinking husband, who is a truck driver, and her two daughters. Mary has been referred to therapy by her younger daughter's social worker after the daughter reported that Mary slapped her upon discovering that she had had an abortion. Mary, a devout Catholic, is strongly opposed to abortion. The therapist in this case is Sarah, a 34-year-old single White Anglo-Saxon Protestant woman, who was born and raised in an upper-class New England family.

The process of relationship formation for Sarah and Mary was initially difficult, partly because of class and ethnic differences; however, they eventually worked through these conflicts. Tyler et al.'s (1991) assessment of the relationship-building process for the dyad follows:

Mary and Sarah did not address several important characteristics of their dyadic relationship that were influencing their patterns of gains and losses. The first issue was their race. Because they were both White, race did not appear to be a salient therapy variable. Yet their *Whiteness* did influence how they related to one another, since it provided a context for convergence around their shared enculturated values and cultural expectations and norms. (p. 220; italics in original)

Thus, neither Mary nor Sarah openly brought into treatment how they understood the nature of social status in North American society and what attributes denoted power in this social system. Both women believed (but did not discuss) that a person's power is measured by how much he or she has acquired in terms of education, income, and social class.

Thus, we see that race in White client/counselor dyads proceeds often with unstated assumptions about similarity and the meaning of group membership. Too many White therapists and supervisors do not think race is an issue for White clients. In a recent study, Ochs (1994) explored the incidence of racial issues in therapy involving White dyads. She found that, although the majority of therapists did not think race was a concern for their clients, close to 25% reported that 5–30% of their clients raised racial issues. These issues spanned many aspects of life: school, work, dating, neighborhood, socializing, affirmative action, and White identity. Ochs (1994) concludes:

In general, the findings in this study seem to indicate an incidence rate and level of concern about handling White clients' racial issues that cannot be dismissed as negligible. In addition, there is little evidence that White counselors are receiving training that they consider relevant to helping White clients with racial issues. (p. 311)

RACIAL ISSUES IN SUPERVISION

A section on clinical applications would not be complete without a discussion about supervision. It is during the course of supervision that trainees and professionals learn to apply the didactic and interpersonal skills needed for therapeutic practice. Scholars (e.g., Blocher, 1983; Cook, 1994; Hunt, 1987; Leong & Wagner, 1994; Peterson, 1991) who write about what supervision is and how it should be conducted may disagree on some issues (see Robiner & Schofield, 1990, for references), but they agree that this is an extremely important and powerful relationship—one that involves several roles and goals for the supervisor and supervisee. Supervisors are vested with the power and responsibility, by their institutions and training programs, to evaluate, influence, and judge trainees. They are also supposed to provide to the less skilled, inexperienced, and less knowledgeable student therapist the skill, knowledge, and personal awareness, to help the client in a professional and ethical manner.

During small group or individual supervision, many mental health professionals learn how to conceptualize client concerns and problems, diagnose patients, and acquire skills in clinical treatment and patient management. It is often in the context of supervision that theory is applied to practice; trainee's learn how to integrate techniques, theory, and interpersonal interventions. The supervisor challenges the student to apply newly acquired knowledge, by providing structure, support, and feedback. Together these aspects of supervision help the trainee learn new and more complex ways of thinking and responding to clients. The trainee eventually learns to be innovative and to integrate the various aspects of information he or she has to intervene in the client's life (Blocher, 1983).

Leong and Wagner (1994) recently reviewed the literature on cross-cultural supervision. They identified three groups of studies. The first involved only passing reference to cross-cultural supervision with the greater focus on other aspects of counseling supervision. The next group of articles drew upon the clinical experience of the authors to identify problems and solutions to cultural difference in supervision and clinical practice. The last group of articles are described as theoretical in focus in that they attempted to offer integration of the issues that arise in supervision in general and cross-cultural supervision in particular. The review authors assessed the theoretical models of supervision for inclusion of demographic, cognitive, and personality factors in the description of cross-cultural supervision.

The first group of articles indicates that supervisors must encourage supervisees to explore their own background. They also suggest that supervisors must address issues of race and culture early in the relationship. Last, it is argued that they should actively work to promote difference in the agency or program through staff development and the recruitment of racially diverse staff members. Another perspective from this group involved discussions of individual difference in terms of similarity; that is, supervisors would have supervisees focus on points of convergence rather than divergence. These perspectives according to Leong and Wagner (1994) lack theory, developmental considerations, specifics, or empirical support.

The second group emphasized clinical experiences and identifies potential problems and solutions in coping with racial differences in clinical practice and supervision. Most of these articles tended to focus on Black and White interactions, usually a Black client and a White or Black therapist. One author (Hunt, 1987) believed that relationship formation was of critical importance and thought that the supervisee's emotional reactions to the client's cooperation or lack thereof was the first consideration. The supervisor should explore with the supervisee the source of his or her reactions. The supervisor then explores with the supervisee his or her biases regarding the client, in particular, how the client is affected by the counselor's feelings and beliefs. The supervisor then suggests more appropriate responses that the trainee practices in the hopes that the therapeutic relationship can be strengthened and made more productive. Writers in the second group went beyond the initial aspects of the supervisory relationship and offered recommendations for how better to cope with cultural issues in the supervision process from beginning to end.

Leong and Wagner describe the next group as addressing cross-cultural supervision as a parallel process to therapy and that the same issues, such as avoidance of the topic of racial or cultural difference, overemphasis, and underemphasis, may arise in both treatment and supervision. The supervisor has the responsibility to guard against these difficulties and he or she must also help the counselor focus on himself or herself so that the counselor can learn how to be an effective therapist. The tasks of self-learning and cultural learning can often conflict and compete for attention in the supervisory relationship. The supervisor clearly needs to have appropriate training in order to provide the type of guidance necessary. He or she should, in the absence of training, seek consultation and encourage the trainee to do so as well.

Other models described by Leong and Wagner suggest that questioning the myth of sameness in both the therapy and supervisory relationships is of crucial importance. They all contend that supervisees should develop, during the course of supervision, from no awareness of race and ethnic issues in treatment to exploring these issues in greater depth. These authors offer developmental models that chart this progress and warn that supervisors should create safe environments for such growth and development. The review of the cross-cultural literature suggests that much more needs to be done to prepare supervisors for their roles. Currently a lot of work seems to be associated with dealing with racial difference during the same time that supervisees are trying to learn how to provide effective treatment. As Bernard (1994) points out "supervision is not an appropriate place for an awareness of multicultural dynamics to begin—not for the trainee and especially not for the supervisor" (p. 160).

Leong and Wagner (1994) conclude their review with several observations. The first is the recognition that very little is known about cross-cultural supervision. They recommend that more work be done to increase our knowledge. The second is related to what is known. In this regard, they state that, based on empirical evidence reviewed, it seems safe to conclude that (a) race can have a profound influence on the supervisory process, particularly in terms of trainee's expectations for supervisor characteristics like empathy, respect, and congruence; (b) race can influence a trainee's perception of supervisor liking; and (c) there are some circumstances under which race does not seem to influence supervision. Beyond these we can only speculate about the cross-cultural counseling supervision process. (p.128)

These authors join me when they ask that future researchers and scholars abandon nonpsychological or categorical conceptualizations of race and ethnicity and begin to use race as a psychological construct. An example of the usefulness of psychological constructs for understanding supervision is provided by Cook (1994) who has described how racial identity might influence the supervisory process.

Cook employed the interactional process model, described in Chapter 8 and reviewed above, to delineate racial issues that might arise in supervision. She points out that while either supervisee or supervisor can raise the issues of race in therapy or the supervisory relationship, how the supervisor responds will determine the depth of the discussion. When the supervisee feels that the supervisor does not recognize race as an important aspect of treatment or supervision, the supervisee may be reluctant to explore such issues for fear of a negative evaluation. Cook points out that the racial identity ego statuses exhibited by either supervisor or supervisee may vary. "The racial identity attitudes of the supervision partner, circumstances in the clinical agency, or other factors might trigger a particular ego status, making it more prominent than the other" (p. 135). Cook describes two types of supervisory pairs *parallel* and *crossed.* In the parallel pairs, both participants have the same level of racial identity. Crossed pairs can be of two types, *progressive* or *regressive.* In the progressive supervisory pair, the more powerful person has the more advance racial identity attitudes, while in the regressive, the person in power has a less advanced racial identity ego status. Cook holds that the power of the supervisor shapes and directs the way race will be dealt with in therapy and in supervision. She states:

The power dynamics in supervision are such that the supervisor holds the most social power in the supervisory relationship. Due to the professional credentials of supervisors, their evaluative role, and their responsibility for clients welfare, they are "ascribed" the highest power in the supervisory relationship. (p. 136)

Given the supervisor's power, his or her racial identity attitudes may shape the racial attitudes and behavior of the supervisee and, indirectly, the client. If the supervision pair is progressive, the supervisor may help the supervisee to advance in his or her racial identity development. In contrast, in a regressive pair, the supervisee

> might suppress his or her racial identity attitudes. If the supervisee either expresses or suppresses his or her attitudes in supervision, he or she is likely to do the same in therapy. Therefore, the supervisor is in a position to influence either consciously or unconsciously, the degree to which each individual involved in supervision is open in expressing his or her racial identity attitudes. (p. 136)

Thus, to the extent that supervisors and supervisees develop in their racial identity, the greater the likelihood that race will be dealt with in therapy and incorporated into the therapeutic process. However, Peterson (1991) contends that the agency or clinic has a responsibility to create a climate in which race can be a valued part of supervision because the supervisor is a representative of the agency or clinic.

SUMMARY

I have explored several central concerns that often arise when clinicians attempt to apply the racially based theoretical models. I have tried to show how the use of the propositions that comprise the Racially Inclusive Model of Psychotherapy shift the nature of the questions asked in applying the model and how the model exposes erroneous assumptions about race in psychotherapy. In the next chapter, I describe the various elements needed for assessing racial components in treatment.

CHAPTER 14

Assessing Race Using the Racially Inclusive Model in Clinical Treatment

This chapter focuses on integrating racial identity data into the assessment and treatment of a client. In the first part of the chapter, I discuss client assessment and some of its components. Within each component is a description of the race and racial identity aspects that should be included and considered. In the second part of the chapter, brief case studies contrast the traditional approaches with the racially inclusive approach. These cases illustrate how race and racial identity can be blended into the assessment and treatment planning process.

CLIENT ASSESSMENT

When assessing a client, generally the clinician gathers information about the client's presenting problem and its etiology, the person's medical history and family background, and personal characteristics. The clinician combs through this information looking for critical and relevant factors that might have contributed to the issues presented. In addition, the clinician must determine whether the client has the personal resources to bring about the desired change. Lastly, the therapist creates an intervention plan based on the information obtained during the assessment process and the clinician's judgment about the client's psychosocial functioning.

In most clinical settings, information gathering begins with a description of the client and an assessment of his or her problem. Typically, the description of the client consists of demographic data such as race, age, gender, marital status, birth order, education, and occupational level. In addition, a therapist often assesses other variables, including physical appearance, grooming, style of dress, body movement, use of gestures, style of speaking, and type and manner of expression. Finally, the clinician's impressions of the patient's emotional responses and cognitive style are incorporated in the client description and conceptualization.

Although the client description appears to be objective and straightforward, both the client's and the therapist's racial identity resolution affects perceptions, affective states, and behavior. The impact of one's racial identity on the client description is important to understand and address because it may result in an inaccurate initial assessment. Recall the study by Jones (1982), where White clinicians tended to evaluate Black clients as more psychologically disturbed than White clients (see Chapter 10). A client's racial identity status is associated with investment in either White American cultural patterns or his or her own racial group's cultural patterns. Consequently, the client's presentation of the problem and his or her perceptions of the therapist are likely to be influenced. A clinician's racial identity status also influences the interpretation of the information presented and his or her perception of the client. For example, the information that a therapist selectively attends to is influenced by the clinician's level of racial identity. In order to appropriately assess for racial influences and racial identity resolutions, a clinician must consider psychosocial, systemic, and personal factors.

Psychosocial Factors

As noted in Chapter 4, a young person's racial identity is most strongly influenced by his or her parents and family. Parental and familial influences diminish as a child matures, whereas peer relationships, school experiences, and messages from the media and other institutions gain importance. Therefore, a systems-oriented perspective is necessary in patient assessment.

A *systems-focused perspective* requires that the client's self-identity and psychological functioning be assessed at several levels, with the recognition that each level interacts with the others. With this perspective, one must consider the patient's *personal* (e.g., skin color, hair type) and *psychological* (e.g., maturity, coping mechanisms, interactional style) influences while gathering information. The psychological resolution, as it pertains to race, includes understanding how race is incorporated in a person's personality. Additionally, a therapist must determine the nature of the psychosocial influences that, in part, shaped the client's personal and psychological make-up (Helms, 1990).

The important *psychosocial* influences are parents, family, friends and peers, schools, churches, the media, and other social institutions. Families and social institutions in turn are affected by *systemic* or macrosystem forces that are expressed through ideologies, political views, political and social climates, economic circumstances, and so forth. Personal qualities, intrapsychic dispositions, and psychosocial and systemic forces taken together create a person's racially based worldview, which operates as the primary information processing center for internal and external information, especially racial data. The racial worldview also subconsciously organizes this information into consistent patterns or templates about the self and others in general and about one's racial group membership (Helms, 1994; Helms & Piper, 1994).

Messages about race are transmitted from the environment to the individual and are based on group-level attributes, rather than individual attributes such as talent and particular ways of interacting.

> On a national level, to the extent that a person appears to share the group characteristic of Whiteness, he or she is considered to be superior to others who do not share that characteristic and, conversely to the extent that the person shares the group characteristics of Blackness, he or she is considered to be inferior to those who do not share the characteristic. A person's first knowledge of how her or his racial characteristics are likely to be evaluated by society is transmitted by these various communications. (Helms, 1990, p. 87)

Psychosocial influences can affect one's racial worldview in numerous ways, depending on how race is addressed, dealt with, valued, or avoided. One can be taught to value, to devalue, or to deny race, or one can be taught to be confused about race. For instance, using a system-focused perspective to examine sociocultural forces that influence the allocation of resources and one's self-concept can be enlightening. When one's racial group is out of favor, few social and economic opportunities exist. This lack of opportunities restricts the range of possibilities available to a family, introduces a plethora of stressors into familial and interpersonal relationships, and impacts one's self-concept. Similarly, when one's racial group is favored, a greater range of possibilities and resources is likely to exist, and fewer stressors may be present. This situation also influences one's self-concept. Thus, one is able to develop a sense of self that is boundless and unconstricted.

Systemic Forces

Any family, regardless of its socioeconomic resources, has difficulties or obstacles to overcome. Even with a family's unlimited resources, a person's self-worth can be diminished.

Marger (1994) points out the effects of social ranking for racial/ethnic group members:

> The fact that members of one or a few ethnic [or racial] groups maintain most of the important positions of political and economic power, own an inordinate share of the society's wealth, and enjoy the most social prestige is due neither to chance nor to their greater motivation or innate capabilities. Rather, it is a consequence of the integral link between [racial] ethnic stratification and other forms of stratification in

the general distributive system. In short, the [racial] ethnic and class systems are in large measure parallel and interwoven. Where people begin their quest for the society's rewards and what they ultimately achieve very much depends on their [race or] ethnicity.

If a person is fortunate enough to be a member of the dominant (racial) ethnic group, his or her way will not necessarily be unimpeded; success is by no means assured by a favored ethnic [or racial] background. People's class position at birth, even for those of the dominant [racial or] ethnic group, is an overarching factor in determining their eventual wealth, power, and prestige. Thus, not all WASPs in American society, for example, are doctors, lawyers, corporation executives, and high-ranking politicians. But for dominant group members, the ethnic [or racial] factor is removed as an impediment to upward mobility; other factors, both individual and structural, will affect their fortunes, but [race or] ethnicity will not.

In the same way, of course, we should not think that minority status means that a person is automatically relegated to the bottom rungs of the wealth, income, educational, political, and other class hierarchies. But for minorities, the chances of winding up at the bottom are much greater. As we proceed down the [racial or] ethnic hierarchy, we find increasing political powerlessness, lack of economic opportunity, and social discrimination and exclusion. The closer to the bottom of the hierarchy, the more difficult the path to social success in whatever form, regardless of other nonethnic [nonracial] social traits. (pp. 64–65)

Internal feelings of self-worth are influenced by the messages communicated regarding visible characteristics. Thus, it seems that sociocultural and system-visible features carry with them the message that information is also being communicated about the person's internal qualities.

Personal Qualities

In the United States, skin color and other physical features are powerful personal influences. Traditional theories of human development and personality contend that various factors shape one's sense of self-worth. Psychoanalytic or psychodynamic approaches to human development suggest that the self evolves as one negotiates a series of critical conflicts, or as one attaches or fails to attach to significant caregivers. Humanistic theories emphasize the nature of a person's experience of self through interaction with others; behavioral and social learning proponents argue that self-concepts develop in relationship to reinforcements and models. Although these theories differ in specifics, they all posit that a person's sense of self is, in part, due to the nature and quality of his or her relationships and the social and physical environment in which he or she is located. As these influences affect one's self-concept or sense of worth, the manner in which one learns about his or her value often occurs through metacommunications and what is not spoken. The process is less apparent but no less disturbing.

Sociocultural messages may be determined and driven by large societal or systemic forces such as the political climate, economic conditions, and social movements and sentiments (e.g., taking steps to reduce or dismantle discrimination and bias in employment, housing, and education). The combination of sociopolitical, economic, and ideological patterns, historical trends, and institutionalized racism creates numerous obstacles and problems that people in our society must face. The racially inclusive model, offers a useful framework for assessing and working through many of these obstacles and difficulties.

An individual typically develops racial pride when receiving messages that actively promote racial awareness and emphasize its value and importance. If a child is exposed to a variety of racial/cultural traditions through friends and social institutions, he or she is likely to develop a multiracial worldview. However, one's racial identity is also shaped by how others respond, react, and regard his or her race.

> If one is exposed to a mixed race world through socialization, and . . . significant role models consider race to be a normal and desirable part of themselves as well as others, it is likely that the person . . . will develop a positive and pluralistic racial identity. (Helms, 1990, p. 87)

Conversely, if a person is taught to devalue or avoid race, or to see his or her own race as well as others' in negative terms, then a healthy or advanced level of racial identity is unlikely. Whites subconsciously feel positive about their race because they belong to the predominant racial group in the United States (McIntosh, 1995).

In addition, when systemic and psychosocial messages about race are contradictory, a great deal of psychic and social energy is required to grasp and to process them. The use of this extra energy to grapple with mixed racial messages may result in a personality that emphasizes race. That is, one's racial worldview affects a wider range of thoughts, actions, and feelings. Because, for the most part, people of color receive conflicting messages about race from internal and external sources, they are likely to have racial worldviews that influence their lifestyles and thoughts to a greater degree than would be true of Whites (Helms, 1990). Adolescence is considered to be the developmental period during which racial issues become especially salient, particularly with respect to dating and peer relationship. Many mental health trainees have reported that racial divisions in schools and social relationships were most evident and powerful during their adolescence. Based on indirect messages, these trainees learned, as adolescents, not to violate society's racial norms about dating, engaging in social activities, and having a racially mixed network of friends. For instance, the experience might be described this way: "I knew every day when I went to the lunch room that I could no longer acknowledge or interact with my [Black, White, Asian] friend because you were expected to stay with your own group. I was deeply angry and upset by this, but would not act differently."

Because adolescence is an important developmental period in general and appears to be significant in one's racial development, a clinician might inquire specifically about issues that are or were salient during this period. Specifically, a therapist should listen for cues about the role of race when asking the client about peer relationships, school life, struggles with independence, occupational choices, and parental relationships.

A therapist who is trying to understand a client's worldview should explore either directly or indirectly other extrafamilial roles and relationships. For instance, the clinician may ask: "Do you attend church?" "Do you participate in church groups?" "Did you participate in recreational activities and, if so, what was the racial makeup of members in these activities?" and "What messages were communicated to you about race and cross-racial relationships?"

Examples of Racial Assessment

Because a person's racially based worldview is subconscious, eliciting specifics about it is difficult. Instead, a therapist can explore aspects of a client's psychosocial world and determine whether and how a client was exposed to people from various racial groups. Two cases are presented here, to underscore how societal factors can affect an individual's racial worldview.

Jim, a 23-year-old White male, grew up in a racially integrated community. His parents frequently entertained neighbors and had friends from various racial groups who were well respected and professionally more advanced than Jim's parents. Jim attended a racially heterogeneous school and had many interpersonal relationships with people from different racial groups. Jim's exposure to a multiracial environment and, more importantly, Jim's parents taught him about being White, its meaning, and its significance; he learned to value his own race and that of others without racist undertones. Jim sought treatment because he was having difficulty interacting with other Whites who, he found, were uncomfortable with their own race.

In contrast, consider the case of Janet, a 21-year-old third-generation Asian woman, presented by Sue and Sue (1990). Janet came for therapy suffering from a severe depressive reaction manifested by feelings of worthlessness, suicidal ideation, and an inability to concentrate. She was unable to recognize the cause of her depression throughout the initial interviews. However, much light was shed on problems when the therapist noticed an inordinate amount of hostility directed towards him.

> When inquiries were made about the hostility, it became apparent that Janet greatly resented being seen by a Chinese psychologist. Janet suspected that she had been assigned a Chinese therapist because of her own race. When confronted with this fact, Janet openly expressed scorn for "anything which reminds me of Chinese." Apparently, she felt very hostile towards Chinese customs and especially the Chinese male, whom she described as introverted, passive, and sexually unattractive. Further exploration revealed a long-standing history of attempts to deny her Chinese ancestry by associating only with Caucasians. When in high school, Janet would frequently bring home White boyfriends which greatly upset her parents. It was as though she blamed her parents for being Chinese, and she used this method to hurt them.
>
> During her college career Janet became involved in two love affairs with Caucasians, both ending unsatisfactorily and abruptly. The last breakup occurred four months ago when the boy's parents threatened to cut off financial support for their son unless he ended the relationship. Apparently, objection arose because of Janet's race.
>
> Although not completely consciously, Janet was having increasing difficulty with denying her racial heritage. The breakup of her last torrid love affair made her realize that she was Chinese and not fully accepted by all segments of society. At first she vehemently and bitterly denounced the Chinese for her present dilemma. Later, much of her hostility was turned inward against herself. Feeling alienated from her own subculture and not fully accepted by American society, she experienced an identity crisis. This resulted in feelings of worthlessness and depression. It was at this point that Janet came for therapy. (pp. 204–205)

The psychosocial and systemic influences in Janet's life resulted in a racial worldview that denied her race. It is also quite possible, while not specifically mentioned, that Janet received messages from the media and other social institutions that being Asian meant that one was inferior. In contrast, Jim, given his social environment, might have a worldview that sees race as a positive and conscious aspect of personality, rather than one of White racial superiority. Yet, his worldview is in contrast with other Whites, so he experiences psychological and social discomfort.

Because Janet's therapist had an advanced level of racial identity, race was recognized as a factor in her anger, depression, and hostility. A therapist who was color-blind may not have considered race as contributing to Janet's symptoms and would have provided Janet with little relief.

These cases illustrate various system-focused perspectives, but it is not apparent how the racially inclusive assessment approach differs from the traditional assessment and treatment. The next section compares the two approaches by drawing on a published case.

CLINICAL ASSESSMENT AND TREATMENT: THE TRADITIONAL APPROACH VS. THE RACIALLY INCLUSIVE APPROACH

Traditional concepts for understanding race in psychotherapy have been limited because they have excluded systemic variables and have considered race as unimportant to the therapeutic process. For instance, according to traditional approaches, if a person of color attempts to reconcile contradictory social and psychological messages and feelings of self-worth as a racial being, he or she is considered resistant and pathological.

Waite (1968) described the course of treatment with Diane, a 17-year-old Black middle-class adolescent. He was helping her to overcome what, in the clinical literature, was called the "nigger complex," defined as "a phobia about acting out any of the fabled attributes which are . . . in the stereotype of the nigger" (p. 427).

This case was selected to demonstrate how racial differences could be used in treatment. According to Waite, Diane's treatment was "aimed at freeing up the adolescent patient's ego restrictions so that she may undertake again the developmental tasks of adolescence" (p. 427). As suggested earlier, race was seen as a distraction from the central issues of development and, as is standard, Waite focused on transferential reactions when assessing the client. However, a therapist often relates his or her countertransferential feelings and thoughts to the client's racial group and rarely, if ever, to his or her own racial group membership.

Waite (1968) reported not only how racial discussions in treatment assisted the patient in numerous ways, but also how they functioned as resistance. He felt that race helped the patient understand herself, her fears, and her "self-imposed limitations," but also hindered therapeutic objectives. The clinician's interpretation of these discussions was that the effects of race were self-imposed and race did not have any societal basis.

According to Waite, non-White clients manifest the following psychological resistances: (a) resistance to the working alliance, based on racial differences between the clinician and the client; (b) racial mythology or the "nigger complex" (i.e., avoidance of societal stereotypes); (c) a superficial identification with the White therapist's racial attitudes; and (d) race as a specific resistance. To get a sense of the four forms of resistance, here are relevant examples from Diane's case.

Diane used racial difference as a way to resist the working alliance: she responded to the therapist's concern about being White by stating that his race was unimportant to her. Later in the treatment, Diane declared that she thought the White therapist could not understand her because he could not comprehend what it was like to be Black. Her assertion was emphatically denied by the therapist, who stated, "My reply emphasized that we could only understand her life as a Negro if she talked about it, including her feelings about working with a white therapist" (Waite, 1968, p. 429). According to Waite, his interpretation helped Diane to focus on her feelings about "being a Negro" by discussing the types of experiences Black public figures and other Blacks encountered. It should be noted that the emphasis is on the person of color, not the therapist.

Diane often referred to race or Black life in terms that were unfamiliar to the therapist. The therapist interpreted this behavior as a test, which apparently he passed. Waite (1968) observed:

> During this period the [therapeutic] emphasis was on the interpretation of those aspects of the patient's verbalizations which reflected resistant motives against working together. These frequently had to do with racial issues. Gradually, she brought more and more of her personal concerns into the therapy with fewer references to race. (p. 429)

Interestingly, Waite did not consider race to be a personal concern. Diane's ability to delay gratification and her experiences in integrated settings, coupled with the therapist's ability to share his own racial attitudes, helped her benefit from his interventions.

Waite (1968) reported that Diane used the second form of resistance, emphasizing racial stereotypes, after the therapeutic alliance was established. He described it this way: "The emphasis was on the Negro as discourteous, impulsive, aggressive, shiftless, and helpless. Although Diane made it clear that the history of enslavement by whites was a contributing factor, she emphasized that for her, being Negro equated bad" (p. 429). Diane seemed to be reporting accurate stereotypes of Black people, and she seemed to be trying to cope with these systemic and psychosocial influences. Waite concluded that Diane's "externalization" of these negative Black characteristics was evidence of her resistance to the treatment. He described this behavior as resistance to change, "gradually, becom[ing] aware that she was avoiding her own specific feelings of badness and proclivity for self-debasement by discussing racial myths" (p. 430). Eventually, he stated, she was able to shift again to personal material.

The third form of resistance, the client's identification with the White therapist's racial attitudes, appeared in the treatment when Diane shared specific complaints, particularly about her parents' moderate racial attitudes. Also, she began to consider and to view riots and other racial conflicts as being equally attributable to Whites and to Blacks. According to Waite (1968), she noticed the "difficulties her friends were having dating Caucasians. She perceived that her own Uncle Tom attitudes clearly conflicted with her efforts to reexamine, reject, and realign her parental introjects and her wish for greater affective involvement in the world" (p. 430).

Waite thought her struggle with "civil rights questions" was an appropriate adolescent activity aimed at developing a unique ego identity. He reported that she often asked, and he shared, his views on complex racial issues; however, Waite did not publish what his views were. As Diane became more active in civil rights and acquired more knowledge about her heritage, her grades improved and she began to participate in extracurricular activities.

The final form of resistance, described as race-specific, became apparent when Diane would shift topics, without warning, to a race-related experience. Waite (1968) acknowledged that Diane's new racial awareness represented important and significant personal growth:

> [Diane's growth] appeared to come about because of her increased emotional freedom from her parents and a superficial identification with the therapist's general attitudes towards this country's racial conflicts. But despite its "positive" attributes there were indications that it was serving the function of resistance. (p. 430)

Waite believed that Diane simply took on a false persona that blocked treatment and led to termination. Recall from Chapter 10 that in White counselor/Black client dyads, Black clients at higher levels of racial identity (Immersion–Emersion and Internalization) felt understood by their White counselors (at lower levels of racial identity) but did not experience any symptom relief, an experience that could lead to termination.

According to Waite, client change is understood through observing and using resistances to increase self-understanding and various types of transference. The specific forms of resistance and other contributing factors that appear in therapy will be patient-specific.

In addition to describing and analyzing Diane's treatment, Waite discussed his efforts to increase his knowledge of Blacks and his empathic capacity. The primary strategy he used was to read novels that involved Black characters. Based on his effort, Waite warned of two dangers that might arise when therapists use cultural attributes in treatment. One danger is that it is impossible to "define a set of cultural attributes which apply to nearly all members of a particular minority group. The psychological energies invested in this kind of interest can serve the purposes of countertransference resistances" (Waite, 1968, p. 432). The second danger is that one should be cautious and read novels about minorities only sparingly. Waite's concerns are accurate if one assumes that all people in a racial group are the same psychologically.

Diane's case will now be examined using the racially inclusive perspective, which moves beyond the traditional transferential and countertransferential explanations of racial influences in psychotherapy. Using the racially inclusive approach and its underlying assumptions would have led to different interpretations of Diane's behavior and possibly to a different therapeutic outcome. For instance, Waite thought that race was an obstacle to treatment and was relieved when Diane moved to topics perceived to be unrelated to race, but he also insisted that she talk about "being a Negro." Apparently, race was discussed primarily to reduce Diane's resistance so they could move to more significant, intrapsychic concerns. In contrast, the racially inclusive model assumes that race is an integral part of one's personality. Therefore, racial identity, as expressed by one's racial worldview, is thought to influence an individual's image of himself or herself and others. Also, racial identity theory assumes that a therapist's racial identity will interact with that of the client. Thus, a therapist with an advanced level of racial identity would have recognized Diane's struggle as an attempt to consciously integrate race into her personality rather than as resistance.

Using the systemic elements of assessment described earlier in this chapter would have shown that the systemic and psychosocial messages Diane received about her race were negative. Diane's family had done well in terms of socioeconomic status—in part, because they de-emphasized or denied their Blackness. In addition, Diane's peers denied the significance of race in their interactions with her, except when cross-racial dating was at issue. Although Diane began to believe that race was important in her personal life and interpersonal relationships, she received conflicting messages from society at large and from her family and peers, and struggled to reconcile these messages. Waite (1968) observed these dynamics:

> Her family was one of the first Negro families to move into a previously all-White neighborhood. Although belonging to Negro organizations, neither parent was especially active in the civil rights movement. Diane belonged to the local NAACP youth group, but here again the attitude was more of "belonging" than of working actively for change. (p. 428)

Thus, early in the treatment, Waite was unable to engage Diane in the work of integrating race into her identity structure. Diane openly confronted the conflicting systemic and psychosocial messages she received from society, peers, and her parents, and she tried to reconcile their meaning to her own life.

At first, she began to internalize the negative societal messages, but these stereotypes seemed to conflict with her own self-perceptions. To some extent, this process was encouraged by the therapist as a way to set race aside or dismiss it, rather than to facilitate her racial understanding.

Racial identity theory posits that both the client and the therapist are members of racial groups, with their own identity resolutions and racial worldviews. Waite talked only about sharing with Diane his attitudes about racial conflicts; he did not reveal these attitudes to his readers. One can only speculate, therefore, about his level of racial identity development. He was able to raise the issue of racial conflict, so he had developed beyond the Contact level, but because he interpreted Diane's discussion of race as resistance, one might surmise that he had not developed beyond the Disintegration level. It is likely that he was confused by race, as suggested by his wanting to move beyond race and by his being unaware of its meaning and symbols. Assuming he was confused about race, it follows that he was unable to integrate race into Diane's treatment. Remember, an integration of race means that a therapist does not ask a client whether race matters but, instead, assesses how it matters.

Waite was not alone in his confusion about race; Diane also seemed confused about her racial identity when she entered treatment. Diane's belief that the White therapist could not understand her suggests that she may have been in the searching phase of Encounter. Thus, she was trying not only to develop a distinct personal identity, but also to integrate her own racial worldview.

Assuming that the therapist was at the Disintegration level and Diane was in Encounter, then their relationship is categorized as parallel: the therapist and client were at the same racial identity level. Waite's introduction of racial issues early in the treatment suggests that he might have been confused and unaware of race's influence in the psychotherapy, in his own personality, and in Diane's. Waite evaluated Diane using two sources: (a) White Euro-American standards and (b) the knowledge he had gained from reading novels written about Black characters. The novels he selected may have been irrelevant to Diane's experiences; she lived in a predominantly White community, and race was marginalized in her home environment.

During the course of treatment, with little assistance from the therapist, Diane's level of racial identity evolved from Encounter to Immersion–Emersion, and finally to Internalization. When the therapeutic relationship shifted from parallel to regressive, Diane terminated treatment. Had the work with Diane been guided by the Racially Inclusive Model of Psychotherapy, perhaps the therapist would have considered his own beliefs, attitudes, and experiences as a White person rather than simply sharing his attitudes about racial conflicts. Also, racial identity theory does not hold that race is an obstacle to treatment through resistance. The Racially Inclusive Model of Psychotherapy holds that race is an important core aspect of one's identity and, as such, should be incorporated into a person's personality structure.

SUMMARY

In the initial portion of this chapter, I described the various components of a racially based assessment in which the clinician considers and includes information about psychosocial, systemic, and personal aspects of a person's racial worldview. Clinicians should, during the course of assessment and treatment planning, conceptualize the patient at all relevant levels using a systems perspective. In this way, a clearer understanding of the numerous racial influences can be incorporated in an evaluation of the patient's profile. The clinician can consider these factors and integrate them with his or her preferred treatment strategies. That is, the racial assessment should be used in conjunction with existing theories and interventions. The second part of the chapter illustrated how these factors can facilitate treatment and problem conceptualization. However, it is important to have a way for educators and clinicians to learn the various propositions of the racially inclusive model. The next chapter outlines a training program that will meet this objective.

CHAPTER 15

Race and Psychotherapy: Training Applications

This chapter gives an overview of a training approach to prepare mental health professionals for implementing the Racially Inclusive Model of Psychotherapy. Training in the helping professions has become increasingly concerned with the race and culture of its constituents. This concern is reflected in the attempts by a great number of training programs to devise ways to prepare their students to effectively work with racially diverse populations (Allison, Crawford, Echemendia, Robinson, & Knapp, 1994; Bernal & Castro, 1994).

Training programs most frequently respond to the call for providing racially and culturally competent mental health professionals by adding a course focused on cultural diversity, cross-cultural mental health, or some variant of these topics. Typically, the added course is not required and it is the only offering that focuses on working with diverse populations. According to Bernal and Castro's (1994) longitudinal study of applied psychology training programs, "a substantial proportion of programs lack the structural basics of minority training. For example, 39% of accredited clinical programs still have no minority related courses, 74% of programs do not require even one minority course for completion of the doctorate" (p. 803). Allison et al. (1994) found, in a survey of applied psychology graduates (clinical, counseling, and school), that "more than 70% of the respondents indicated that they had received additional training regarding these [working with cultural difference] topics after obtaining their degrees" (p. 795).

It is important to put this training experience into perspective. The minimum training period for a mental health professional is two years for master's degrees, and the maximum is approximately five years for doctoral degrees. In a two-year program, a student may be required to take 20 courses, which include practice-oriented courses (e.g., field placement, practica) and didactic classes. In doctoral level training, approximately 40 courses may be required. Racially or culturally focused training usually accounts for, at best, two courses within a 20- to 40-course training program, and, for many programs, no such training exists.

A recent study (Hills & Strozier, 1992) found that 89% of the doctoral level counseling psychology programs in the United States offer at least one course that has a cultural focus. Bernal and Castro (1994) report that 40% of the 104 clinical programs they surveyed had no course focused on racial or cultural issues, 35% had one course, 14% had two, and some 9% had more than two. In many cases if courses do exist in programs they are not required for graduation.

Courses that teach traditional models of personality and human development dominate mental health training programs; psychodynamic and cognitive-behavioral models were most prominent in a recent study (Mayne, Norcross, & Sayette, 1994). Trainees, regardless of race, are taught to apply traditional notions of human development and personality to racial issues in psychotherapy. Moreover, practica, externships, and internship supervision also usually operate without a consideration of race. To use traditional psychodynamic constructs (e.g., transference and countertransference) when trying to understand and explain race, in effect, limits its importance and places blame on the victims of racism (see Chapter 4). However, a training approach that integrates traditional and racially inclusive principles, as presented in this book, would delimit many of the shortcomings previously described. Such a training model would require that both faculty and students explore the propositions of the racially inclusive model. In addition, the faculty would have to understand the various perspectives described in the cross-cultural and antiracist training literature.

This chapter provides an overview of a training model that could be of use to students and professionals who wish to negotiate and cope with issues of race and racial identity, and to be able to use the racially inclusive model when delivering services. First, I review cross-cultural training approaches and their assumptions. Next, I describe a series of courses and strategies that should be required because they are critical when training mental health professionals (e.g., social workers, guidance counselors, teachers, psychiatrists, and psychologists) to have at least minimal racial and cultural competence.

CROSS-CULTURAL TRAINING APPROACHES

As noted in the introduction and throughout the text most traditional teachers and those who teach what is called multicultural, diversity, or cross-cultural courses are guided by fundamental assumptions about cultural differences. For many, these assumptions are covert, yet they result in distinctly different training strategies. I contend that five common approaches guide psychological training: (a) Universal, (b) Ubiquitous, (c) Traditional

(Anthropological), (d) Race-Based, and (e) Pan-National (Carter & Qureshi, 1995).

Universal Approach

The universal or etic approach to culture equates difference with individual differences; its proponents assume that all people are human beings, and that differences within one group (intragroup) are greater than differences between groups (intergroup). It is espoused explicitly by traditional theories and practice (Sue et al., 1982; Sue & Sue, 1990). The universal approach does not deny the existence of race or culture, but focuses primarily on the shared human experience and secondarily on incorporating culture-specific knowledge. The main assumption underlying the universal approach is that there is a human bond that supersedes all experience. On this basis, then, individuals are human beings first, and members of racial, ethnic, or gender groups second. Therefore, individual differences are paramount. Thus, when our identity is associated with reference groups, all possible groups unique to the person should be considered in such a way as to capture the individual's uniqueness.

Mental health training based on the universal approach to culture would teach trainees about "special populations" from a unifying perspective, in an attempt to bring everyone together into the "melting pot" or "salad bowl." The universal approach would, perhaps ultimately, do away with salient domains of difference (i.e., differences that emerge from and through being socialized within the framework of a particular racial group). Finally, the universal perspective has the advantage of reminding us that humans have many common characteristics and attributes and that all people are unique individuals. The disadvantage of this approach is that it implicitly downplays sociopolitical history and intergroup power dynamics by assuming no one group membership has more meaning than any other. Its aim is to enable a clinician to overlook differences or to see clients primarily as individuals (Carter & Qureshi, 1995).

Ubiquitous Approach

The ubiquitous approach to culture is essentially a liberal position. Virtually all forms of social or group identity and/or shared circumstances are treated as cultural. Culture can be a function of affectional orientation, geography, income level, military experience, and so forth. A person can belong, then, to multiple groups and cultures, which would be situationally determined according to the specific group with which the individual was participating (Ridley, Mendoza, Kanitz, Angermeier, & Zenk, 1994).

The assumption of the ubiquitous approach is that any human difference resulting from a group or shared experience, regardless of its nature, can be considered cultural. It equates social group affiliations or domains of differences within a dominant or superordinate culture as representing distinct cultures. In this way, if a person develops a particular socially based identity such as class or age, then this, according to the ubiquitous perspective, is culture. The ubiquitous approach attempts to include groups that traditionally have been denigrated and ignored. Thus, mental health training that uses this approach insists that differences be acknowledged, celebrated, and "accepted." By defining the various "domains of difference" as "cultural," each domain is legitimized and differences are not seen as pathological. At the same time, the ubiquitous approach can lead to an avoidance and denial of groups' sociopolitical histories and intergroup power dynamics. Paradis (1981) proposes training objectives that aim to increase a trainee's awareness of his or her and others' cultures, as well as to unearth and discard stereotypical and prejudicial attitudes associated with differences of all sorts.

Traditional (Anthropological) Approach

The traditional or anthropological approach defines difference as country, wherein individuals share a common language, kinship, history, mores, values, beliefs, symbols, epistemology, cultural artifacts, and so forth (Christensen, 1989; Copeland, 1983; Leong & Kim, 1991; Nwachuku & Ivey, 1991; Parker, Bingham, & Fukuyama, 1985; Parker, Valley, & Geary, 1986). Culture, then, is not a matter of social differences or domains of difference; instead, an individual is a member of a cultural group by birth, upbringing, and environment.

The traditional approach suggests that one is a member of a particular culture by accident of birth, not by any psychological process. The advantage of this type of assumption is that it reminds us that many cultural traditions are maintained and sustained within geographical boundaries. Moreover, it highlights that culture is learned through socialization and that society's institutions reinforce the meanings of behavior, thought, and feelings learned through family. However, this approach de-emphasizes similar or different processes that occur within a particular country.

Proponents of the traditional approach assume that exposure to a culture or to cultural knowledge is the primary key to effective cross-racial therapy. The idea is that one person or family is representative of the entire group (see Howard, 1991). Nwachuku and Ivey (1991) talk of using "cultural informants" to develop cultural knowledge. Parker, Valley, and Geary's (1986) Multifaceted approach, Parker, Bingham, and Fukuyama's (1985) Ethnic Student Training Group, Leong and Kim's

(1991) Intercultural Sensitizer, and Nwachuku and Ivey's (1991) Culture-specific approach all emphasize increasing the clinician's knowledge of the client's culture. In part, the traditional (anthropological) perspective attempts to help trainees become comfortable with culturally different clients. This approach, however, considers race to be a "false" construct (i.e., biologically speaking) and minimizes the role of racism among the culturally different.

Race-Based Approach

The race-based approach, as described in the introduction and throughout the text, assumes that race is a social construct, a concept that is ignored by other approaches. Christensen (1989) defines race as "an arbitrary classification of populations conceived in Europe, using actual or assumed genetic traits to classify populations of the world into a hierarchical order, with Europeans superior to all others" (p. 275). I argue that race is central to cultural groupings in the United States and is the superordinate locus of culture through which racial groups are identified. People are classified into races and consequently cultural groups by skin color, language, and physical features (see Chapter 3). The race-based approach does not reject the approach to culture proffered by other approaches; however, in the final analysis, culture is interactively defined with an eye to sociopolitical history and intergroup power dynamics. Race-based theorists hold that the definitive aspects of culture, for example, cultural values (see Carter, 1991), vary according to psychologically and socially grounded racial categories.

The race-based approach assumes that the experience of belonging to a racial group transcends all other experiences in the United States. Because race is perhaps the most visible of all "cultural differences" and because of the history of racial segregation and racism in the United States, race has been and continues to be the ultimate measure of social exclusion and inclusion (Marger, 1994). Race is relevant because it is visible, and the rules and bounds of social and cultural interaction are determined by visibility (Copeland, 1983; Kovel, 1984; Ridley, 1995). Proponents of the race-based view believe that race as culture should not be seen as many ethnicities, culture-generally speaking, or diversities; it needs to be understood directly as the most significant difference. To deny its importance is to ignore American sociopolitical history and the fact that our society and culture are constructed on the basis of racial divisions.

The race-based perspective assumes that intergroup power dynamics are important, so that the White (or Conformity or Pre-encounter) counselor enjoys the fruits of dominant group membership (McIntosh, 1995). As such, this counselor has a vested interest in the status quo, which sees people of color as deprived, inferior, or deviant, rather than as different

(Midgette & Meggert, 1991; Ponterotto & Casas, 1991; Sue & Sue, 1990). Consequently, all people who are White-identified seem to have no interest in developing a consciousness of racial inequities inherent in the status quo, or in creating social or psychological change (Prilleltensky, 1989). Hence, proponents of the race-based approach stress raising people's consciousness about racism and racial identity development (Carter, 1990b; Helms, 1990, 1994; Katz, 1985; McRae & Johnson, 1991).

The advantage of this perspective is that it considers the importance of sociopolitical and historical dynamics on current events. It also introduces psychological variability (i.e., racial identity) to racial groups such that membership alone does not determine cultural affiliation. The disadvantage of this view is that it requires a deeply personal and potentially painful journey and soul-searching for each person to become comfortable with his or her racial socialization. In addition, it is difficult to address race as a social issue when it is treated as invisible in the social structure.

Pan-National Approach

This perspective views race and oppression in the global context and as definitive of culture. Where the race-based approach conceives of culture as racially circumscribed in the context of North American sociopolitical history, the pan-national perspective holds that racial group membership determines one's experience of oppression regardless of geographical boundaries.

Proponents of the psychology of oppression (e.g., Bulhan, 1985) focus on the role played by the imposition of European social theory on non-European peoples. The psychology of oppression, as its name indicates, concentrates on the relationship between oppression and psychosocial functioning and development. Culture is understood interactively, wherein the cultures of the oppressor and the oppressed have developed in relation to each other. According to this approach, because of the violence of colonialism, slavery, and their legacies, oppressed non-European people become alienated from themselves and their cultures, and Whites develop a culture based on violence. The upshot of this interaction is a worldwide sociopolitical context that is fundamentally alienating to oppressed people. In this regard, "the paramount tasks of psychology and psychiatry are to unravel the relation of the psyche to the social structure, to rehabilitate the alienated, and to help transform social structures that thwart human needs" (Bulhan, 1985, p. 195).

A pan-national training program would thematize oppression and reject approaches that deny anti-African, anti-Asian, or anti-Indian power dynamics inherent in European psychology. Trainees would be required to understand and emancipate themselves from Eurocentric psychology as a first step. Thus, scholars who teach and train from the pan-national perspective advocate knowledge of ancient history and shared racially and culturally based characteristics and experiences.

This view's assumption allows for a broad understanding of race as it relates to oppression throughout the world, and demonstrates how groups are connected by color and the experience of oppression. Its disadvantage is that, when viewing oppression as the primary racial connection, one can overlook the role of other important reference groups such as religious and class variation (Carter & Qureshi, 1995).

TRAINING FOR RACIAL-CULTURAL COMPETENCE

As is apparent from the preceding chapters, I believe that race is equivalent to culture in the United States and therefore find it imperative that students and professionals learn about the history of racism in the United States and the racially determined social order. As noted above, even when programs offer cultural training, racial issues and racism comprise only a small part of the course offerings. In that context, students will not learn much about racial factors and their influence in psychotherapy. Racial-cultural competence cannot be acquired in one course. A series of classes is needed to equip trainees with knowledge and skills that will result in minimum racial-cultural competence.

Racial-cultural competencies within the context of an academic training program should be acquired through didactic courses as well as experiential practica. In the context of institutional and organizational training, competencies can be acquired through in-service training sequences or a customized consultation arrangement. In this section, I describe a training program that incorporates the Racially Inclusive Model of Psychotherapy to teach cross-racial competencies.

The Training Components

Didactic courses can provide a racial-cultural context for learning. Such context-focused courses (i.e., not specific to race or culture) usually are core psychology topical areas taught without a racial-cultural focus. However, it is possible to include information about racial-cultural issues in introductory, developmental, and organizational psychology, research methods, psychopathology, and psychological testing/assessment courses. For instance, initial courses which focus on psychotherapeutic techniques and interventions could be taught so trainees learn when and how to use and understand a client's racial worldview. Trainees should be equipped with context-focused strategies that highlight the dominant (i.e., White) racial-cultural patterns of perception, communication, language, relationship styles, activity, and so forth. In this way, all trainees will be able to recognize their own racially determined cultural predispositions.

Context-focused (i.e., not specific to race or culture) courses can provide a basic foundation in psychological, psychiatric, social work, nursing, teaching, and counseling knowledge, while making explicit the racial-cultural context. Content-specific (i.e., specific to race or culture) courses are designed to provide specific content such as psychological and emotional knowledge and experiences aimed at deepening the trainees' or students' grasp of racial issues in society. These types of courses should help a student to understand that race has many expressions and that all individuals have a race and are affected by racism. These courses also should be designed to help students to talk openly about race and about racism and its impact on all people, not just people of color.

Perspectives on Cross-Cultural Psychotherapy

An overview lecture course would be offered that explores different perspectives on race, mental health, and psychotherapy. In this course, the approaches presented previously are used to show the various ways in which mental health theorists have discussed and defined cultural difference and how these notions affect our understanding of wellness and illness. Students explore traditional and cultural assumptions of and perspectives on normal and abnormal behavior, human functioning, and interpersonal relationships. In addition, using these assumptions and perspectives, students examine the various approaches offered by mental health professionals for understanding and coping with racial variation in psychotherapy.

Racism and Mental Health

A offering that focuses on racism and mental health would follow. A principal goal of this course is to show the intellectual foundation of knowledge associated with race and racism and how racism affects both the oppressor and the oppressed, and to increase students' ability to discuss racial issues with less emotionalism, which often characterizes such discussions. The course begins with an examination of American cultural practices. This exploration is comparative and highlights specific American cultural patterns, including philosophy, thinking, language, and activity. Next, the course provides a historical overview focusing on Asian, Latin, and African contributions to humankind. This overview demonstrates that these groups had complex and elaborate civilizations long before the rise of European powers. The overview is followed by an examination of racial inequality in the United States, specifically the relative influences of class and race in the history and development of racism in the United States. The purpose of this material is to teach students the critical role of race in historical events. In particular, the material describes structural and institutionalized relationships in the colonies and the early United States, wherein Blacks, Hispanics, and Indians were relegated to low social status, and Whites, depending on ethnicity, were accorded greater access to positions of power and status. The historical information is enriched by adding readings on the impact of racism on White Americans such as the edited book by Bowser and Hunt. Recent events that indicate a similar racial/class order are presented, too. These current events are followed by a focused discussion on racism and mental health that incorporates the material presented in Chapters 2 and 3. Thus far, the material provides the foundation for introducing the racial identity theory, which offers a way to comprehend feelings of confusion and hopelessness and can move people toward a more meaningful understanding of race and racism. The racial identity theory and its corresponding research are presented so that students learn that psychological variability occurs within each racial group. Finally, the idea of relationship types is added to the complexity of the racially inclusive framework. Video presentations and small group discussions supplement the didactic material.

Racial-Cultural Experiences and Practica

These didactic courses would be complemented by a racial-cultural counseling lab experience that consists of a small and a large group discussion, lectures, and skill-building sessions. The small group would follow Johnson's (1990) "C" group model, in which students share responses to a structured interview about the salience of various reference group identities (e.g., race, gender, and ethnicity).

The course is experiential, skill-oriented, and didactic. It is intended to provide insight into the role of racial and social factors in the development of relationships in counseling. The focus of the class is on the individual participant as a racial person who brings to his or her counseling relationships a network of personal and social identities and group affiliations that can serve as both barriers and resources in the development of effective counseling relationships.

The laboratory experience consists of group experiences including a small group in which students use a structured interview and observe intergroup relationship dynamics. The small group activities and experiences are understood in terms of the dynamics associated with gender, class, race, and ethnicity. Students are provided with on-going feedback (of the type given in clinical supervision) in small groups, skill sessions, and in comments to individual journal entries. The skill building component of the course uses simulated counseling sessions focused on the reference groups noted above. Within the roles of counselor and client each student is evaluated with respect to each other's competence in handling the various reference group issues that are introduced in the simulated sessions.

The lecture portion of the course provides a conceptual framework on racial-cultural counseling and discusses how the various reference group identities are interrelated. In particular, students learn how race as a clear visible marker is used to group people according to social class, religion, and ethnicity. The lecture is also intended to be a place where all students can raise questions and clarify any aspect of the course that is not clear or confusing. It is also the place where assigned readings are discussed.

The course requires that students show minimum competence in racial-cultural counseling. The emphasis on competence, which is focused on reference group issues, is weighted heavily on showing basic counseling competence such as: the ability to listen; check your perceptions; reflect, thoughts, feelings, and experiences; focus and lead the interviewee; express and recognize emotions and feelings in oneself and others; show empathy; and receive and respond to feedback and supervision from instructors and other students. Students must attend each class and complete all assignments on time. Students must also demonstrate a significant level of personal and professional development regarding their understanding and ability to incorporate reference group issues, at both a group and a personal level, into their counseling interactions in group and skill sessions. This means each student must show racial-cultural counseling competence in several ways:

1. Demonstrate through personal journals and in group sessions that he or she understands the meaning and significance of his or her various reference group memberships (e.g., race). In addition, students must show in their journals the ability to explore reference group issues through dialogue with his or her group leader and the course professor.

2. Demonstrate how to communicate, understand, and interact with others in one's group with recognition of intergroup issues and power dynamics. Often this means demonstrating one's ability to understand issues from an intergroup and individual perspective. It also means being able to grasp the fact that individuals develop and interact from the vantage point of one's racial group(s) as well as from one's personal point of view. The goal for each student in the small group is two-fold: They are supposed to help, by using counseling skills, the interviewee deepen his or her understanding of his or her reference group memberships. At the same time, they should use the small group interactions to gain further insight into

thier own reference group identities. In the group, the task for each student is to help each other learn. It is expected that each student will show that he or she is capable of coping with difficult emotional issues in skill sessions and the small group in the same way that counselors working with clients must be comfortable interacting with them when clients are struggling with difficult personal material.

3. Students must demonstrate an ability to apply—during skill-building sessions—racial-cultural learning acquired from lecture, group, and personal growth. Essentially, students are being asked to explore and learn about various reference group memberships, such as race, at intellectual and emotional levels and to share some aspects of that process by applying the learning in skill sessions as client and counselor.

The course is designed to teach students how, in the context of counseling supervision and by drawing on their prior learning, it is possible to understand in one's self and others how race influences one's personality (as it interacts with religion, social class, gender, and ethnicity). These reference group memberships also influence perceptions of others and counseling interactions. What is more important, students need to learn how to be competent counselors who understand their clients' complex psychosocial issues.

Ideally, this experiential class would be followed by an advanced practicum in which students would work with clients, under supervision, and participate in a seminar in which they learn to integrate knowledge and practice via case presentations and clinical discussions.

SUMMARY

The core of this training approach is the use of the Racially Inclusive Model of Psychotherapy as a way for students and professionals to learn about themselves as racial people who are shaped by various reference group identities. Through self-learning and development, they would come to appreciate racial and cultural differences as important and valuable aspects of their and another people's identity. The training is also presumed to help promote trainees' racial identity development. In this way, mental health professionals could effectively work in mental health settings and appropriately deal with race and properly use racial identity in conjunction with traditional theories in clinical work. In the absence of systematic training and experience, I doubt whether many mental health professionals could use or even see racial dynamics in psychotherapy (Thompson, Worthington, & Atkinson, 1994).

The racially inclusive training program I propose would have the effect in mental health training and service delivery of including all persons as members of racial groups, thus equipping all mental health professionals with the knowledge and skills that are necessary if one wants to be competent as a clinician. It is apparent from all existing demographic information that people of color are comprising a larger segment of the population. This fact not only suggests that their mental health needs will require attention; it also portends an increase in racial tension in the country. Race is the single most important sociopolitical and mental health issue our society must face and resolve. Mental health professionals could be at the forefront of genuine social change if, but only if, they learn how to understand and cope with racial influences in their own lives and in the lives of their patients.

CHAPTER 16

A Call to the Mental Health Profession

During the course of this book, I have argued that mental health professionals must learn about and value race as part of each person's identity. I have posited that race has been an impediment to psychological health, in part, because it has been attributed almost exclusively to people of color, the victims of individual, institutional, and cultural racism. If the victims are the only ones belonging to a race and they are powerless in the society, then race can be perceived as an undesirable and unimportant factor. The history, structure, and sociopolitical functioning of the United States as it pertains to race must be accepted as something that affects all people. Everyone belongs to a racial group, and race as part of personality need not be associated with negative connotations—it just *is*. Race can be understood by way of racial identity theory, and, by using it, one can grasp race's role in human development as a valued and beneficial component of self. I have stated that race is an aspect of every American's personality, because we all are socialized in a racial context. The racial environment affects the manner in which we are valued and develop a sense of self-worth. All Americans, consciously or subconsciously, must confront and resolve racial dilemmas, and one's level of racial identity influences the way one addresses racial issues, and has implications for one's mental health.

I have tried to show that one's racial identity status has a direct impact on the type of worldview one adopts, and that this worldview, in turn, determines how one perceives and interacts with others. Currently, the training mental health professionals receive does not equip them to understand race and racial identity and their influence on the psychotherapy process. Rather, most are taught through socialization and professional training to ignore race or to substitute race for something else. Denying or ignoring race promotes only confusion and conflict. As mental health professionals, we are taught—and many of us come to believe—that the best way to help change and heal people is to confront the source of distress and learn how it affects them. It is imperative that this model for facilitating change and healing be modified to include, address, and understand race as a psychological factor.

Presently, the way race is treated in mental health practice mirrors the way race is treated in the general society: race is a taboo topic, race is not valued, and race is not discussed. Mental health practitioners have worked hard to convey to people the harmful effects of family or personal secrets. In the American social family, where race is concerned, the family is dysfunctional because race is a taboo topic. To break the boundaries that exist because of race, it is essential that race be discussed, understood, and integrated as an accepted part of our psychosocial development.

Yee et al. (1993) have asked that psychologists confront the meaning of race in psychological practice and research. I extend their call to all mental health professionals and concur with their observation:

> Despite gestures addressing racism, major psychological [and other mental health] associations [and professionals] have neglected the fundamental issue—the need to define race scientifically and designate how it should be used as a psychological concept. Inaction has fostered a void that allows individuals and groups to assume and promulgate their own race meanings and agendas . . . race is treated according to personal and partisan preference with little or no responsibility taken for scientific reference and qualification. (p. 1137)

I hope that the content of this book will help professionals define and understand race as a psychological construct. I also hope that clinicians will begin to integrate race and racial identity assessments into their work, so that race will not simply be listed as a client characteristic. Rather, through the use of the Racially Inclusive Model of Psychotherapy, the clinician should integrate race into his or her understanding of the patient's personality structure and his or her treatment strategies.

Furthermore, training programs need to teach their students and continuing education programs need to be available to instruct practicing professionals about the importance and significance of race in clinical practice. I strongly urge faculty and training staff to incorporate information about race into the training of mental health professionals.

It is my sincere hope that this volume can serve as a step in the direction of understanding race's influence in psychotherapy.

APPENDIX

Measures

INSTRUMENTS

The Black Racial Identity Attitude Scale

The Black Racial Identity Attitude Scale (BRIAS) was adapted by Helms and Parham (1981) from Hall, Cross, and Freedle's (1972) Q-sort procedure for assessing racial identity attitudes. The scale consists of 30 items to which subjects are asked to respond using a five-point Likert scale (1 = strong disagreement, and 5 = strong agreement). The scale is scored by summing the appropriately keyed items such that each subject has an individual scale score for each racial identity attitude. Helms and Parham (1981) found the following reliability coefficients for each scale: Pre-encounter (.67), Encounter, (.72), Immersion–Emersion (.66), and Internalization (.71). Scale intercorrelations were also reported: the Pre-encounter scale was negatively correlated with Encounter ($r = -.46$), Immersion–Emersion ($r = -.42$), and Internalization attitudes ($r = -.17$). The Encounter scale intercorrelations with the Immersion–Emersion and Internalization scales were .62 and .64, respectively. A somewhat lower, but positive intercorrelation, was obtained ($r = .39$) between Immersion–Emersion and Internalization attitudes. The obtained correlations were in a direction that is consistent with the theory underlying the scales.

The White Racial Identity Attitude Scale

The White Racial Identity Attitude Scale (WRIAS) (Helms & Carter, 1990) was designed to assess the five levels of White racial identity attitudes (i.e., Contact, Disintegration, Reintegration, Pseudo-Independence, and Autonomy) proposed by Helms (1984). Helms (1984) hypothesized that White Americans may progress through five stages of racial consciousness. The scale consists of 50 items to which subjects respond using a five-point Likert scale (1 = strongly disagree, 5 = strongly agree). Scores were obtained for each level by summing the responses to the appropriately keyed items. Helms and Carter (1990) reported internal reliability coefficients, from a sample of 506 White college students, for the scales as follows: Contact (.55), Disintegration (.77), Reintegration (.80), Pseudo-Independence (.71), and Autonomy (.67).

Scale intercorrelations were computed also; it was found that the Contact scale was negatively correlated with the Disintegration (r = −.20) and Reintegration (r = −.32) scales. The Contact scale was positively correlated with the Pseudo-Independent scale (r = .49) and the Autonomy scale (r = .39). The Disintegration scale was found to be positively correlated with the Reintegration scale (r = .72) and negatively correlated with the Pseudo-Independence (r = −.52) and the Autonomy scales (r = −.63). The Reintegration scale was negatively correlated with the Pseudo-Independence (r = −.55) and Autonomy scales (r = −.49). The Pseudo-Independence scale was positively correlated with the Autonomy scale (r = .63). The obtained correlations are in a direction that is consistent with the theory underlying the scales (see Carter, in press; Helms, in press, for more information about scoring this measure).

PROCESS MEASURES

Therapist's Intentions

Hill and O'Grady (1985) proposed a therapy process measure of counselor intentions. They defined counselor intention as a "therapist's rationale for selecting a specific behavior, response mode, technique or intervention to use with a client at any given moment within the process of the session" (p. 3). Thus, "counselor intentions" seems to refer to the reason for a therapist's choosing a particular intervention or response. Hill and O'Grady argued that therapists gather a considerable amount of data from various sources (e.g., presenting problem, diagnosis, behavioral observations, and so on). This information is accumulated and assessed quickly and with some degree of sophistication. These data, on the basis of experience and training, are then used to develop counseling goals or intentions. Counselor intentions presumably guide the choice of interventions, according to Hill and O'Grady. The therapist then alters and adjusts his or her interventions in response to the client's overt reactions. The client is presumed to go through a similar process.

If the intention system is to be useful in verifying the Helms (1984) theory regarding the influence of race in the counseling process, then the intention system must be sensitive enough to differentiate across dyads. Hill and O'Grady (1985) described the development of the intention measure and reported results of two empirical studies in which the measure was used. The first study ("Study 1") was a case study, and the other was an examination of the model across theoretical orientations. In Study 1, they found that the intentions used by therapists appeared to correspond with the therapists' descriptions of their therapeutic styles: "Thus, a profile of intention usage can provide a process measure of orientation based on actual cognitive behavior" (p. 10).

General support was found for variation in intentions usage as a function of theoretical orientation. For instance, 7 of the 19 intentions ("clarify," "self-control," "give information," "feelings," "insight," "change," and "therapist needs") differentiated among three theoretical orientations (i.e., psychoanalytic, humanistic, and behavioral). The psychoanalytic therapists used "feelings" and "insight" more frequently; the humanistic therapists used "therapist needs" more often; and behavioral therapists used "change" and "set limits" more frequently.

The results of these two studies suggest that the therapists' intentions system should be useful in assessing differential counselor intentions as proposed by the Helms (1984) model. Helms proposed that counselors with various types of racial identity attitudes use different strategies.

Subjects, acting as therapists, were asked to indicate after each of their speaking turns or statements which of 19 intentions seemed to capture their purpose or the "intent" of the intervention. The 19 intentions are: get information, give information, support, focus, cognitions, feeling, insight, change, challenge, therapist needs, set limits, clarify, hope, cathart, behavior, self-control, reinforce change, resistance, and relationship. Because intentions are presumed to be internal cognitive processes of the therapist, they are difficult to subject to statistical reliability tests. The therapist intentions list was used in conjunction with the client reaction system, which will be described next.

Description of Therapist Intentions (Hill & O'Grady, 1985)

Set limits: To structure, make arrangements, and/or establish goals and objectives.

Get information: To find out specific facts about history, client functioning, etc.

Give information: To educate, give facts, correct misperceptions or misinformation, give reasons for counselor's behavior or procedure.

Support: To provide a warm supportive, empathic environment; to increase trust and rapport and build relationships.

Focus: To help client get back on track, change subject, or structure the discussion if the client has been diffuse or rambling.

Clarify: To provide or solicit more elaboration, emphasis, or specification when client or counselor has been vague, incomplete or confusing.

Hope: To convey the expectation that change is possible and likely to occur.

Cathart: To promote relief from tension or unhappy feelings, to allow the client a chance to let go or talk through feelings and problems.

Cognitions: To identify maladaptive, illogical, or irrational thoughts or attitudes (e.g., "I must be perfect").

Behaviors: To identify and give feedback about the client's inappropriate or maladaptive behaviors and/or its consequences.

Self Control: To encourage the client to own or gain a sense of mastery or control over his/her thoughts, feelings, and behaviors.

Feelings: To identify, intensify, and/or enable acceptance of feelings, to encourage client to become aware of or deepen hidden feelings.

Insight: To encourage understanding of the underlying reasons, dynamics, assumptions, or unconscious motivations for cognitions, behaviors, attitudes, or feelings.

Change: To build and develop new and more adaptive skills, behaviors, or cognitions in dealing with self and others. May be to instill more adaptive assumptive models. May be to give an assessment of opinion about client functioning that will help client see self in new way.

Reinforce change: To give reinforcement or feedback about behavioral, cognitive, or affective attempts at change to enhance the probability that change will be continued or maintained.

Resistance: To overcome obstacles to change or progress.

Challenge: To jolt the client out of a present state; to shake up current beliefs or feelings; to test validity or appropriateness of beliefs, thoughts, feelings, or behaviors.

Relationship: To resolve problems as they arise in the relationship in order to build or maintain a smooth working alliance.

Therapist needs: To protect, relieve, or defend the therapist; to alleviate anxiety. May try to unduly persuade, argue, or feel good or superior at the expense of the client.

Client Reactions

Hill, Helms, Spiegel, and Tichenor (1988) have reported on a system consisting of 19 positive, negative, and neutral client reactions. They described two studies, one of which examined whether the client reaction system was valid and useful; the other study was designed to assess the generalizability of the client reaction system. Their studies suggest that the client reaction system (a) is sensitive to differing types of therapeutic experiences,

(b) is capable of discriminating between experienced and inexperienced counselors, and (c) appears to have content validity in that clients felt the system was representative of their experience in therapy.

Hill et al. (1988) suggest that, like counselor intentions, measures of reliability and interrater reliability may not be appropriate measures of client reactions, because the reactions are measures of "fleeting experience known only to the subject" (p. 22).

Hill et al. (1988) reported that client reactions appear to be able to differentiate between therapy sessions that were experienced as more, or less, challenging to the client. The reaction system is presumed to have content validity because clients indicate that the reaction system does accurately describe their experience. Thus, it appears that the client reaction system is an appropriate measure of client reactions to counselor interventions and allows for examination of the interactional nature of the influence of racial identity attitudes in the counseling process.

The measure consists of the following positive reactions: supported, understood, hopeful, relief, more clear, feelings, negative thoughts or behaviors, better self-understanding, took responsibility, challenged, got unstuck, new perspective, educated, learned new ways to behave. Negative reactions are: miscommunicated, felt worse about myself, felt a lack of direction, ineffective therapist intervention. The neutral reaction was no particular reaction.

Clients were requested to indicate their reactions to each counselor statement or speaking turn. The frequency of the client's various reactions to the counselor's interventions was calculated and used to describe the client's experience of the different types of counseling relationships.

Description of Client Reactions
(Hill, Helms, Spiegel, & Tichenor, 1988)

Supported: I felt accepted and liked by my counselor.

Understood: I felt that my counselor really understood me and knew what I was saying or what was going on with me.

Hopeful: I felt confident, encouraged, and optimistic; like I could change.

Relief: I felt less depressed, anxious, or angry.

More clear: I got more focused about what I was really trying to say.

Feelings: I felt a greater awareness of or deepening of feelings or was able to express myself in a more emotional way.

Negative thoughts or behavior: I became aware of specific thoughts or behaviors which cause problems for me or others.

Better self-understanding: I realized or understood something new about myself which helped me accept and like myself better.

Took responsibility: I felt more responsibility for myself, blamed others less, and realized my part in things.

Challenged: I felt shook up, forced to question myself, or to look at issues I had been avoiding.

Got unstuck: I felt freed up and more involved in what I have to do in counseling.

New perspective: I got a new understanding of another person, situation, or the world.

Educated: I gained greater knowledge or information or learned something I didn't know.

Learned new ways to behave: I got specific ideas about what I can do differently to cope with particular situations or problems.

Miscommunication: I felt that my counselor didn't really hear me, or understood me. I felt confused or puzzled about what my counselor was trying to say. I felt distracted from what I was saying.

Felt worse about myself: I felt sicker, more depressed, out of control, dumb, incompetent, ashamed, or self-conscious. I worried that my counselor would disapprove or not be pleased with me or like me. I wanted to avoid something painful. I felt scared, and overwhelmed about what might happen.

Felt a lack of direction: I felt that my counselor didn't give me enough guidance. I felt impatient, bored or dissatisfied with having to go over the same thing again.

Ineffective counselor intervention: I felt attacked, criticized, judged, ignored, put down or hurt by my counselor. I felt angry, upset, or disturbed about what my counselor was or was not doing. I questioned my counselor's ability or judgement. I felt pressured or that my counselor was too directive and wanted things to go a certain way. I felt doubtful or disagreed with what my counselor said.

No particular reaction: I didn't have a particularly positive or negative reaction to the counselor's statement. The counselor's statement was too short or unclear for me to react. I thought the statement was social conversation.

CASE STUDY PROCESS MEASURES

Counselor Verbal Response System

1. Minimal Encourager: A short phrase that indicates simple agreement, acknowledgment, or understanding. It encourages but does not

request the client to continue talking; does not imply approval or disapproval. May be a repetition of a key word; does not include responses to questions (see Information, below).

2. Silence: A pause of 5 seconds; considered the counselor's pause if it occurs between a client's statement and a counselor's statement or within the client's statement (except after a simple acceptance of the client's statement, e.g., "Yes" pause).

3. Approval/Reassurance: Provides emotional support, approval, or reinforcement. May imply sympathy or tend to alleviate anxiety by minimizing client's problems.

4. Information: Supplies information in the form of data, facts, resources, theory, and so on. May be information specifically related to the counseling process, the counselor's behavior, or arrangements (time, place, fee, and so on). May answer a question. Does not include directions for what the client should do (see Direct Guidance, below).

5. Direct Guidance: Directions or advice that the counselor suggests for the client and counselor together, either within or outside the counseling session. Not aimed at soliciting verbal material from the client (see Closed Question, Open Question, below).

6. Closed Question: Data-gathering inquiries that request a one- or two-word answer, a "yes" or "no," or a confirmation of the counselor's previous statement. The possible client responses to this type of inquiry are typically limited and specific. If statements are phrased in the form of a closed question but meet the criteria for another category, put in the other category.

7. Open Question: A probe requests a clarification of feelings or an exploration of a situation without purposely limiting the nature of the response to a "yes" or "no" or a one- or two-word response. If statements are phrased in the form of an open question but meet the criteria for another category, put in the other category.

8. Restatement: A simple repeating or rephrasing of the client's statement(s) (not necessarily just the immediately preceding statements). Typically contains fewer but similar words and is more concrete and clearer than the client's message. May be phrased either tentatively or as a statement.

9. Reflection: A repeating or rephrasing of the client's statement (not necessarily just the immediately preceding statements). Must contain reference to stated or implied feelings. May be based on previous statements, nonverbal behavior, or knowledge of the total situation. May be phrased either tentatively or as a statement.

10. Interpretation: Goes beyond what the client has overtly recognized. Might take one of several forms: establish connections between seemingly isolated statements or events; interpret defenses, feelings, resistance, or transference (the interpersonal relationship between

counselor and client); indicate themes, patterns, or causal relationships in the client's behavior or personality. Usually gives alternative meanings for old behaviors or issues. If a statement also meets the criteria for a confrontation, put it under confrontation.

11. Confrontation: Contains two parts. The first part may be implied rather than stated and refers to some aspect of the client's message or behavior. The second part usually begins with a "but" and presents a discrepancy. This contradiction or discrepancy may be between words and behavior, between behavior and action, between two things the client has stated, between real and ideal self, between verbal and nonverbal behavior, between fantasy and reality, or between the counselor's and the client's perception.

12. Nonverbal Referent: Points out or inquires about aspects of the client's nonverbal behavior, e.g., body posture, voice tone or level, facial expressions, gestures, and so on. Does not interpret the meaning of these behaviors.

13. Self-Disclosure: Usually begins with an "I." The counselor shares his or her own personal experiences and feelings with the client. Note: Not all statements that begin with an "I" are self-disclosure; the statement must have a quality of sharing or disclosing.

14. Other: Statements that are unrelated to the client's problems, such as small talk or salutations, comments about the weather or current events, disapproval or criticism of the client; or a statement that does not fit into any other category or is unclassifiable because of difficulties in transcription, comprehensibility, or incompleteness.

Client Verbal Response System

1. Simple Responses: A short and limited phrase (typically one or two words). Usually one of three types: (a) indicates agreement, acknowledgment, understanding, or approval of what the counselor has said; (b) indicates disagreement or disapproval of what the counselor has said; or (c) responds briefly to a counselor's question with specific information or facts. (Note: Just because the counselor asks a question, do not automatically put the client's response here. In fact, tend to put it in another category unless it is a very simple response.) Generally, responses in this category do not indicate feelings, description, or exploration of the problem.

2. Requests: Attempts to obtain information or advice or to place the burden or responsibility for solution of the problem on the counselor.

3. Description: Discusses history or events, or indicates relation to the problem in a storytelling or narrative style. The person seems more interested in letting the counselor know what happened rather than in affective responses, understanding, or resolving the problem.

4. Experiencing: Affectively explores feelings, behaviors, or reactions about self or problems, but does not convey an understanding of causality. May indicate a growing awareness of behaviors or problems without necessarily understanding why they have occurred. Does not refer to feelings toward the counselor/counseling situation. (Note: Sometimes listening to the audio tape is helpful to differentiate this category from Description.)

5. Exploration of Client–Counselor Relationship: Indicates feelings, reactions, attitudes, or behaviors related to the counselor or the counseling situation. Does not refer to feelings that are not directed toward the counselor.

6. Insight: Indicates that a client understands or is able to see themes, patterns, or causal relationships in his or her behavior or personality, or in another's behavior or personality. Often has an "aha" quality. Insight statements usually have an appropriate internalization quality, i.e., the client takes the appropriate responsibility rather than assuming too much or blaming the other person or using "shoulds" imposed from outside rather than inside. Statements explaining the "why" of behavior should indicate a logical and reasoned explanation rather than a rationalization. (Note: This may be hard to determine; give the client the benefit of the doubt that he or she is not rationalizing, unless it is an obvious distortion.)

7. Discussion of Plans: Refers to action-oriented plans, decisions, future goals, and possible outcomes of plans. The client seems to have a problem-solving attitude here. Discussion of past plans is not included. Should be actual plans rather than hypothetical ruminations about the various possibilities open to the client in the future (these would fit under Description, above).

8. Silence: A pause of 5 seconds (4 seconds is close enough) is considered the client's pause if it occurs between the counselor's statement and a client's statement, within the counselor's statements, or immediately after a client's simple response.

9. Other: Statements that are unrelated to the client's problem, such as small talk or salutations, comments about weather or events, or any statements that do not seem to fit into other categories, because of difficulties in transcription, comprehensibility, or incompleteness.

RELATIONSHIP MEASURES

The Session Evaluation Questionnaire

The Session Evaluation Questionnaire (SEQ-Form 4) (Stiles & Snow, 1984) consists of 22 bipolar adjective scales that employ a semantic differential format. The SEQ assesses client and counselor ratings of session impact. In other words, the SEQ assesses how the client and counselor experience the relationship and/or session. The scale is composed of two dimensions, Depth and Smoothness, which measure independent evaluative aspects of counselor and client perceptions of the session, and two scales, Positivity and Arousal, which measure aspects of client and counselor postsession affect. The Depth scale assesses the perceived power and value of the session. Smoothness is an evaluation of how the session was experienced; that is, whether the session was pleasant, relaxed, and comfortable. The postsession measure of Positivity reflects the extent to which counselor and client felt confident and happy, and whether there was an absence of fear or anger. Arousal is reflective of feelings of excitement and activity.

Significant positive correlations have been discovered (Stiles & Snow, 1984) between client and counselor ratings on the Depth index ($r = .20$, $p < .001$), which includes the semantic differential scales: bad-good, valuable-worthless, shallow-deep, full-empty, and special-ordinary. Counselor and client ratings of Smoothness also correlated positively ($r = .39$, $p < .001$). Smoothness is composed of the semantic differential scales: safe-dangerous, difficult-easy, unpleasant-pleasant, and rough-smooth. In addition, Stiles found a significant correlation between client and counselor ratings of Positivity ($r = .21$, $p < .001$). The Positivity scale includes the scales: happy-sad, angry-pleased, uncertain-definite, confident-afraid, and friendly-unfriendly. Finally, client and counselor ratings on the arousal index have proven to correlate positively ($r = .10$, $p < .01$). The scale scores ranged from 1 to 7. Participants were asked to place an "X" on each line to show how they felt about the session. Thus, scale scores were derived by computing the mean of the items comprising the scale. Stiles and Snow (1984) reported counselor means for Depth of 4.62 (SD = 1.08), Smoothness 4.01 (SD = 1.12), Positivity 4.54 (SD = .99), and Arousal 4.35 (SD = .99). Client means were 5.06 (SD = 1.00) for Depth, 4.21 (SD = 1.43) for Smoothness, 4.55 (SD = 1.55) for Positivity, and 4.73 (SD = 1.14) for Arousal.

The means and standard deviations for race and gender may be considered comparable. The present sample's subscale means and standard deviations appear to be similar to Stiles and Snow's (1984) sample means and standard deviations.

The SEQ was used to measure the counselors' and clients' experiences of the counseling process or relationship. It added to the client reaction and counselor intention data in that the SEQ was completed by both clients and counselors. Therefore, it provided a way to assess the counseling process as experienced by clients and counselors along the same dimensions (i.e., Depth and Smoothness).

AFFECTIVE MEASURES

The State-Trait Anxiety Inventory (STAI)

The STAI, developed by Spielberger, Gorsuch, and Lushene (1968), consists of two distinct self-report scales and is used to measure the concept of trait anxiety (A-Trait) and state anxiety (A-State). However, only the A-State scale was used and discussed here.

The STAI A-State scale consists of 20 self-statements. Using each of these, respondents are asked to indicate how they feel at a particular moment. Spielberger et al. (1968) used undergraduate students in introductory psychology classes to establish normative data for this scale. Means for the normative group were 36.35 (SD = 9.67) for men and 36.12 (SD = 9.26) for women. As might be anticipated, the test-retest reliability of this scale, which is used for gauging transitory anxiety states, is low, ranging from .16 to .54. Several studies have been conducted to demonstrate the validity of the scale. One study demonstrated that the scale differentiated among subjects ordered along four experimental conditions of stressfulness. In the present study, the STAI was used to determine the levels of anxiety that characterized the various counseling dyads and to examine how the various reactions and intentions related to anxiety.

The Hostility Dimension of the Symptom Checklist-90 Revised Form (Derogatis, 1984)

The Hostility dimension is intended to reflect behavior, thought, or affect that characterizes angry feelings. Six items comprise this dimension. Subjects were requested to indicate or describe how much each item was characteristic of them. The options by which subjects could describe themselves were: 0 = not at all, 1 = a little bit, 2 = moderately, 3 = quite a bit, 4 = extremely. Derogatis reported internal consistency reliability of .84 for the Hostility subscale and test-retest reliability of .78. In the present study, the Hostility subscale was scored by summing the scale values marked by the respondents and dividing the total by the number of items (n = 6). Scores could range from 0 to 4. The Hostility subscale was used as a measure of anger because some regressive and crossed relationships have been hypothesized to be associated with feelings of anger on the part of the client and counselor.

Personal Data Sheet

The Personal Data Sheet, designed for this study, was used to investigate professional characteristics (e.g., years of counseling experience, level of training, and prior training in cross-cultural counseling) of participants. Participants were asked to indicate their age, socioeconomic status, race/ethnicity, educational level, and country of origin.

References

Abel, T. M., Metraux, R., & Roll, S. (1987). *Psychotherapy and culture* (rev. ed.). Albuquerque, New Mexico: University of New Mexico Press.

Aboud, F. E. (1987). The development of ethnic self-identification and attitudes. In J. S. Phinney & M. J. Rotherman (Eds.), *Children's ethnic socialization: Pluralism and development* (pp. 29–51). Newbury Park, CA: Sage.

Acosta, F. X., Yamamoto, J., & Evans, L. A. (1982). *Effective psychotherapy for low-income and minority patients.* New York: Plenum Press.

Adams, W. A. (1950). The Negro patient in psychiatric treatment. *American Journal of Orthopsychiatry, 20,* 305–310.

Adams, W. A. (1970). Dealing with racism in biracial psychiatry. *Journal of the American Academy of Child Psychiatry, 9,* 33–43.

Allen, T. W. (1994). *The invention of the white race: Racial oppression and social control.* London, England: Verso.

Allison, K. W., Crawford, I., Echemendia, R., Robinson, L., & Knapp, D. (1994). Human diversity and professional competence. *American Psychologist, 49*(9), 792–796.

Allport, G. W. (1954). *The nature of prejudice.* Reading, MA: Addison-Wesley.

Andersen, M. L., & Collins, P. H. (1995). *Race, class, and gender: An anthology.* Belmont, CA: Wadsworth.

Atkinson, D. R. (1987). Research on cross-cultural counseling and psychotherapy: A review and update of reviews. In P. Pederson (Ed.), *Handbook of cross-cultural counseling and therapy.* New York: Praeger.

Atkinson, D. R., & Gim, R. H. (1989). Asian-American cultural identity and attitudes toward mental health services. *Journal of Counseling Psychology, 36,* 209–212.

Atkinson, D. R., Morten, G., & Sue, D. W. (1979). *Counseling American minorities: A cross-cultural perspective.* Dubuque, IA: W. C. Brown.

Atkinson, D. R., Morten, G., & Sue, D. W. (1989). *Counseling American minorities: A cross-cultural perspective* (3rd ed.). Dubuque, IA: W. C. Brown.

Atkinson, D. R., Morten, G., & Sue, D. W. (1993). *Counseling American minorities: A cross-cultural perspective* (5th ed.). Dubuque, IA: W. C. Brown.

Atteneave, C. (1982). American Indians and Alaska native families: Emigrants in their own homelands. In M. McGoldrick, J. K. Pearce, & J. Giordano (Eds.), *Ethnicity and family therapy* (pp. 55–83). New York: Guilford Press.

Atwell, I., & Azibo, D. A. (1991). Diagnosing personality disorders in Africans using the Azibo nosology: Two case studies. *The Journal of Black Psychology, 17*(2), 1–23.

Austin, L. N., Carter, R. T., & Vaux, A. (1990). The role of racial identity in black students' attitudes toward counseling and counseling centers. *Journal of College Student Development, 31*(3), 237–243.

Axelson, J. A. (1993). *Counseling and development in a multicultural society.* Pacific Grove, CA: Brooks/Cole Publishing Co.

Babad, E. Y., Birnbaum, M., & Benne, K. D. (1983). *The social self* (Vol. 144). Beverly Hills, CA: Sage.

Banks, G. (1972). The effects of race on one-to-one helping interviews. *Social Service Review, 45,* 137–146.

Banks, H. C. (1975). The Black person as client and as therapist. *Professional Psychology, 8,* 470–475.

Banks, J. A. (1988). *Multiethnic education* (2nd ed.). Newton, MA: Allyn & Bacon.

Banks, W. (1977). Group consciousness and the helping professions. *Personnel and Guidance Journal, 55,* 319–330.

Basch, M. F. (1980). *Doing psychotherapy.* New York: Basic Books.

Beaton, S. R. (1974). The function of "colorblindness." *Perspectives in Psychiatric Care, 12,* 80–85.

Bell, R. L. (1971). The culturally deprived psychologist. *The Counseling Psychologist, 2,* 104–107.

Berman, J. (1979). Counseling skills used by black and white male and female counselors. *Journal of Counseling Psychology, 26,* 81–84.

Bernal, M. E., & Castro, F. G. (1994). Are clinical psychologists prepared for service and research with ethnic minorities? *American Psychologist, 49*(9), 797–805.

Bernard, J. M. (1994). Multicultural supervision: A reaction to Leong and Wagner, Cook, Priest, and Fukuyama. *Counselor Education and Supervision, 34*(2), 159–171.

Bernard, V. W. (1953). Psychoanalysis and members of minority groups. *Journal of the American Psychoanalytic Association, 1,* 256–267.

Betancourt, H., & Lopez, S. R. (1993). The study of culture, ethnicity, and race in American psychology. *American Psychologist, 48*(6), 629–637.

Bevis, W. M. (1921). Psychological traits of the southern Negro with observations as to some of his psychoses. *American Journal of Psychiatry, 1,* 69–78.

Blocher, D. G. (1983). Toward a cognitive developmental approach to counseling supervision. *The Counseling Psychologists, 11*(1), 27–34.

Block, C. J., Roberson, L., & Neuger, D. (1995). White racial identity theory: A framework for understanding reactions toward interracial situations in organizations. *Journal of Vocational Behavior, 46,* 71–88.

Bowser, B. P., & Hunt, R. G. (Eds.). (1981). *Impacts of racism on white Americans.* Newbury, Park. CA: Sage.

Boyd-Franklin, N. (1989). *Black families in therapy: A multisystems approach.* New York: Guilford Press.

Bradby, D., & Helms, J. E. (1990). Black racial identity attitudes and white therapist cultural sensitivity in cross-racial therapy dyads: An exploratory study. In J. E. Helms (Ed.), *Black and white racial identity attitudes: Theory, research, and practice* (pp. 165–176). Westport, CT: Greenwood Press.

Branch, C. W., & Newcombe, N. (1986). Racial attitude development among young black children as a function of parental attitudes: A longitudinal and cross-sectional study. *Child Development, 57,* 712–721.

Branch, C. W., & Newcombe, N. (1988). The development of racial attitudes in young black children. *Annals of Child Development, 5,* 125–154.

Brislin, R. W. (Ed.). (1990). *Applied cross-cultural psychology.* Newbury Park, CA: Sage.

Brookins, C. C. (1994). The relationship between Afrocentric values and racial identity attitudes: Validation of the belief systems analysis scale on African American College students. *Journal of Black Psychology, 20,* 104–128.

Brown, L. B. (1950). Race as a factor in establishing a casework relationship. *Social Casework, 31,* 91–97.

Bulhan, H. A. (1985). Black Americans and psychopathology: An overview of research and theory. *Psychotherapy: Theory, Research, and Practice, 22*(2), 370–378.

Calnek, M. (1970). Racial factors in the countertransference: The black therapist and the black client. *American Journal of Orthopsychiatry, 40,* 39–46.

Carter, R. T. (1988). *An empirical test of a theory on the influence of racial identity attitudes on the counseling process within a workshop setting.* Doctoral dissertation, University of Maryland, 1987. *Dissertation Abstracts International, 49,* 431A.

Carter, R. T. (1990a). Does race or racial identity attitudes influence the counseling process in black/white dyads? In J. E. Helms (Ed.), *Black and white racial identity attitudes: Theory, research, and practice* (pp. 145–164). Westport, CT: Greenwood Press.

Carter, R. T. (1990b). The relationship between racism and racial identity among white Americans: An exploratory investigation. *Journal of Counseling and Development, 69,* 46–50.

Carter, R. T. (1990c). Cultural value differences between African-American and white Americans. *Journal of College Student Development, 31,* 71–79.

Carter, R. T. (1991). Racial identity attitudes and psychological functioning. *Journal of Multicultural Counseling and Development, 19,* 105–115.

Carter, R. T. (in press). Exploring the complexity of racial identity measures. In G. R. Sodowsky & J. Impara (Eds.), *Multicultural assessment.* Lincoln, NB: Buros Institute of Mental Measurement.

Carter, R. T., & Cook, D. A. (1992). A culturally relevant perspective for understanding the career paths of visible racial/ethnic group people. In Z. Liebowitz & D. Lea (Eds.), *Adult career development* (2nd ed., pp. 192–217). Washington, DC: National Career Development Association.

Carter, R. T., & Goodwin, A. L. (1994). Racial identity and education. In L. Darling-Hammond (Ed.), *Review of research in education* (pp. 291–336). Washington, DC: American Education Research Association.

Carter, R. T., Gushue, G. V., & Weitzman, L. M. (1994). White racial identity development and work values. *Journal of Vocational Behavior, 44,* 185–197.

Carter, R. T., & Helms, J. E. (1987). The relationship of black value-orientation to racial identity attitudes. *Measurement and Evaluation in Counseling and Development, 19,* 185–195.

Carter, R. T., & Helms, J. E. (1988). The relationship between racial identity attitudes and social class. *Journal of Negro Education, 57*(1), 22–30.

Carter, R. T., & Helms, J. E. (1990). White racial identity attitudes and cultural values. In J. E. Helms (Ed.), *Black and white racial identity: Theory, research, and practice* (pp. 105–118). Westport, CT: Greenwood Press.

Carter, R. T., & Helms, J. E. (1992). The counseling process as defined by relationship types: A test of Helms' interactional model. *Journal of Multicultural Counseling and Development, 20,* 181–201.

Carter, R. T., & Parks, E. E. (1994). White racial identity and psychological functioning. Submitted to the *Journal of Counseling Psychology.*

Carter, R. T., & Qureshi, A. (1995). A typology of philosophical assumptions in multicultural counseling and training. In J. G. Ponterotto, J. M. Casas, L. A. Suzuki, & C. M. Alexander (Eds.), *Handbook of Multicultural Counseling* (pp. 239–260). Newbury Park, CA: Sage.

Casas, J. M., & Vasquez, J. T. (1989). Counseling the Hispanic client: A theoretical and applied perspective. In P. B. Pedersen, J. G. Draguns, W. L. Lonner, & J. E. Trimble (Eds.), *Counseling across cultures* (3rd ed., pp. 177–204). Honolulu: University of Hawaii Press.

Chestang, L. (1984). Racial and personal identity in the black experience. In B. White (Ed.), *Color in a white society.* Silver Spring, MD: NASW Publications.

Christensen, C.P. (1989). Cross-cultural awareness development: A conceptual model. *Counselor Education and Supervision, 28,* 270–287.

Claney, D., & Parker, W. M. (1988). Assessing white racial consciousness and perceived comfort with black individuals: A preliminary study. *Journal of Counseling and Development, 67,* 449–451.

Clark, A., Hocevar, D., & Dembo, M. H. (1980). The role of cognitive development in children's explanations and preferences for skin color. *Developmental Psychology, 10,* 591–599.

Clark, K. B. (1965). *Dark ghetto.* New York: Harper & Row.

Clark, K. B. (1988). *Prejudice and your child.* Middletown, CT: Wesleyan University Press.

Cohen, A. I. (1974). Treating the black patient: Transference questions. *American Journal of Psychotherapy, 28,* 137–143.

Comas-Diaz, L., & Griffith, E. E. H. (1988). *Clinical guidelines in cross-cultural mental health.* New York: John Wiley.

Comas-Diaz, L., & Jacobsen, F. M. (1991). Ethnocultural transference and countertranference in the therapeutic dyad. *American Journal of Orthopsychiatry 6*(3), 392–402.

Comer, J. P. (1980). White racism: Its root, form, and function. In R. L. Jones (Ed.), *Black psychology* (2nd ed., pp. 361–366). New York: Harper & Row.

Conant, J. B. (1961). *Slums and suburbs.* New York: McGraw-Hill.

Cook, D. A. (1994). Racial identity and supervision. *Counselor Education and Supervision, 34*(2), 132–141.

Cook, D. A., & Helms, J. E. (1988). Visible racial/ethnic group supervisees' satisfaction with cross-cultural supervision as predicted by relationship characteristics. *Journal of Counseling Psychology, 33,* 168–174.

Cooper, S. (1973). A look at the effect of racism on clinical casework. *Social Casework, 54,* 78–84.

Copeland, E. J. (1983). Minority populations and traditional counseling programs: Some alternatives. *Counselor Education and Supervision, 21,* 187–193.

Cross, D. E., Long, M. A., & Ziafka, A. (1978). Minority cultures and education in the United States. *Education and Urban Society, 10,* 263–276.

Cross, W. E. (1978). The Cross and Thomas models of psychological Nigrescence. *Journal of Black Psychology, 5,* 13–19.

Cross, W. E. (1980). Models of psychological Nigrescence: A literature review. In R. L. Jones (Ed.), *Black psychology* (2nd ed., pp. 81–89). New York: Harper & Row.

Cross, W. E. (1991). *Shades of black.* Philadelphia: Temple University Press.

Cross, W. E., Parham, T. A., & Helms, J. E. (1991). The stages of black identity development: Nigrescence models. In R. L. Jones (Ed.), *Black psychology* (3rd ed., pp. 319–338). Berkeley, CA: Cobb & Henry.

Cross, W. E., Parham, T. A., & Helms, J. E. (in press). Nigrescence revisited: Theory and research. In R. L. Jones (Ed.), *Advances in Black psychology* (Vol. 1). Berkeley, CA: Cobb & Henry.

Crystal, D. (1989). Asian-Americans and the myth of the model minority. *Social Casework, 70,* 405–413.

Curry, A. (1964). Myth, transference, and the black therapist. *Psychoanalytic Review, 51,* 7–14.

Dennis, R. M. (1981). Socialization and racism: The white experience. In B. P. Bowser & R. G. Hunt (Eds.), *Impacts of racism on white Americans* (pp. 71–85). Beverly Hills, CA: Sage.

Denton, S. E. (1986). *A methodological refinement and validation analysis of the developmental inventory of black consciousness.* Unpublished doctoral dissertation, University of Pittsburgh.

Derogatis, L. R. (1984). *SCL-90-R: Administration, scoring and procedures manual II.* Baltimore: Clinical Psychometric Research.

Devereux, G. (1951). Three technical problems of the psychotherapy of Plains Indian patients. *American Journal of Psychotherapy, 5,* 411–423.

Dillard, J. M. (1983). *Multi-cultural counseling.* Chicago: Nelson Hall.

D'Souza, D. (1992). *Illiberal education: The politics of race and sex on campus.* New York: Random House.

Dufrene, P. M., & Coleman, V. D. (1994). Art and healing for Native American Indians. *Journal of Multicultural Counseling and Development, 22*(3), 145–152.

Edsall, T. B., & Edsall, M. D. (1991, May). Race. *The Atlantic Monthly,* pp. 53–86.

Erikson, E. H. (1959). Identity and the lifecycle Monograph 1. *Psychological Issues.* New York: International Universities Press.

Erikson, E. H. (1963). *Childhood and society* (rev. ed.). New York: Norton.

Erikson, E. H. (1968). *Identity: Youth and crisis.* New York: Norton.

Evarts, A. B. (1913). Dementia precox in the colored race. *Psychoanalytic Review, 1,* 388–403.

Fairchild, H. H. (1991). Scientific racism: The cloak of objectivity. *Journal of Social Issues, 47*(3), 101–115.

Fleming, J. (1984). *Blacks in college.* San Francisco: Jossey-Bass.

Fooks, G. M. (1973). Dilemmas of black therapists. *Journal of Non-White Concerns, 1,* 181–190.

Frankenberg, R. (1993). *White women race matters: The social construction of whiteness.* Minneapolis, MN: University of Minnesota Press.

Franklin, A. J., Carter, R. T., & Grace, C. (1993). An integrative approach to psychotherapy with Black/African Americans: The relevance of race and culture. *Comprehensive handbook of psychotherapy integration* (pp. 465–479). New York: Plenum Press.

Fredrickson, G. M. (1971). *The black image in the white mind: The debate on Afro-American character and destiny.* New York: Harper & Row.

Fredrickson, G. M. (1989). *The arrogance of race.* Middletown, CT: Wesleyan University Press.

Fry, P. S., Kropf, G., & Coe, K. J. (1980). Effects of counselor and client racial similarity on the counselor's response patterns and skills. *Journal of Counseling Psychology, 27,* 130–137.

Gardner, L. H. (1971). The therapeutic relationship under varying conditions of race. *Psychotherapy: Theory, Research, and Practice, 8,* 78–87.

Garfield, S. L. (1978). Research on client variables in psychotherapy. In S. L. Garfield & A. E. Bergin (Eds.), *Handbook of psychotherapy and behavior change* (2nd ed., pp. 191–232). New York: John Wiley.

Garfield, S. L., & Bergin, A. E. (1978). *Handbook of psychotherapy and behavior change* (2nd ed.). New York: John Wiley.

Garfield, S. L., & Bergin, A. E. (1986). *Handbook of psychotherapy and behavior change* (3rd ed.). New York: John Wiley.

Garrett, J. T. & Garrett, M. W. (1994). The path of good medicine: Understanding and counseling Native American Indians. *Journal of Multicultural Counseling and Development, 22*(3), 134–144.

Gibbs, J. T. (1990). Biracial adolescents. In J. T. Biggs & L. N. Huang (Eds.), *Children of color: Psychological interventions with minority youth* (pp. 322–350). San Francisco: Jossey-Bass.

Gibbs, J. T., & Moskowitz-Sweet, G. (1991). Clinical and cultural issues in the treatment of biracial and bicultural adolescents. *Families in Society: The Journal of Contemporary Human Services, 72(10),* 579–592.

Giddings, P. (1984). *When and where I enter.* New York: Bantam.

Goodman, M. (1952). *Race and awareness in young children.* Cambridge, MA: Addison-Wesley.

Gotunda, N. (1991). A critique of "Our Constitution is color-blind." *Stanford Law Review, 44*(1), 1–73.

Gould, S. J. (1981). *The mismeasure of man.* New York: Norton.

Green, B. A. (1985). Considerations in the treatment of black patients by white therapists. *Psychotherapy, 22*(2), 389–393.

Green, B. A. (1993). Psychotherapy with African American women: Integrating feminist and psychodynamic models. *Journal of Training and Practice in Professional Psychology, 7*(1), 49–66.

Green, E. M. (1914). Psychosis among Negroes: A comparative study. *Journal of Nervous and Mental Disorders, 41,* 697–708.

Greenson, R. R. (1965). The working alliance and transference neurosis. *Psychoanalytic Quarterly, 34,* 151–181.

Grier, W. H. (1967). When the therapist is Negro and some effects on the treatment process. *American Journal of Psychiatry, 123,* 1587–1591.

Grier, W. H., & Cobbs, P. M. (1968). *Black rage.* New York: Bantam.

Griffith, M. S. (1977). The influence of race on the psychotherapeutic relationship. *Psychiatry, 40,* 27–40.

Grove, K.J. (1991). Identity development in interracial, Asian/white late adolescents: Must it be so problematic? *Journal of Youth and Adolescence, 20*(6), 617–628.

Guthrie, R. V. (1976). *Even the rat was white: A historical view of psychology.* New York: Bantam.

Hall, G. S. (1904). *Adolescence.* New York: Appleton.

Hall, W. S., Cross, W. E., & Freedle, R. (1972). Stages in the development of black awareness: An empirical investigation. In R. L. Jones (Ed.), *Black Psychology* (1st ed., pp. 156–165). New York: Harper & Row.

Harper, F. (1973). What counselors must know about the social sciences of black Americans. *Journal of Negro Education, 42,* 109–116.

Harrington, M. (1963). *The other America.* Baltimore: Penguin.

Hayes, W. A. (1991). Radical black behaviorism. In R. L. Jones (Ed.), *Black psychology* (3rd ed., pp. 65–78). New York: Harper & Row.

Heine, R. W. (1950). The Negro patient in psychotherapy. *Journal of Clinical Psychology, 16,* 373–376.

Helms, J. E. (1984). Toward an explanation of the influence of race in the counseling process: A black–white model. *The Counseling Psychologist, 12,* 153–165.

Helms, J. E. (1986). Expanding racial identity theory to cover counseling process. *Journal of Counseling Pschology, 33*(1), 62–64.

Helms, J. E. (Ed.). (1990). *Black and white racial identity: Theory, research, and practice.* Westport, CT: Greenwood Press.

Helms, J. E. (1992). *Race is a nice thing to have.* Topeka, KS: Content Communications.

Helms, J. E. (1994). Racial identity and "racial" constructs. In E. J. Trickett, R. Watts, & D. Birman (Eds.), *Human diversity* (pp. 285–311). San Francisco: Jossey-Bass.

Helms, J. E. (in press). Towards an approach for assessing racial identity. In G. R. Sodowsky & J. Impara (Eds.), *Multicultural assessment.* Lincoln, NB: Buros Institute of Mental Measurement.

Helms, J. E., & Carter, R. T. (1986). Manual for the Visible Racial/Ethnic Identity Attitude Scale. In R. T. Carter, B. R. Fretz, & J. R. Mahalik (Eds.), *An exploratory investigation into the relationship between career maturity, work role salience, value-orientation, and racial identity attitudes.* Paper presented at the 94th annual convention of the American Psychological Association, Washington, DC.

Helms, J. E., & Carter, R. T. (1990). The development of the White Racial Identity Inventory. In J. E. Helms (Ed.), *Black and white racial identity attitudes: Theory, research, and practice* (pp. 145–164). Westport, CT: Greenwood Press.

Helms, J. E., & Carter, R. T. (1991). Relationships of white and black racial identity attitudes and demographic similarity to counselor preferences. *Journal of Counseling Psychology, 38*(4), 446–457.

Helms, J. E., & Parham, T. A. (in press). The development of the Racial Identity Attitude Scale. In R. L. Jones (Ed.), *Handbook of tests and measurements for black populations* (Vols. 1–2). Berkeley, CA: Cobb & Henry.

Helms, J. E., & Piper, R. E. (1994). Implications of racial identity theory for vocational psychology. *Journal of Vocational Behavior, 44,* 124–138.

Henderson, G. (Ed.). (1986). *Understanding and counseling ethnic minorities.* Springfield, IL: Charles C. Thomas.

Herring, R. D. (1995). Developing biracial ethnic identity: A review of the increasing dilemma. *Journal of Multicultural Counseling and Development, 23,* 29–38.

Herring, R. G. (1994). The clown or contrary figure as a counseling intervention strategy with Native American Indian clients. *Journal of Multicultural Counseling and Development, 22*(3), 153–164.

Highlen, P. S., & Hill, C. E. (1984). Factors affecting client change in counseling. In S. Brown & R. Lent (Eds.), *Handbook of counseling psychology* (pp. 334–396). New York: John Wiley.

Hill, C. E. (1986). An overview of the Hill Counselor and Client Verbal Responses Modes Category Systems. In L. S. Greenberg & W. M. Pinsol (Eds.), *The psychotherapeutic process: A research handbook.* New York: Guilford Press.

Hill, C. E., Greenwald, C., Reed, K. R., Charles, D., O'Farrell, M., & Carter, J. (1981). *Manual for the Counselor and Client Verbal Response Category Systems.* Columbus, OH: Marathon Consulting and Press.

Hill, C. E., Helms, J. E., Spiegel, S. B., & Tichenor, V. (1988). Development of a system for categorizing client reactions to therapist interventions. *Journal of Counseling Psychology, 35,* 27–36.

Hill, C. E., & O'Grady, K. (1985). List of therapist intentions illustrated in a case study and with therapists of varying theoretical orientations. *Journal of Counseling Psychology, 32,* 3–22.

Hill, C. E., Thames, T. B., & Rardin, D. (1979). A comparison of Rogers, Perls, and Ellis on the Hill Counselor Verbal Response Category System. *Journal of Counseling Psychology, 26,* 198–203.

Hill, R. B. (1972). *The strengths of black families.* New York: Emerson Hall.

Hills, H. I., & Strozier, A. L. (1992). Multicultural training in APA-approved counseling psychology programs: A survey. *Professional Psychology: Research and Practice, 23*(1), 43–51.

Hines, P. M., & Boyd-Franklin, N. (1982). Black families. In M. McGoldrick, J. K. Pearce, & J. Giordano (Eds.), *Ethnicity and family therapy.* New York: Guilford Press.

Howard, G. S. (1991). Culture tales: A narrative approach to thinking, cross-cultural psychology, and psychotherapy. *American Psychologist, 46,* 1187–1197.

Hunt, P. (1987). Black clients: Implications for supervision of trainees. *Psychotherapy, 24*(1), 114–119.

Ivey, A. E., Ivey, M. B., & Simek-Downing, L. (1980). *Counseling and psychotherapy: Integrating skills, theory, and practice* (2nd ed.). Englewood Cliffs, NJ: Prentice-Hall.

Jackson, A. M. (1973). Black identity development. *MEFORM: Journal of Educational Diversity and Innovation, 2,* 19–25.

Jackson, A.M. (1983). Treatment issues for black patients. *Psychotherapy: Theory, Research, and Practice, 2*(2), 143–151.

Jackson, A. M. (1990). Evolution of ethnocultural psychotherapy. *Psychotherapy, 27*(3), 428–435.

Jarvis, E. (1844). Insanity among the colored population of the free states. *American Journal of the Medical Sciences, 7,* 71–83.

Jaynes, G. D., & Williams, R. M. (Eds.). (1989). *A common destiny: Blacks in American society.* Washington, DC: National Academy Press.

Jencks, C. (1992). *Rethinking social policy: Race, poverty, and the underclass.* Cambridge, MA: Harvard University Press.

Jenkins, A. H. (1991). A humanistic approach to black psychology. In R. L. Jones (Ed.), *Black psychology* (3rd ed., pp. 79–88). New York: Harper & Row.

Jenkins, Y. M. (1985). The integration of psychotherapy-vocational interventions: Relevance for black women. *Psychotherapy, 22*(2), 394–397.

Jensen, A. R. (1969). How much can we boost IQ and scholastic achievement? *Harvard Education Review, 39,* 1–123.

Jensen, A. R. (1995). Psychological research and race differences. *American Psychologist, 50*(1), 41–42.

Jensen, A. R., & Johnson, F. W. (1994). Race and sex differences in head size and IQ. *Intelligence, 18,* 309–333.

Johnson, D. J. (1992). Racial preference and biculturality in biracial preschoolers. *Merrill-Palmer Quarterly, 38*(2), 233–244.

Johnson, S. D. (1990). Toward clarifying culture, race, and ethnicity in the context of multicultural counseling. *Journal of Multicultural Counseling and Development, 18*(1), 41–50.

Jones, A., & Seagull, A. A. (1977). Dimensions of the relationship between the black client and white therapist. *American Psychologist, 32,* 850–855.

Jones, E. E. (1978). Effects of race on psychotherapy process and outcome: An exploratory investigation. *Psychotherapy: Theory, Research, and Practice, 15,* 226–236.

Jones, E. E. (1982). Psychotherapists' impressions of treatment outcome as a function of race. *Journal of Clinical Psychology, 38,* 722–731.

Jones, J. M. (1972). *Prejudice and racism.* New York: Random House.

Jones, J. M. (1981). The concept of racism and its changing reality. In B. P. Bowser & R. G. Hunt (Eds.), *Impacts of racism on white Americans* (pp. 27–49). Beverly Hills, CA: Sage.

Jones, R. L. (1991). *Black psychology* (3rd ed.). Berkely, CA: Cobb & Henry.

Kardiner, A., & Ovesey, L. (1951). *The mark of oppression.* New York: Norton.

Karp, J. P. (1981). The emotional impact and a model for changing racist attitudes. In B. P. Bowser & R. G. Hunt (Eds.), *Impacts of racism on white Americans* (pp. 87–96). Beverly Hills, CA: Sage.

Katz, J. H. (1985). The sociopolitical nature of counseling. *The Counseling Psychologist, 13*(4), 615–624.

Katz, J. H., & Ivey, A. E. (1977). White awareness: The frontier of racism awareness training. *Personnel and Guidance Journal, 55*(8), 485–488.

Katz, P. A. (1982). Development of children's racial awareness and intergroup attitudes. In L. G. Katz (Ed.), *Current topics in early childhood education* (Vol. 4, pp. 17–54). Norwood, NJ: Ablex.

Katz, P. A., & Zalk, S. R. (1978). Perceptual concomitants of racial attitudes in urban grade school children. *Developmental Psychology, 14,* 447–461.

Kennedy, J. (1952). Problems posed in the analysis of black patients. *Psychiatry, 15,* 313–327.

Kernberg, O. F., Selzer, M. A., Koenigsburg, H. W., Carr, A. C., & Applebaum, A. H. (1980). *Psychodynamic psychotherapy of borderline patients.* New York: Basic Books.

Kim, S. C., Lee, S. U., Chu, K. H., & Cho, K. J. (1989). Korean-Americans and mental health: Clinical experiences of Korean-American mental health services. *Asian American Psychological Association Journal, 13,* 18–27.

Kitano, H. H. L. (1989). A model for counseling Asian Americans. In P. B. Pedersen, J. G. Draguns, W. L. Lonner, & J. E. Trimble (Eds.), *Counseling across cultures* (3rd ed., pp. 139–152). Honolulu: University of Hawaii Press.

Klein, M. (1952). *Developments in psychoanalysis.* London: Hogarth Press.

Kluckhohn, F. R., & Strodtbeck, F. L. (1961). *Variations in value orientations.* Evanston, IL: Row, Peterson.

Kochman, T. (1989). Black and white cultural styles in pluralistic perspective. In B. R. Gifford (Ed.), *Test policy and test performance: Education, language, and culture* (pp. 259–294). Boston: Klumer Associate Publishers.

Kovel, J. (1984). *White racism.* New York: Columbia University Press.

LaFromboise, T. D., Trimble, J. E., & Mohatt, G. V. (1990). Counseling intervention and American Indian tradition: An integrative approach. *The Counseling Psychologist, 18,* 628–654.

Leong, F. T. L. (1986). Counseling and psychotherapy with Asian-Americans: Review of the literature. *Journal of Counseling Psychology, 33*(2), 196–206.

Leong, F. T. L., & Kim, H. H. W. (1991). Going beyond cultural sensitivity on the road to multiculturalism: Using the intercultural sensitizer as a counselor training tool. *Journal of Counseling and Development, 70,* 112–118.

Leong, F. T. L., & Wagner, N. S. (1994). Cross-cultural counseling supervision: What do we know? What do we need to know? *Counselor Education and Supervision, 34*(2), 117–131.

Lin, J. C. H. (1994). How long do Chinese Americans stay in psychotherapy. *Journal of Counseling Psychology, 41*(3), 288–291.

Lind, J. E. (1913). The dream as a simple wish-fulfillment in the Negro. *Psychoanalytic Review, 1,* 295–300.

Lipsky, S. (1978). Internalized oppression. *Black Reemergence, 5*–10.

Locke, D. C. (1994). *Increasing multicultural understanding.* Newbury Park, CA: Sage.

Loevinger, J. (1976). *Ego development.* San Francisco, CA: Jossey-Bass.

Loevinger, J. (1979). The idea of the ego. *Counseling Psychologist, 8,* 3–5.

Looney, J. (1988). Ego development and black identity. *Journal of Black Psychology, 15*(1), 41–56.

Majors, R., & Nikelly, A. (1983). Serving the black minority: A new direction for psychotherapy. *Journal of Non-White Concerns, 11,* 143–151.

Marger, M. N. (1991). *Race and ethnic relations* (2nd ed.). Belmont, CA: Wadsworth.

Marger, M. N. (1994). *Race and ethnic relations* (3rd ed.). Belmont, CA: Wadsworth.

Martin, J. K., & Nagayama-Hall, G. C. (1992). Thinking black, thinking internal, thinking feminist. *Journal of Counseling Psychology, 39,* 509–514.

Mayne, T. J., Norcross, J. C., & Sayette, M. A. (1994). Admission requirements, acceptance rates, and financial assistance in clinical psychology programs. *American Psychologist, 49*(9), 806–811.

Mays, V. M. (1985). The black American and psychotherapy: A dilemma. *Psychotherapy, 22*(2), 379–388.

McCaine, J. (1986). *The relationships of conceptual systems to racial and gender identity, and the impact of reference group identity development on interpersonal styles of behavior and levels of anxiety.* Unpublished doctoral dissertation, University of Maryland, College Park.

McDavis, R. J., & Parker, M. (1977). A course on counseling ethnic minorities: A model. *Counselor Education and Supervision, 17,* 146–149.

McGoldrick, M., Pearce, J. K., & Giordano, J. (Eds.). (1982). *Ethnicity and family therapy.* New York: Guilford Press.

McIntosh, P. (1995). *White privilege and male privilege: A personal account of coming to see correspondences through work in women's studies.* In M. L. Andersen & P. H. Collins (Eds.). *Race, class and gender: An anthology* (2nd ed.). Belmont, CA: Wadsworth.

McRae, M. B., & Johnson, S. D., Jr. (1991). Toward training for competence in multicultural counselor education. *Journal of Counseling and Development, 70,* 131–135.

Meichenbaum, D., & Cameron, R. (1982). Cognitive behavior modification: Current issues. In G. T. Wilson & C. M. Franks (Eds.), *Contemporary behavior therapy: Conceptual and empirical foundations.* New York: Guilford Press.

Midgette, R. J., & Meggert, S. S. (1991). Multicultural counseling instruction: A challenge for faculties in the 21st century. *Journal of Counseling and Development, 70*(1), 136–141.

Miller, P. H. (1993). *Theories of developmental psychology* (3rd ed.). New York: W. H. Freeman and Co.

Mitchell, S. L., & Dell, D. M. (1992). The relationship between black students' racial identity attitudes and participation in campus organizations. *Journal of College Student Development, 33,* 39–43.

Munford, M. B. (1994). Relationship of gender, self-esteem, social class, and racial identity to depression in blacks. *Journal of Black Psychology, 20,* 143–156.

Murry, C., & Hernstein, R. J. (1994). *The bell curve.* New York: Free Press.

Myers, D. (1989). *Psychology* (2nd ed.). New York: Worth Publishing Inc.

Nagayama-Hall, G., & Malony, H. N. (1983). Cultural control in psychotherapy with minority clients. *Psychotherapy, 20*(2), 131–142.

Njeri, I. (1991, January 13). Call for census category creates interracial debate. *Los Angeles Times,* E1, E9–11.

Nwachuku, U. T., & Ivey, A. E. (1991). Culture-specific counseling: An alternative training tool. *Journal of Counseling and Development, 70,* 106–111.

Ochs, N. (1994). The incidence of racial issues in white counseling dyads: An exploratory survey. *Counselor Education and Supervision, 33*(4), 305–313.

Ordway, J. (1973). Some consequences of racism for whites. In C. Willie, B. Brown, & B. Kramer (Eds.), *Racism and mental health.* Pittsburgh: University of Pittsburgh Press.

Orlinsky, D. E., & Howard, K. I. (1978). The relations of process to outcome in psychotherapy. In S. L. Garfield & A. E. Bergin (Eds.), *Handbook of psychotherapy and behavior change* (2nd ed., pp. 283–330). New York: John Wiley.

Ornstein, A. (1982). The education of the disadvantaged: A 20-year review. *Educational Researcher, 24,* 197–211.

Ottavi, T. M., Pope-Davis, D. P., & Dings, J. G. (1994). The relationship between White racial identity attitudes and self-reported multicultural competencies. *Journal of Counseling Psychology, 41,* 149–154.

Overmier, K. (1990). Biracial adolescents: Areas of conflict in identity formation. *The Journal of Applied Social Sciences, 14*(2), 157–176.

Papajohn, J., & Spiegel, J. P. (1975). *Transactions in families.* San Francisco: Jossey-Bass.

Paradis, F. E. (1981). Themes in the training of culturally effective psychotherapists. *Counselor Education and Supervision, 21,* 136–151.

Parham, T. A. (1989). Cycles of psychological nigrescence. *The Counseling Psychologist, 17,* 187–226.

Parham, T. A., & Helms, J. E. (1981). The influence of black students' racial identity attitudes on preference for counselor's race. *Journal of Counseling Psychology, 28,* 250–257.

Parham, T. A., & Helms, J. E. (1985a). Attitudes of racial identity and self-esteem in black students: An exploratory investigation. *Journal of College Student Personnel, 26*(2), 143–147.

Parham, T. A., & Helms, J. E. (1985b). Relation of racial identity attitudes to self-actualization and affective states of black students. *Journal of Counseling Psychology, 32,* 431–440.

Parham, T. A., & Williams, P. T. (1993). The relationship of demographic and background factors to racial identity attitudes. *Journal of Black Psychology, 19*(1), 7–24.

Parker, W. M., Bingham, R. P., & Fukuyama, M. (1985). Improving cross-cultural effectiveness of counselor trainees. *Counselor Education and Supervision, 24,* 349–352.

Parker, W. M., & McDavis, R. J. (1983). Attitudes of blacks toward mental health agencies and counselors. *Journal of Non-White Concerns, 11,* 89–99.

Parker, W. M., Valley, M. M., & Geary, C. A. (1986). Acquiring cultural knowledge for counselors in training: A multifaceted approach. *Counselor Education and Supervision, 26,* 61–71.

Parloff, M. B., Waskow, I., & Wolfe, B. E. (1978). Research on therapist variables in relation to process and outcome. In S. L. Garfield & A. E. Bergin (Eds.), *Handbook of psychotherapy and behavior change* (2nd ed., pp. 233–282). New York: John Wiley.

Pedersen, P. B. (Ed.). (1987). *Handbook of cross-cultural counseling and therapy.* Westport, CT: Greenwood Press.

Peregory, J. J. (1993). Transcultural counseling with American Indians and Alaskan Natives: Contemporary issues for consideration. In J. McFadden (Ed.), *Transcultural counseling: Bi-lateral and international perspectives* (pp. 163–191). Alexandra, VA: American Counseling Association.

Peterson, F. K. (1991). Issues of race and ethnicity in supervision: Emphasizing who you are, not what you know. *Clinical Supervisor, 9*(1), 15–31.

Pettigrew, T. F. (1981). The mental health impact. In B. P. Bowser, & R. G. Hunt (Eds.), *Impacts of racism on white Americans.* Newbury Park, CA: Sage.

Phinney, J. S., & Rotheram, M. J. (Eds.). (1987). *Children's ethnic socialization: Pluralism and development.* Newbury Park, CA: Sage.

Piaget, J. (1952). *The origins of intelligence in children.* New York: International Universities Press.

Piaget, J., & Inhelder, B. (1968). *Memory and intelligence.* London, England: Routledge Press.

Pinderhughes, C. A. (1973). Racism and psychotherapy. In C. Willie, B. Kramer, & B. Brown (Eds.), *Racism and mental health.* Pittsburgh: University of Pittsburgh Press.

Pinderhughes, E. (1982). Afro-American families and the victim system. In M. McGoldrick, J. K. Pearce, & J. Giordano (Eds.), *Ethnicity and family therapy.* New York: Guilford Press.

Pinderhughes, E. (1989). *Understanding race, ethnicity, and power: The key to efficacy in clinical practice.* New York: Free Press.

Piskacek, V., & Golubs, M. (1973). Children of interracial marriage. In I. R. Stuart & L. E. Abt (Eds.), *Interracial marriage: Expectations and reality.* New York: Grossman.

Pomales, J., Claiborn, C. D., & LaFromboise, T. D. (1987). Effects of black students' racial identity on perceptions of white counselors varying in cultural sensitivity. *Journal of Counseling Psychology, 33,* 57–61.

Ponterotto, J. C., & Casas, J. M. (1991). *Handbook of racial/ethnic minority counseling research.* Springfield, IL: Charles C. Thomas.

Ponterotto, J. C., Casas, M. J., Suzuki, L. A., & Alexander, C. M. (Eds.). (1995). *Handbook of multicultural counseling.* Thousand Oaks, CA: Sage.

Pope-Davis, D. B., & Ottavi, T. M. (1992). The influence of white racial identity attitudes on racism among faculty members: A preliminary examination. *Journal of College Student Development, 33*(5), 389–394.

Pope-Davis, D. B., & Ottavi, T. M. (1994). The relationship between racism and racial identity among white Americans: A replication and extension. *Journal of Counseling and Development, 72,* 293–297.

Porter, J. (1971). *Black child, white child: The development of racial attitudes.* Cambridge, MA: Harvard University Press.

Poston, C. W. S. (1990). The biracial identity development model: A needed addition. *Journal of Counseling and Development, 69,* 153–155.

Poussaint, A. F. (1984). Benefits of being interracial. *The Council on Interracial Books for Children, Children of Interracial Families, 15*(6).

Prilleltensky, I. (1989). Psychology and the status quo. *American Psychologist, 44,* 795–802.

Proshansky, H. (1966). The development of intergroup attitudes. In L. W. Hoffman & M. L. Hoffman (Eds.), *Review of child development research* (Vol. 2). New York: Russell Sage Foundation.

Prudhomme, C., & Musto, D. F. (1973). Historical perspectives on mental health and racism in the United States. In C. V. Willie, B. M. Kramer, & B. S. Brown (Eds.), *Racism and mental health.* Pittsburgh: University of Pittsburgh Press.

Pyant, C. T., & Yanico, B. J. (1991). Relationships of racial identity and gender role attitudes to black women's psychological well-being. *Journal of Counseling Psychology, 38,* 315–322.

Ramsey, P. G. (1987). Ethnicity and the young child. In J. S. Phinney & M. S. Rotheram (Eds.), *Children's ethnic socialization: Pluralism and development.* Newbury Park, CA: Sage.

Ramsey, P. G., Vold, E. B., & Williams, L. R. (1989). *Multicultural education: A source book.* New York: Garland.

Remington, G., & DaCosta, G. (1989). Ethnocultural factors in resident supervision: Black supervisor and white supervisees. *American Journal of Psychotherapy, XLIII*(3), 389–404.

Richardson, T. & Helms, J. E. (1994). The relation of the racial identity attitudes of black men to perceptions of parallel counseling dyads. *Journal of Counseling and Development, 73*(2), 172–177.

Ridley, C. R. (1995). *Overcoming unintentional racism in counseling and therapy.* Thousand Oaks, CA: Sage.

Ridley, C. R., Mendoza, D. W., Kanitz, B. E., & Angermeier, L., Zenk, R. (1994). Cultural sensitivity in multicultural counseling: A perceptual schema model. *Journal of Counseling Psychology, 41,* 125–136.

Riegel, K. (1976). The dialectics of human development. *American Psychologists, 31,* 689–700.

Robiner, W. N. & Scofield, W. (1990). References on supervision in clinical and counseling psychology. *Professional Psychology Research and Practice, 21*(4), 297–312.

Root, M. P. (1985). Guidelines for facilitating therapy with Asian American clients. *Psychotherapy, 22,* 349–356.

Root, M. P. (1990). Resolving "other" status: Identity development of biracial individuals. In L. S. Brown & M. P. Root (Eds.), *Diversity and complexity in feminist therapy* (pp. 185–206). New York: Harrington Park Press.

Riessman, F. (1962). *The culturally deprived child.* New York: Harper & Row.

Rotheram, M. J., & Phinney, J. S. (1987). Ethnic behavior patterns as an aspect of identity. In J. S. Phinney & M. J. Rotheram (Eds.), *Children's ethnic socialization: Pluralism and development.* Newbury Park, CA: Sage.

Rothenberg, P. S. (1995). *Race, class, and gender in the United States* (3rd ed.). New York: St. Martin Press.

Rushton, P. J. (1995a). Construct validity, censorship, and the genetics of race. *American Psychologist, 50*(1), 40–41.

Rushton, P. J. (1995b). *Race, evolution, and behavior: A life history perspective.* New Bruswick, NJ: Transaction.

Sager, C. J., Brayboy, T. L., & Waxenberg, B. R. (1972). Black patient-white therapist. *American Journal of Orthopsychiatry, 42,* 415–432.

St. Clair, H. (1951). Psychiatric interview experiences with Negroes. *American Journal of Psychiatry, 108,* 113–119.

Samuels, A. S. (1972). The reduction of interracial prejudice and tension through group therapy. In H. I. Kaplan & B. J. Sadock (Eds.), *New models for group therapy.* New York: Dutton.

Sattler, J. M. (1977). The effects of therapist-client similarity. In A. S. Gurman & A. M. Razin (Eds.), *Effective psychotherapy: A handbook of research* (pp. 252–290). New York: Pergamon.

Schachter, J. S., & Butts, H. F. (1968). Transference and countertransference in interracial analysis. *Journal of the American Psychoanalytic Association, 16,* 792–808.

Seward, G. H. (1972). *Psychotherapy and culture conflict in community mental health* (2nd ed.). New York: Ronald Press.

Shon, S. P., & Ja, D. Y. (1982). Asian families. In M. McGoldrick, J. K. Pearce, & J. Giordano (Eds.), *Ethnicity and family therapy.* New York: Guilford Press.

Sims, W. E. (1981). Humanizing education for culturally different and exceptional children. In W. E. Sims & B. Bass de Martinez (Eds.), *Perspectives in multicultural education* (pp. 1–16). New York: University Press of America.

Smedley, A. (1993). *Race in North America: Origin and evolution of a world view.* Boulder, CO: Westview Press.

Solberg, V. S., Ristma, S., Davis, B. J., Tata, S. P., Jolly, A. (1994). Asian-American students' severity of problems and willingness to seek help from university counseling centers: Role of previous experience, gender, and ethnicity. *Journal of Counseling Psychology, 41*(3), 275–279.

Solinger, R. (1992). *Wake up, little Susie.* New York: Routledge.

Sommers, V. (1964). The impact of dual cultural membership on identity. *Psychiatry, 27,* 332–344.

Spiegel, J. P. (1982). An ecological model of ethnic families. In M. McGoldrick, J. K. Pearce, & J. Giordano (Eds.), *Ethnicity and family therapy* (pp. 31–51). New York: Guilford Press.

Spielberger, C. D., Gorsuch, R. L., & Lushene, R. E. (1968). *The State-Trait Anxiety Inventory (Preliminary Test Form X).* Tallahassee: Florida State University.

Spurlock, J. (1973). Some consequences of racism for children. In C. V. Willie, B. M. Kramer, & B. S. Brown (Eds.), *Racism and mental health.* Pittsburgh: University of Pittsburgh Press.

Stanfield, T. H. (1985). The ethnocentric basis of social science knowledge production. In E. W. Gordon (Ed.), *Review of research in education* (pp. 387–415). Washington, DC: American Educational Research Association.

Steele, S. (1990). *The content of our character: A new vision of race in America.* New York: Harper Perennial.

Stephan, C. W., & Stephan, W. G. (1989). After intermarriage: Ethnic identity among mixed-heritage Japanese-Americans and Hispanics. *Journal of Marriage and the Family, 51,* 507–519.

Stewart, E. C., & Bennett, A. (1991). *American cultural patterns: A cross-cultural perspective* (2nd ed.). Yarmouth, ME: Intercultural Press.

Stiles, W. B., & Snow, J. S. (1984). Counseling session impact as viewed by novice counselors and clients. *Journal of Counseling Psychology, 31,* 3–12.

Strupp, H. H. (1992). The future of psychodynamic psychotherapy. *Psychotherapy, 29,* 21–27.

Sue, D. W. (1981). *Counseling the culturally different: Theory and practice.* New York: John Wiley & Sons.

Sue, D. W. (1994). Asian American mental health and help-seeking behavior: Comment on Solberg et al. (1994), Tata and Leong (1994), and Lin (1994). *Journal of Counseling Psychology, 41*(3), 292–295.

Sue, D. W., Bernier, J., Durran, A., Feinberg, L., Pedersen, P., Smith, E., & Vasquez-Nuttal, E. (1982). Position paper: Cross-cultural counseling competencies. *The Counseling Psychologist, 10*(2), 45–52.

Sue, S., Fujino, D. C., Hu, L., Takeuchi, D. T., & Zane, N. (1991). Community mental health services for ethnic minority groups: A test of the cultural responsiveness hypothesis. *Journal of Consulting and Clinical Psychology, 59,* 533–540.

Sue, D. W., & Sue, D. (1990). *Counseling the culturally different: Theory and practice* (2nd ed.). New York: John Wiley.

Sue, S., & Sue, D. W. (1971). Chinese-American personality and mental health. *Amerasia Journal, 1,* 36–49.

Szasz, T. S. (1971). The Negro in psychiatry: An historical note on psychiatric rhetoric. *American Journal of Psychotherapy, 25,* 469–471.

Tata, S. P., & Leong, F. T. L. (1994). Individualism-collectivism, social-network orientation, and acculturation as predictors of attitudes toward seeking professional psychological help among Chinese Americans. *Journal of Counseling Psychology, 41*(3), 280–287.

Taub, D. J., & McEwen, M. K. (1992). The relationship of racial identity attitudes to autonomy and mature interpersonal relationships in black and white undergraduate women. *Journal of College Student Development, 33*(5), 439–446.

Terkel, S. (1992). *Race.* New York: Free Press.

Thomas, A., & Sillen, S. (1972). *Racism and psychiatry.* New York: Carol Publishing Group.

Thomas, C. (1971). *Boys no more.* Beverly Hills, CA: Glencoe Press.

Thomas, M. B., & Dansby, P. G. (1985). Black clients: family structures, therapeutic issues, and strengths. *Psychotherapy, 22*(2), 398–406.

Thomason, T. C. (1991). Counseling Native Americans: An introduction for non-Native American counselors. *Journal of Counseling and Development, 69*(4), 321–327.

Thompson, C. E., & Jenal, S. T. (1994). Interracial and intraracial quasi-counseling interactions when counselors avoid discussing racial issues. *Journal of Counseling Psychology, 41*(4), 484–491.

Thompson, C. E., Worthington, R., & Atkinson, D. R. (1994). Counselor content orientation, counselor race, and Black women's cultural mistrust, and self-disclosures. *Journal of Counseling Psychology, 41,* 155–161.

Thompson, J. R. (1987). *The process of psychotherapy: An integration of clinical experience and empirical research.* Lanham, MD: University Press of America.

Tizard, B., & Phoenix, A. (1993). *Black, white, or mixed race: Race and racism in the lives of young people of mixed parentage.* London: Routledge.

Tokar, D. M., & Swanson, J. L. (1991). An investigation of the validity of Helms' (1984) model of white racial identity development. *Journal of Counseling Psychology, 38,* 296–301.

Triandis, H. C., & Lambert, W. W. (Eds.). (1980). *Handbook of cross-cultural psychology* (Vols. 1–6). Boston: Allyn & Bacon.

Trimble, J. E. (1976). Value differences among American Indians: Concerns for the concerned counselor. In P. Pederson, W. J. Lonner, & J. G. Draguns (Eds.), *Counseling across cultures* (3rd ed., pp. 65–81). Honolulu: University Press of Hawaii.

Trimble, J. E., & Fleming, C. M. (1989). Providing counseling services for Native American Indians: Client, counselor, and community characteristics. In P. B. Pedersen, J. G. Draguns, W. J. Lonner, & J. E. Trimble (Eds.), *Counseling across cultures* (3rd ed., pp. 177–204). Honolulu: University of Hawaii Press.

Tsui, P., & Schultz, G. L. (1985). Failure of rapport: When psychotherapeutic engagement fails in the treatment of the Asian client. *American Journal of Orthopsychiatry, 55,* 561–569.

Turner, S., & Armstrong, S. (1981). Cross-racial psychotherapy: What the therapists say. *Psychotherapy: Theory, Research, and Practice, 18,* 375–378.

Tyler, F. B., Brome, D. R., & Williams, J. E. (Eds.). (1991). *Ethnic validity, ecology and psychotherapy: A psychosocial competence model.* New York: Plenum Press.

Vaughn, G. M. (1987). A social psychological model of ethnic identity development. In J. S. Phinney & M. J. Rotheram (Eds.), *Children's ethnic socialization: Pluralism and development* (pp. 56–72). Newbury Park, CA: Sage.

Vontress, C. E. (1969). Cultural barriers in the counseling relationship. *Personnel and Guidance Journal, 48,* 11–17.

Vontress, C. E. (1970). Counseling blacks. *Personnel and Guidance Journal, 48,* 713–719.

Vontress, C. E. (1971). *Counseling Negroes.* Boston: Houghton Mifflin.

Waite, R. R. (1968). The Negro patient and clinical theory. *Journal of Consulting and Clinical Psychology, 32*(4), 427–433.

Watts, R. J. (1992). Racial identity and preferences for social change strategies among African Americans. *Journal of Black Psychology, 18*(2), 1–18.

Watts, R. J., & Carter, R. T. (1991). Psychological aspects of racism in organizations. *Group and Organizational Studies, 16*(3), 328–344.

West, C. (1993). *Race matters.* Boston: Beacon Press.

Wilkerson, I. (1992, June 21). Two neighborhoods and a wall called race. *New York Times,* p. 1.

Willie, C. V., Kramer, B. M., & Brown, B. S. (1973). *Racism and mental health.* Pittsburgh: University of Pittsburgh Press.

Wilson, G. T. (1986). Social psychological concepts in the theory and practice of behavior therapy. In P. Eelen (Ed.), *Behavior therapy: Beyond the conditioning framework.* Hillsdale, NJ: Erlbaum.

Wilson, G. T., & Agras, S. (1992). The future of behavior therapy. *Psychotherapy, 29*(1), 39–43.

Winn, N. N., & Priest, R. (1993). Counseling biracial children: A forgotten component of multicultural counseling. *Family Therapy, 20*(1), 28–36.

Yee, A. H., Fairchild, H. H., Weizmann, F., & Wyatt, G. E. (1993). Addressing psychology's problem with race. *American Psychologist, 48*(11), 1132–1140.

Author Index

Subject Index